# BUCHAREST

## ILLUSTRATED GUIDE

## O EDIȚIE LITERA

Left **Boats on Cişmigiu Lake**   Centre **Concert on Verona Terrace**   Right **VW and bicycle**

PRIMĂRIA MUNICIPIULUI
BUCUREŞTI

**Address:**
Splaiul Independenţei nr. 291–293
sector 6
cod poştal 060042

**Address CIDRC
(Registratura PMB)**
Casierie PMB:
Regina Elisabeta, nr. 42,
Phone: 021 302 15 15

Phone: 0800 800 868

# Contents
## Bucureşti. Ghid ilustrat

*Previous page –* **Mogoşoaia Palace**

Left **Miorița Fountain**  Centre **Librecht House**  Right **Spătarul Mihai Cantacuzino, Colțea Hospital**

Contents

Left **CEC Palace**  Centre **The Statue of Gh. C. Cantacuzino, Icoanei Garden**  Right **Smârdan Street**

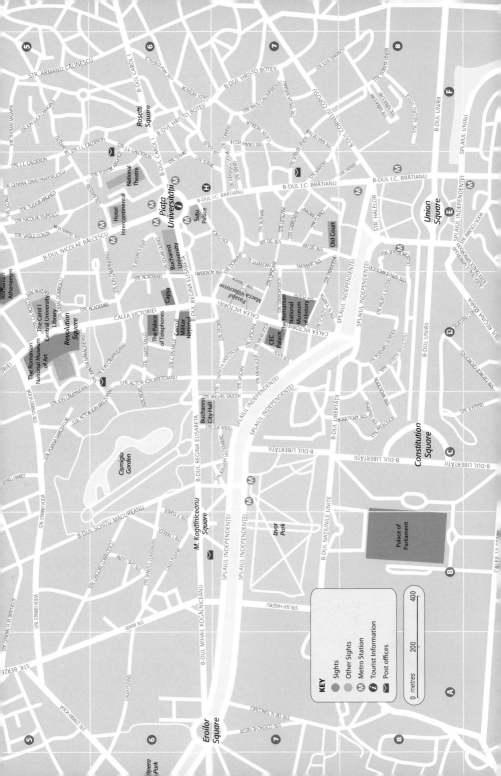

# BUCHAREST
## touristic guide

BUCHAREST

# Bucharest Highlights

*With a history of more than 500 years and capital of Romania since 1859, Bucharest is a city that concentrates more than 3 million people every day. The "Little Paris" of the inter-war period was ravaged by mass destruction in the communist period, when historic monuments, especially churches, were demolished. Embarked on a continuous search for architectural identity and still subject to often inappropriate transformations, the city nevertheless conceals buildings that are genuine jewels, and places well worth visiting.*

### Lipscani

A fascinating and vibrant area, thronging with tourists, where 17th century buildings *(right)* can be found alongside modern restaurants and pubs *(pp. 10–11)*. It has been undergoin extensive renovation for the last few years.

### Palace of Parliament

Popularly known as the House of the People, this imposing building *(above)* is the second largest in the world after the Pentagon and is a symbol of the communist period *(pp. 12–13)*.

### Calea Victoriei

Calea Victoriei (Victory Avenue) is the city's most beautiful thoroughfare. It runs through the centre of the city from Victory Square to United Nations Square. In the time of Constantin Brâncoveanu it was called the Mogoşoaia Deck, as it was paved with tree trunks *(pp. 14–15)*.

### Romanian Athenaeum

Built at the end of the 19th century, partly by public subscription, it is an illustrious concert venue. The building is one of the most beautiful in Bucharest *(pp. 18–19)*.

*Previous pages – **Stavropoleos Church, architectural detail***

### The Romanian National Museum of Art

Housed in the former royal palace, the museum has three major collections: European Art, Old Romanian Art, and Modern Romanian Art. Among the attractions are works by Brâncuşi, Rembrandt, Monet and El Greco *(pp. 20–23)*.

### Cişmigiu Garden

Designed by German landscape architect O. Mayer, the oldest and most beautiful park in Bucharest *(see photo below)* was laid out as a public garden in 1847–1860 *(pp. 28–29)*.

### Village Museum

Located in Herăstrău Park and covering an area of 30 hectares, the open-air museum *(above and below)* recreates the atmosphere of a typical Romanian village. It was inaugurated in 1936 in the presence of King Carol II *(pp. 30–33)*.

0 — metres — 300

### Caru' cu bere (The Beer Dray)

The most famous restaurant in Bucharest is housed in a particularly beautiful late-19th-century historic monument *(pp. 34–35)*.

### Stavropoleos Church

A small but extraordinarily beautiful church *(above)* situated on Lipscani Street. It was built in the Byzantine style in 1724 by a Greek monk named Ioannikos *(pp. 36–37)*.

### The Romanian National Museum of History

The museum *(above)* has more than 650,000 exhibits, the most precious of which are the Dacian gold bracelets from the Pietroasa hoard and a copy of Trajan's Column *(pp. 26–27)*.

Bucharest

# Lipscani

The commercial heart of old Bucharest, Lipscani developed around the Princely Court, now on Franceză Street, the oldest street in Bucharest. Nowadays, the area is part of the cultural and tourist trail, and teems with art galleries, antiques shops, cafés, pubs, and restaurants. Since 1990, it has been partly restored, but most of the old buildings are still awaiting renovation.

Bas-relief,
Glassmakers' Court

🔘 **The Lipscani district stretches between University Square and Union Square and is flanked by Victory Avenue and I.C. Brătianu Boulevard.**

The historic centre includes 97 historic monuments and 120 atmospheric buildings (many built in the 19th century in the Renaissance, Neoclassical and Neo-Baroque styles), which were nationalised by the communist authorities in 1948. The Lipscani area is impressive for its host of atmospheric places evocative of the 17th century.

## Highlights

1. The Old Court mediaeval ensemble
2. Palace of the Dacia Insurance Comp.
3. Manuc's Inn
4. The Linden Inn
5. Church of the Annunciation
6. The NBR Palace
7. Chrissovelloni Bank
8. Glassmakers' Court
9. Macca-Villacrosse Passage
10. Stavropoleos Church

### 1 The Old Court mediaeval ensemble
Here you can see fragments of buildings from successive epochs of the Princely Court, from the 15th to 17th centuries. ◈ 31 Franceză St

### 2 Palace of the Dacia Insurance Company
It was built in 1874, on the foundations of the Filipescu Inn. A medallion of Mihai Eminescu and a marble plaque commemorate the fact that the great poet worked here for two years as editor of the Timpul newspaper. ◈ 19 Lipscani St

### 3 Manuc's Inn (Hanul lui Manuc)
Built in 1808 at the behest of Manuc Bey, an Armenian merchant and diplomat, the inn has lost its former grandeur. It used to have 15 vaulted cellars, 23 shops, and 107 guest rooms on the upper storey. In 1812, it was here that the Peace Treaty between Russia and the Ottoman Empire was signed. Restored to the Cantacuzino family, the inn has recently been renovated. ◈ 62 Franceză St

### 4 The Linden Inn (Hanul cu Tei)
One of the few historic inns (1833) still to exist in Bucharest and the only one preserved in its original form. Situated between Blănari and Lipscani streets, it is an enchanting spot, with art galleries and shops.

### 5 Church of the Annunciation

One of the oldest buildings in Bucharest, the Church of the Annunciation (also called the Old Court Church) was built in 1559. The murals are by Constantin Lecca and Mişu Popp.

◈ *33 Franceză St*

### 6 The NBR Palace

The National Bank of Romania Palace *(below)* was built in 1883–1885, in the French Neoclassical style.

The murals are by G.D. Mirea, N. Grigorescu, and E. Voinescu. In the niches of the façade there are statues symbolising Agriculture, Industry, Commerce, and Justice.

◈ *25 Lipscani St*

### 7 Chrissovelloni Bank

Now the Bucharest Municipality branch of the NBR, it was designed by G.M. Cantacuzino and built between 1923 and 1928. It is a felicitous combination between the fascinating image of an Italian Renaissance palazzo and the modern functionality of a bank.

◈ *16 Lipscani St*

### 8 Glassmakers' Court

One of Bucharest's jewels, here guest craftsmen, watched by tourists, make glass using centuries-old techniques.

◈ *9 Şelari St*

### 9 Macca-Villacrosse Passage

The most beautiful covered passage in Bucharest links Lipscani and Calea Victoriei. It was designed by Felix Xenopol and completed in 1891. It is named after the Greek merchant Mihalake Macca and Xavier Villacrosse, the capital's chief architect (1840–1850).

### 10 Stavropoleos Church

Situated near the National Museum of History and Caru' cu bere restaurant, the church was built by the Greek monk Ioannikos in 1774 and remains an architectural jewel even today. The inner courtyard was restored by architect Ion Mincu. There is a detailed description on pp. 36–37.

◈ *4 Stavropoleos St*

## Origin of the Name

In 1750, Uliţa Mare (Main Alley) was renamed Lipscani after the merchants who sold wares, in particular cloth from Lipsca (Leipzig) on this street. Trade flourished and Lipscani became famous abroad. Even today, the streets are named after various merchant guilds: Blănari (Furriers), Căldărari (Coppersmiths), Şelari (Saddlers), Zarafi (Bankers),

Lipscani

# Palace of Parliament

*The Palace of Parliament (also known as the House of the People) was built on what was once Spirii Hill (now Arsenalului Hill) starting with 1983. More than 7 km² of old Bucharest were destroyed during communism, including historic monuments such as Văcărești Monastery. The gigantic House of the People is mentioned three times in the Book of Records: second-largest as surface area; largest and most expensive civil administrative building; and heaviest structure ever built. Since 1994, it has housed the Chamber of Deputies and the Senate, and since 2004, the west wing has been home to the National Museum of Contemporary Art (MNAC). The palace is open to visitors.*

*Palace of Parliament, view from United Nations Boulevard*

**⊘ Palace of Parliament**
- 2–4 Izvor St
- Open to visitors daily, 10-16; for guided tours, phone 021 311 3611
- Entry only with an identification document
- Entrance fee: 25 lei, standard tour; 15 lei, panoramic city view from the terrace; 10 lei tour of basement
- www.cdep.ro
- Partial access for the disabled

**MNAC**
- 2-4 Izvor St, Wing E4/entrance via Calea 13 Septembrie
- Open Wed.–Sun., 10–18
- Entrance fee: 5 lei
- Izvor or Piaţa Unirii Metro stations, buses 136 and 385
- www.mnac.ro

## Top 10 Features

1. 13 Septembrie Entrance
2. The Hall of Human Rights
3. The Hall of Union
4. The Nicolae Bălcescu Room
5. The Nicolae Iorga Room
6. The Alexandru Ioan Cuza Room
7. The Ion I. C. Brătianu Room
8. The Gallery of Honour and the Official Entrance Hall
9. The C.A. Rosetti Room
10. MNAC

### 1 13 Septembrie Entrance
The blue glass cupola that caps the staircase is a copy of the one at the Hermitage. One original feature is the symmetry between the ceiling and the floor motif, inspired by a mosaic discovered at Histria.

### 2 The Hall of Human Rights
With a surface area of 625 m², the hall is completely panelled with native wood essences. The impressive chandelier weighs two tonnes and is the second largest in the building.

### 3 The Hall of Union
The immense carpet (1,100 m²), which covers the central part of the hall on special occasions, weighs around three tonnes. 35 people are required to unroll it.

### 4 The Nicolae Bălcescu Room

In this room it can be found the only material not of Romanian origin: the mahogany of the doors, which was a gift to Nicolae Ceaușescu from President Mobutu of Zaire (now the Democratic Republic of Congo.

### 5 The Nicolae Iorga Room

Decorated using the same essences of wood for the ceiling and walls, mainly oak, the room bearing the name of the great historian Nicolae Iorga has art déco furnishings and floral paintings by native artists.

### 6 The Alexandru Ioan Cuza Room

The room is named after the ruler who accomplished the Union of 1859 and is one of the most imposing in the palace: it is the tallest (20 m) and has the second largest surface area (2,040 m²).

### 7 The Ion I.C. Brătianu Room

Here you can admire the red velvet curtains embroidered with gold and silver thread, made by the nuns of Agapia and Văratec convents.

### 10 MNAC

Inaugurated in October 2004, the National Museum of Contemporary Art promotes the cutting edge of Romanian and foreign art. Temporary exhibitions and educational programmes are held here.

### 8 The Gallery of Honour and the Official Entrance Hall

The floor in the central area imitates a white, beige, red and black carpet and is made of marble. The two monumental staircases have 16 m high windows with drapes weighing no less than 250 kg.

### 9 The C.A. Rosetti Room

An auditorium that combines cubist and Art Déco features. The huge chandelier weighs three tonnes.

## Impressive Dimensions

The huge building covers 330,000 m² and has 12 storeys, 8 underground levels, and around 1,000 rooms. It was built using: 1,000,000 m³ of marble 5,500 tonnes of cement 7,000 tonnes of steel 20,000 tonnes of sand 900,000 m³ of various essences of wood 3,500 tonnes of crystal 200,000 m³ of glass 2,800 chandeliers 220,000 m³ of carpets 3,500 m³ of leather.

# Calea Victoriei

One of the oldest thoroughfares in Bucharest, in the 18th century it was called the Mogoșoaia Deck, as it was paved with tree trunks. Its present name dates from the end of the Independence War, in 1878. In 1882, it was here that the city's first electrical installations were fitted, in front of the Royal Palace. Stretching 2,700 metres, between Victory Square and United Nations Square, the avenue is regarded as the capital's most elegant street.

*Capșa*

🕐 Have coffee and cakes at Casa Capșa, reliving the inter-war charm of this famous café.

You can take lunch at the National Military Club restaurant. The food is decent and the prices are low.

There is also an elegant hotel at the Capșa. Find out more at www.capsa.ro

## Highlights

1. Enescu Palace
2. Vernescu Palace
3. Kretzulescu Church
4. Revolution Square
5. Athénée Palace Hotel
6. Casa Capșa
7. The CEC Palace
8. The National Military Club
9. The Palace of Telephones
10. The Carol I Central University Library

### Enescu Palace
Designed by architect Ioan D. Berindei for Grigore Cantacuzino, known as "the Nabob", and built between 1901 and 1903, the palace was inherited by the future wife of composer George Enescu, who bequeathed it as a museum in her will. ◈ *141 Calea Victoriei*

### Vernescu Palace
Built around 1820, the building was restored by architect Ion Mincu and painter G.D. Mirea in the 19th century. It is now home to a famous casino. ◈ *133 Calea Victoriei*

### Biserica Kretzulescu
It was built in 1722 by Logothete Kretzulescu, a son-in-law of Constantin Brâncoveanu. The murals are by Gh. Tattarescu. ◈ *47 Calea Victoriei*

### Revolution Square
Revolution Square (Piața Revoluției) is a symbolic place: it was here that Ceaușescu gave his last speech, on 21 December 1989, before fleeing by helicopter. Before 1989, it was called Palace Square, after the former Royal Palace, now the National Museum of Art.

### Athénée Palace Hotel
Designed by Th. Bradeau and built in 1912, it was the first building in Bucharest to use reinforced concrete. ◈ *1–3 Episcopiei St*

*The Romanian Athenaeum and The National Museum of History, described on the following pages, are also located on Calea Victoriei.*

### The CEC Palace

**7** The eclectic CEC Palace was designed by French architect Paul Gottereau and built in 1900 on the site of a 16th century church that had been rebuilt by Constantin Brâncoveanu. Alexandru Ioan Cuza passed the law establishing the National Savings Bank (CEC). It is planned to turn the palace into a museum. ⬥ *13 Calea Victoriei*

### The Palace of Telephones

**9** Romania's first tall building (52.5 m) with a metal framework was built in the 1930s on the site of the former Oteteleşanu terrace. The architects were Americans Walter Froy and Louis Week and Dutchman E. van Saanen-Algy. ⬥ *37 Calea Victoriei*

### The Carol I Central University Library

**10** The library was designed by French architect Paul Gottereau and built in 1893. It was inaugurated by Carol I in 1895. Extended in 1911 and modernised since 1989, the CUB is the country's most extensive university library. ⬥ *121–127 Calea Victoriei*

### Casa Capşa

**6** Opened in 1886 by renowned confectioner Grigore Capşa, it was a meeting place for artists, politicians, writers, and journalists. After 1932, it was the semi-official café of Bucharest's writers and artists. ⬥ *36 Calea Victoriei*

### The National Military Club

**8** The palace was built in 1910–13 on the marshy site of the Sărindar Monastery, as a club for officers of the Bucharest garrison. You can visit the Marble, Gothic, and Norwegian Halls. ⬥ *1 Constantin Mille St*

### Grigore Capşa

One of twelve brothers from a family of Aromanians, Grigore Capşa served his apprenticeship as a pastry-maker and confectioner in Paris.
In 1852, he opened the Capşa Confectionery Shop, which won awards in Paris and Vienna.
He invented the Joffre, a cake named in honour of the French marshal when he visited Bucharest.

# Romanian Athenaeum

*Built by public subscription between 1886 and 1888, following the famous "Give a leu for the Ateneu" campaign, the building was designed by French architect Albert Galleron as a "palace of science and the arts." The building's circular form made use of the existing foundations, which had been intended for a circus. The Athenaeum, which has exceptional acoustics, is home to the George Enescu Philharmonic and the festival of the same name, which transforms Bucharest into the capital of classical music once every two years.*

*The concert hall*

🍴 **After concerts, you can dine at the nearby Ateneu Bistro, an intimate and pleasant local restaurant.**
*3 Episcopiei St*

• *Nos. 1–3 Benjamin Franklin St*
• *021 3150 024 021 3152 567*
• *For concerts, visit www.fge.org.ro*

## Top 10 Features

1. Impressive Architecture
2. George Enescu Philharmonic
3. Concert Hall
4. Concert Organ
5. Concert Hall Cupola
6. Monumental Staircase
7. Fresco
8. Medallions of the Voievodes
9. Statue of Eminescu
10. George Enescu Festival

### 1 Impressive Architecture
Built in the Neoclassical style on a site belonging to the Văcărescu family, the Athenaeum has decorative features typical of late-19th-century French architecture. Inspired by Greek temples, the building has a colonnade on which rests a triangular fronton.

### 2 George Enescu Philharmonic
The Athenaeum is home to the George Enescu Philharmonic. The Romanian Philharmonic Society was founded in 1868 and has given concerts in the Athenaeum since its inauguration on 5 March 1889.

### 3 Concert Hall
The hall is 28.5 m in diameter, 16 m in height, and a seating capacity of 800, out of which 500 seats in the stalls and 52 in the boxes.

### 4 Concert Organ
At the initiative of George Enescu, money was raised in 1935 to build a concert organ.

*Previuos pages – **The Macca-Villacrosse Arcade***

### Fresco

  An emblem of the Athenaeum, the fresco was painted by Costin Petrescu between 1933 and 1938 and depicts 25 episodes from national history, beginning with the Emperor Trajan's conquest of Dacia. The fresco is 3 m wide and 70 m long. The funds were raised by public subscription.

### Statue of Mihai Eminescu

 In front of the Athenaeum there is a statue of the national poet Mihai Eminescu (1850–1889) by Romanian sculptor Gh. Anghel.

### Concert Hall Cupola

At the wish of Alexandru Odobescu, the ceiling of the Concert Hall was decorated with animal, vegetal and anthropomorphic motifs in gilded polychrome relief, reminiscent of characters from Romanian folklore.

### George Enescu Festival

The international festival was founded in 1958, three years after the death of the great composer. After a period of hiatuses, it resumed in 2003 and is held every two years, usually in September. Over the years, a number of major figures from the world of classical music have participated: Arthur Rubinstein, David Oistrach, Kurt Masur, Herbert von Karajan, Sergiu Celibidache.

### Give a *Leu* for the *Ateneu*!

The fund-raising campaign with the above mentioned slogan was initiated by naturalist Constantin Esarcu (1836–1898) at the end of the nineteenth century. A national lottery was held, which sold 500,000 one-leu tickets. The campaign became a lesson in national unity and meant the awakening of the national consciousness.

### Monumental Staircase

The central part of the beautiful lobby has twelve stucco columns. Four monumental pink Carrara marble staircases lead to the concert hall. Each staircase has a brick column in the centre and forms a balcony overlooking the rotunda.

### Medallions of the Voievodes

The Athenaeum is circular, with a peristyle of six Ionic columns in front. Beneath the peristyle you can see the mosaic heads of five Romanian voievodes: Neagoe Basarab, Alexander the Good, Carol I, Vasile Lupu, and Matei Basarab.

# The Romanian National Museum of Art

The former Royal Palace, designed by architect N. Nenciulescu and built between 1930 and 1937 partly on the site of the old palace of Carol I, has housed the Romanian National Museum of Art since 1948. Like the University Library, the museum suffered during the revolution of December 1989. Eighty per cent of the building was damaged and hundreds of artworks were destroyed. It was not until 2000 that the museum reopened its doors, when the Gallery of European Art was inaugurated.

Alonso Cano,
*The Flagellation of Christ*

⏺ **The museum holds regular temporary exhibitions.**

**MNAR**
- 49–53 Calea Victoriei
- 021 313 30 30
- Open: Wed.–Sun. 11–19 (May–Sep.), 10–18 (Oct.–Apr.) Closed Mon., Tue., 1 and 2 Jan., the 1st and 2nd days of Easter, the 1st and 2nd days of Pentecost, 1 May, 15 Aug., 25 and 26 Dec.
- Entry fee: 8 lei to the Gallery of European Art, 10 lei to the National Gallery, 50% reduction for schoolchildren, students and seniors.
- Disabled access
- www.mnar.arts.ro

## Highlights

1 Former Royal Palace
2 Gallery of European Art
3 Gallery of Old Romanian Art
4 Gallery of Modern Romanian Art
5 Lapidarium
6 Drawings and Engravings Cabinet
7 Decorative Art
8 Oriental Art
9 Auditorium
10 Programmes for the public

### Former Royal Palace

The current look of the palace dates from renovations carried out during the reign of Carol II (1930–1940). On the night of 6–7 December 1926, a calamitous fire swept through the upper storey of the central wing, destroying the Throne Room, Hall of Festivities, Silver Hall, Ladies' Salon, Minor Celebrations Hall, Honorary Luncheon Hall, the Red Cross Office and storeroom, and the Staircase of Honour. Rebuilding work was completed in 1942, and the palace became a symbol of the National Renaissance Carol II wished to inaugurate when he returned to Romania.

### Gallery of European Art

The gallery houses around 3,000 works, including canvases by famous artists Domenico Veneziano, Bronzino, Tintoretto, Rembrandt, Rubens, Monet, Sisley, Rodin, Claudel, El Greco, and Francisco Zurbaran.

### Gallery of Old Romanian Art

The most significant collection of its kind in Romania, with more than 9,500 works, including icons, frescos, tapestry, manuscripts, books, silverware, jewellery, woodcarvings, stone sculptures, and ceramics.

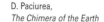

D. Paciurea,
*The Chimera of the Earth*

### 4 Gallery of Modern Romanian Art

The most valuable collection in Romania, with more than 8,500 paintings and 2,500 sculptures. Around 700 works are currently exhibited, dating from the early 19th century to the great classics and the 1960s.

Lucas Cranach, *Venus and Cupid*

Pieter Brueghel the Younger, *Summer*

### 7 Decorative Art

The vast collection comprises around 11,500 items, including embroidery, ceramics, miniatures, furniture, silverware, tin items, and bronzes.

### 8 Oriental Art

More than 3,000 works of Islamic, Chinese and Japanese art, including Iranian carpets, paintings on silk, and jade carvings.

### 9 Auditorium

The auditorium has high-performance technical equipment and is used for concerts, film showings, symposia and conferences.

El Greco, *The Marriage of the Virgin*

### 10 Programmes for the public

The "Bird Concealed in Stone" workshop, dedicated to Brâncuși, "An Hour for Art", and "Artwork under the Magnifying Glass" are just a few of the museums interactive programmes.

### 5 Lapidarium

The sculptures you can admire here originally belonged to monuments of old Romanian architecture, no longer extant: tombstones, door and window setting, columns, capitals.

### 6 Drawings and Engravings Cabinet

A collection of more than 17,000 drawings and 40,000 engravings. In December 1989, the drawings storeroom was destroyed in a fire and a large number of works were lost forever.

Nicolae Grigorescu, *A Flower among Flowers*

### A love story

One of the reasons Grigorescu left France was because of unrequited love. The Romanian artist was in love with one of the daughters of François Millet, probably Marguerite, whom he hoped eventually to marry. His humble circumstances caused him to renounce his love for the master's daughter and to distance himself from the artists' colony at Barbizon.

Left **Th. Aman**, *Soirée*   Centre **Şt. Luchian**, *Decorative Panel*   Right **I. Iser**, *Family of Tartars*

# Other masterpieces

**1** *Venus and Cupid,*
**Lucas Cranach the Elder**
The painting comes from the collection of King Carol I and dates from around 1520. The two mythological figures are sinuous in the elegance of their lines.

**2** *The Four Seasons,*
**Pieter Brueghel the Younger**
It is supposed that these four canvases were painted between 1622 and 1635. Each one evokes the labours of the season illustrated.

**3** *The Adoration of the Shepherds,* **El Greco**
This 3 m high canvas was painted in 1600 for a church in Madrid. As in the museum's other two El Grecos, the strong, cold colours are vivid and the brushwork emphatic.

**4** *Haman before Esther,*
**Rembrandt and workshop**
Painted by Rembrandt and his pupils between 1660 and 1665, the painting covers another one with the same subject, which had been made by the master around 1635. The monumental composition (236 x 186 cm) was inspired by the Old Testament Book of Esther.

*Rodin, The Bronze Age*

**5** *Camille/The Green Dress,*
**Claude Monet**
Painted in 1866, this French Impressionist painting was purchased in 1914 by collector Anastasie Simu.

**6** *The Kiss,*
**Auguste Rodin**
This is one of the great sculptor's best-known works, created at the end of the 19th century. You may also admire The Bronze Age, another masterpiece *(below)*.

**7** *Decorative Panel,*
**Stefan Luchian**
It seems that the painting was part of a cycle of seasons created around 1901. The stylisation of form, the abundance of vegetal elements, and the pastel tones are features of the Art Nouveau style.

**8** *At the Seaside,*
**Nicolae Grigorescu**
A seascape from 1881–1882, in which Grigorescu comes close to Impressionism in the emphasis he places on vibrations of light.

**9** *Danaid,* **Brâncuși**
Exhibited for the first time in 1914, the sculpture was probably made in 1908. The stone is unpolished, preserving its original texture.

**10** *The Chimera of the Earth,*
**Dimitrie Paciurea**
This is one of the Bucharest sculptor's outstanding works, created in 1927–1928. It is part of a highly original series of chimaeras.

## Moments in the History of the Building

1 1812–1815 A residence is built for Dinicu Golescu the Stolnik on the site of the future palace

2 1837 Prince Al. Ghika transforms the residence into a ceremonial palace

3 1859–1866 It becomes the residence of Alexandru Ioan Cuza

4 10 May 1866 Carol of Hohenzollern-Sigmaringen moves into the main building

5 1882 The Royal Palace is fitted with electrical lighting

6 1882–1906 The palace is extended and modernised by architects Paul Gottereau and Karl Liman

7 1926 Queen Maria directs the rebuilding of the upper storey of the central wing after it was destroyed by fire

8 1930–1937 Carol II begins reconstruction and extension work on the palace

9 1944 A new wing of the palace is partly destroyed in the April bombing raid

10 1950 The Museum opens to the public

# Constantin Brâncuși
## (1876–1957)

*Brâncuși is undoubtedly the best known and most admired Romanian artist. Originally from Hobița (Gorj), he trained at the School of Fine Arts in Bucharest, and finished his education at the famous École Nationale Supérieure des Beaux Arts in Paris. After graduating, he went o work in the Auguste Rodin's studio, but withdrew a few months later, realising that "nothing grows in the shadow of great trees." He decided to make his own way in the world capital of culture at that time: Paris. Brâncuși's biography is inseparable from his art, and he spent his entire life perfecting himself. His friends from the time, Marcel Duchamp, Man Ray, and Amedeo Modigliani, have left numerous accounts of how the Romanian artist used to work from dawn to dusk in his white studio in the Impasse Ronsin. Thanks to these labours, he is now recognised as the greatest sculptor of the 20th century. His works are exhibited in all the world's great museums: the Pompidou Centre in Paris (where the artist's studio has been reconstructed), MoMA, and the Guggenheim.*

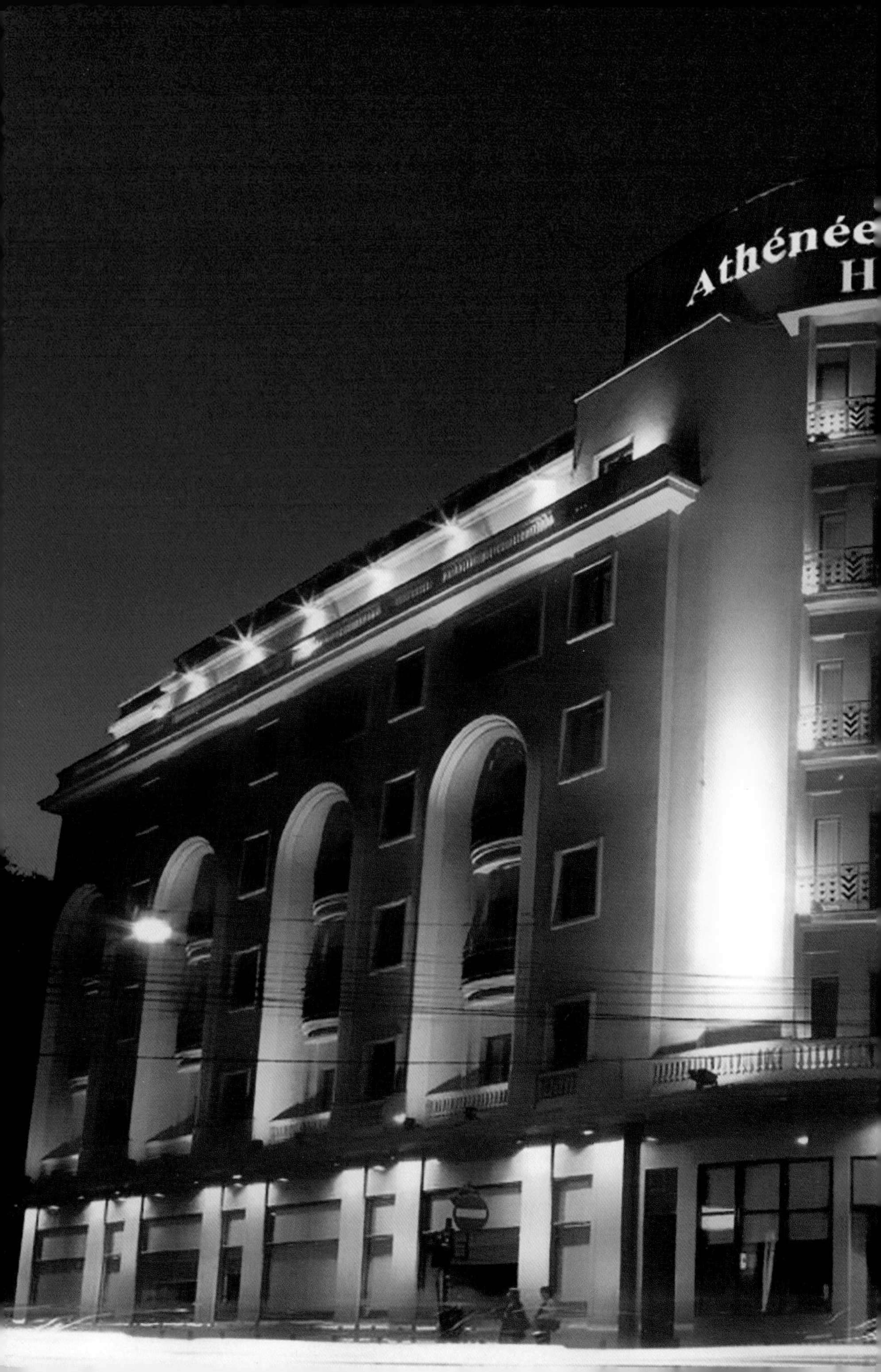
Athénée

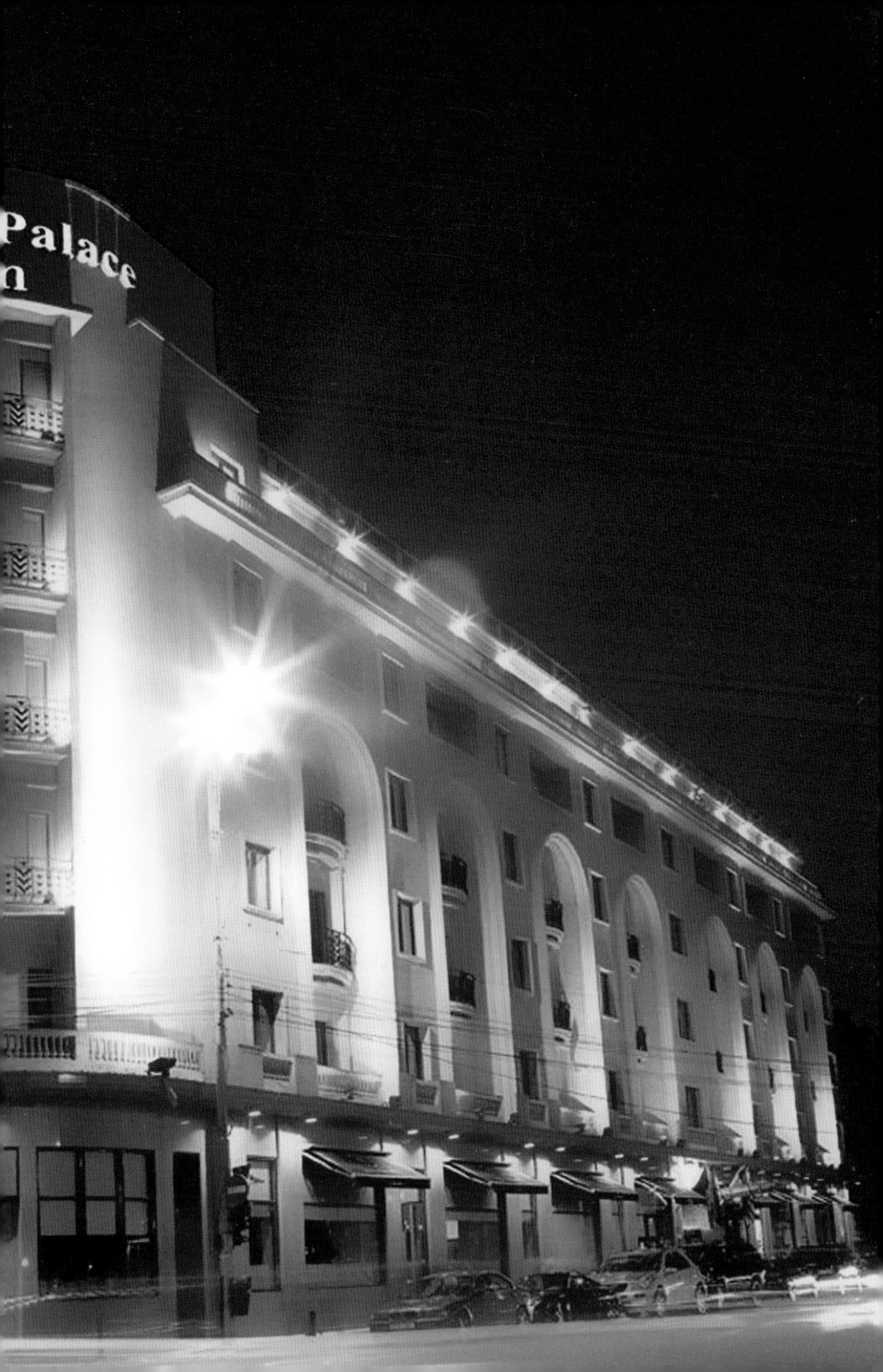
Palace
n

# The Romanian National Museum of History

Inaugurated in 1972, the RNHM is one of the most prestigious institutions of Romanian culture. The museum is housed in a historical monument, formerly the Post Office Palace, designed by architect Al. Săvulescu (1847–1902) and built between 1894 and 1899. The collections include more than 650,000 objects (archaeology, history, numismatics, philately), which are constantly enriched by donations, purchases, and new archaeological discoveries. Since 2003, the building has been undergoing reconsolidation and refurbishing, scheduled for completion in 2014–2015. Thus, only two sections of the permanent exhibition are currently open to visitors: the Historic Treasure and the Lapidarium.

*RNMH*

⚙ Year after year, the museum organises archaeological digs at numerous sites and over the last decade it has become one of the main institutions involved in conservational archaeological research.

• 12 Calea Victoriei
• 021 3158 207
• Wed.–Sun., 10–18 (Apr.–Oct.), 9–17 (Nov.–Mar.)
• Closed Mon., Tue.
• Entry fee: 8 lei (valid one day), reductions for various categories of visitors
• Free entry on the 26th of each month
• www.mnir.ro

## Highlights

1. Romanian Historic Treasure
2. Cernavodă Thinker and Sitting Woman
3. Hinova Hoard
4. Dacian Hoards
5. Dacian Gold Bracelets
6. Copy of Trajan's Column
7. Pietroasa Hoard
8. Engolpion Cross and Ring from Dinogetia-Garvăn
9. Liturgical Banner of Stephen the Great
10. Crowns of the Kings and Queens of Romania

### Romanian Historic Treasure
1 A chronological exhibition of more than 3,000 items made from metal and precious stones, including the oldest gold artefacts to have been created on the territory of what is now Romania, in the 5th millennium B.C.

### The Cernavodă Thinker and Sitting Woman
2 The two figures *(above)* were discovered in a tomb at Cernavodă in 1956. Made from burnt clay, the figurines depict a seated man and woman, who strike a contemplative pose. They are remarkable examples of the Neolithic art that developed in the Lower Danube region in the 5th millennium B.C.

### The Hinova Hoard
3 The hoard was discovered in 1980 in a late-Bronze Age/early-Iron Age tomb. It consists mainly of jewellery (a diadem, bracelets, necklaces) and weighs almost 5 kg.

### Dacian hoards
4 Sumptuous hoards have been unearthed in ancient Dacian burial mounds. In its collections, the museum preserves an impressive number of discoveries from Aghighiol, Băiceni-Cucuteni, Bunești-Averești, Peretu, Poroina, and elsewhere.

### Dacian Gold Bracelets

The 13 Dacian gold bracelets (1st century B.C.–1st century A.D.) recovered to date are part of a series of 24 similar pieces, from five hoards that were illegally unearthed by gangs of treasure-hunters at Sarmizegethusa Regia between 1999 and 2001. These objects *(left)* are among the most spectacular archaeological discoveries to have been made in Romania in the last 170 years. The 13 pieces weigh more than 12 kg in total.

### Copy of Trajan's Column

Trajan's Column was erected in Rome between 107 and 113 A.D. after the Dacian Wars and is the work of architect Apollodorus of Damascus. The Copy in Bucharest *(right)* is the best to have been produced in the last two centuries.

Commissioned during the inter-war period, it was conserved in the Vatican until 1967, and was subsequently brought to Bucharest and installed in the museum in 1972.

### Engolpion Cross and Ring from Dinogetia-Garvăn

Both pieces are from a Byzantine hoard discovered a few decades ago in Dobrogea. The engolpion with sapphires and opals *(right)*, as well as the gold ring, both worked in filigree, were probably made in a workshop in Constantinople and belonged to a high functionary or cleric.

### Pietroasa Hoard

Known as the Hen with the Golden Chicks, this hoard was accidentally discovered by two peasants in 1837. Of the 22 initial pieces, the Romanian state has been able to recover only 12. The pieces preserved in the museum's collection weigh 18.8 kg. The name was inspired by the stylised bird forms of the fibulae. The hoard dates from the early 5th century, when the Ostrogoths occupied the region of the Carpathians and Lower Danube.

### Liturgical Banner of Stephen the Great

A highly rare example of Byzantine embroidery, from the 15th century, measuring 1.24 by 0.95 m and depicting St George. Although it used to be believed this was Stephen the Great's battle standard, the banner in fact had a ceremonial religious role, as it is embroidered with a prayer to St George. It was brought back from Mount Athos in 1917, with the help of France, and was restored in the museum's laboratories in 2011.

### Crowns of the Kings and Queens of Romania

The Crown of King Carol I was made using steel from a cannon captured in the Independence War in 1877. At his coronation in Alba Iulia in 1922, King Ferdinand wore the same steel crown, while Queen Maria's crown *(below)* was created specially for the occasion by French jeweller Felize using solid gold. Felize.

# Cişmigiu Garden

*Located in the heart of the capital, Cişmigiu is the oldest and most beautiful park in Bucharest. It was once a grove, with a lake fed by natural springs, which was first mentioned in the reign of Matei Basarab, when it was called "the Pond of Dura the merchant". The history of the current name goes back to the 18th century. Around 1770, Alexandru Ipsilanti, the ruler of Wallachia, ordered the construction of two drinking fountains. The first was near what is now the entrance to the park, on the side adjacent to Ştirbei Vodă Street. Behind it was built the house of the head of the works: Dumitru Suiulgi-Başa, the Great Cişmigiu (director of drinking fountains or "cişmele").*

*Eminescu's Spring*

🍴 Take lunch or dinner at the famous Monte Carlo Restaurant.

There are a number of terraces on the shore of the lake.

In summer, it is possible to hire a boat. In winter, the lake becomes a skating rink.

"Cişmigiu is a stroll where without paying a penny, / Idle folk come to gawp, ever so many."
*Alexandru Sihleanu (1834–1857)*

## Highlights

1. Oldest Public Garden
2. A Garden According to the European Fashion
3. Central Lake
4. Roman Round
5. Monte Carlo Restaurant
6. Eminescu's Spring
7. Newspaper Kiosk
8. Sissi Stefanidi Spring
9. Rose Garden
10. Exotic Birds

### 1 Oldest Public Garden

Around 1830, Russian General Pavel Kiseleff ordered the insalubrious marsh to be drained and a public garden to be laid out. The work was carried out during the reign of Prince Gheorghe Bibescu. The architect was Karl Friedrich Wilhelm Meyer, the former director of the Imperial Gardens in Vienna. The park was officially opened in 1854.

### 2 A Garden According to the European Fashion

Cişmigiu was in the style of an English park. 30,000 trees were planted, grottos, flowerbeds and bridges were made, and 100 oak benches were provided. Toward the end of the 19th century, Cişmigiu could be regarded as one of the most beautiful parks in Europe.

### Central Lake

Meyer transformed the former pond into a lake with a drainage system to allow it to be cleaned easily. In the middle of the lake was a fountain. A year later, the lake dried up because of the rubbish thrown into it by the cobblers who had workshops in the area!

### Monte Carlo Restaurant

Built by the famous architec Ion Mincu, destroyed by bombs in the World War II, the restaurant *(bottom left)* has been completely rebuilt and is now a tourist attraction. In the 1960s, Maria Tănase used to sing here.

### Newspaper Kiosk

The newspaper kiosk *(below)* at the entrance of the garden is a replica of the one installed by the municipality in 1878.

### Sissi Stefanidi Spring

The sculpture, created by Ion Dimitriu-Bîrlad, depicts a mother grieving for her daughter, emptying water from a pitcher. The statue was made at the request of the Stefanidi family,at the death of their daughter.

### Rose Garden

Consisting of stonewalls, wooden pergolas and iron chains for the exhibition of hanging roses, the garden is unique in the diversity of its dendrological material.

### Roman Round

Near Schitu Măgureanu St can be found the so-called Roman Round, which has busts of famous Romanian writers, including Eminescu, Odobescu, Maiorescu, Caragiale, Creangă, Hasdeu, Bălcescu and others.

### Eminescu's Spring

Not far from Știrbei Vodă Boulevard, the spring is said to have once had the best water in the capital. The poet Mihai Eminescu lived nearby and often came here to drink.

### Exotic Birds

In summer the lake by the Eminescu Spring is home to more than 100 exotic birds: black and white swans, mandarin ducks, Canadian geese, and peacocks.

# Village Museum

The Dimitrie Gusti National Village Museum stretches over 30 hectares and currently features 322 structures. The museum recreates the traditional atmosphere of the Romanian rural community. It was inaugurated on 10 May 1936 in the presence of King Carol II, at the same time as the inauguration of Herăstrău Park, of which it is part.

### Auriferous Rock Mill
A machine from Transylvania dating from 1925 and brought to the museum in 1950. It is made up of nine hammers that fall rhythmically, crushing the gold-bearing ore.

The entrance to the Village Museum

## Highlights

1. Typical Houses
2. Huts
3. Auriferous Rock Mill
4. Watermills and Windmills
5. Fishery
6. Church from the Village of Răpciuni
7. Wallachian Inn
8. Oil Press
9. Wooden Church from Maramureş
10. "Vâltoare"

### Typical Houses
The houses exhibited were dismantled and rebuilt piece by piece. The oldest dates from the 17th century (Zapodeni, Vaslui County), the most recent from the 20th century (Soveja, Vrancea County). Writer Victor Ion Popa designed the layout.

At Easter, Whitsun, the Feast of Ss Peter and Paul, the Feast of St Demetrios, Christmas, and Dragobete, the museum holds fairs that bring together craftsmen from all over the country. Visitors can admire, buy, and sample traditional Romanian crafts, food, and drinks.

At the entrance, there is a souvenir shop and a soft-drinks stand.

• 28-30 Kiseleff Chaussée
• 021 317 91 10
• Open: Mon. 9–17, Tue.–Sun. 9–19
• Entrance fee: 6 lei; schoolchildren and students: 1.5 lei
• www.muzeul-satului.ro

### Huts
The museum also has three sunken earth huts, all dating from the 19th century and typical of the Moldavia and Oltenia regions (main photo).

### Watermills and Windmills
Nine watermills and three windmills (below) from the 19th century are exhibited. They were used for milling cereals and pumping water.

### 5 Fishery

A structure for the sorting, processing and temporary storage of fish, this is another of the museum's interesting features. Originally from Jurilovca in Tulcea County, it dates from 1929.

### 7 Wallachian Inn

The La Bariera Inn was brought from Vălenii de Munte in the Prahova region. Built at the beginning of the 19th century, the inn was frequented by merchants. Legend says that Alexandru Ioan Cuza once visited the inn. Visitors to the museum can eat lunch here.

### 9 Wooden Church from Maramureş

The church is from the village of Dragomireşti and dates from 1722. Remarkable are the decorative features on the arched posts of the open porch, as well as the steep roof with its so-called "double hem".

### 10 Vâltoare

The "vâltoare" uses the power of mountain streams to wash fabrics. The water is channelled into a pool, in which woollen rugs are whirled around, making them thicker and fluffier.

### A Unique Museum

When the museum was founded, there were already two other open-air museums in Europe: the Skansen Museum (Stockholm) and the Bigdo Museum (Lillehamer). In 1929, the Ethnographic Museum of Transylvania opened in Cluj. The museum in Bucharest proved to be the most original from the outset, thanks to the work of folklorist and sociologist Dimitrie Gusti. He periodically allowed families of peasants to live in the museum.

### 6 Church from the Village of Răpciuni

The church dates from 1773 and was brought to the museum in 1958, after the village of Răpciuni (Neamţ County) was moved to make way for the Bicaz Reservoir.

### 8 Oil Press

The museum has two hydraulic oil presses, used for processing pumpkin, hemp, and sunflower seeds. One is from the village of Romoşel (Hunedoara County), the other from the Alba region (Zlatna), both dating from the 19th century. The second looks older, and is housed in a thatched wooden structure.

*Following pages* – **House from the Village Museum**

# Caru' cu bere (The Beer Dray)

*With a history of more than one hundred years, the beer hall on Stavropoleos Street is a place laden with tradition. Every object tells its own story, and the architecture is a reminder of why Bucharest used to be called the Little Paris. The murals, stained glass windows, and carved balustrades are distinctive features. A hundred years ago, the festive atmosphere, which still lives, attracted leading fi gures of the day, including famous writers. Over the years, the building has undergone a number of alterations: after the World War I it was extended, in 1948 it was nationalised (and the interior decorations were whitewashed over), and in 1964 it was restored. Restored again in 2006, the restaurant has become one of the city's top attractions.*

*The Beer Dray sign*

⏱ **You can find special lunch menus at low prices. Reservations required.**

- *5 Stavropoleos St*
- *021 313 75 60*
  *0726 282 373*
- *Open: Mon.–Thur., Sun. 8–24, Fri. and Sat. 8–2*
- *www.carucubere.ro*

## Highlights

1. A Historic Monument
2. Fairytale Interior
3. Film Set
4. Old Man Ghiță
5. The Cellar
6. Culinary Specialties
7. The Beer
8. Beer Dray Mici
9. Souvenir Shop
10. The Clock

### 1 A Historic Monument

The original location of the beer hall was in the Zlătari Inn on Podul Mogoşoaiei. The present beer hall was designed by Austrian architect Siegfried Kofczinsky, commissioned by merchant Nicolae Mircea, the first owner, and was built between 1875 and 1892.

### 2 Fairytale Interior

Both the façade and the interior are in the Neo-Gothic style. The furniture and woodwork have been restored to their original splendour, and are made from wood joined without nails.

### 3 Film Set

The distinctive atmosphere from a bygone age has attracted many Romanian directors, and a number of important films have been shot here: *Two Tickets*, *Telegrams* and *Darclée*.

### 4 Old Man Ghiță

The beer hall's symbol is Old Man Ghiță and his lamp. He keeps watch from behind the wooden balustrade on the right of the main hall. A cellarman by trade, for decades he kept going down in the all-time famous cellar hidden away among the beer and wine barrels.

### 6 Culinary Specialties

For more than a century, the Beer Dray has been renowned in Bucharest for its delicious culinary specialties. Hot dogs with horseradish and pork with stewed cabbage are among the gastronomic attractions nowadays. In the photograph: stuffed cabbage leaves with polenta and sour cream.

STR. STAVROPOLEOS

### 7 The Beer

Even today, the main attraction is, of course, the beer, made since 1879 to a unique and still undisclosed recipe.

### 8 Beer Dray *Mici*

Another culinary attraction are the famous Romanian *mici*, made according to a secret recipe since the inter-war period, it is said.

### 10 The Clock

A feature as original as the beer, the clock has been tirelessly telling the time since the first customer entered the beer hall in 1879.

## Beer in the Romanian Countries

Beer is attested since the olden days in the Romanian Countries. For example, in the 16th century, a foreign traveller related that at the court of Vasile Lupu, in Moldavia, beer was held in high esteem. But brewing did not begin in earnest until after 1800. It was a German who opened the first brewery, in 1809. The word halbă (beer mug) comes from the German halbes liter. "Ţap" ("he-goat"), a smaller mug, takes its name from a renowned German brewer by the name of "Bock" (he-goat, in German)!

### 5 The Cellar

Opened in 1930, the cellar is now like a museum. Beer mugs from various epochs are exhibited here, and you can also listen to live music.

### 9 Souvenir Shop

Here you can buy Beer Dray mugs, plates, and teapots engraved with the name of the beer hall.

# Stavropoleos Church

*Hidden among tall buildings behind the Romanian National Museum of History, there stands a small but spectacular church, whose name, Stavropoleos, comes from the Greek Stauropolis (City of the Cross). Stavropoleos dates from 1724, when a Greek monk founded an inn and church on this site. In 1726, Ioannikos was appointed Metropolitan of Stavropoleos. The names of the builders have unfortunately been lost, and only that of Iordan, the stucco maker, has survived down the centuries.*

**Porch**
**3** The church porch was carved by master stonemasons from the Brâncoveanu period. Particularly impressive are the vegetal decorations, the floral band, and the columns. The porch combines the Baroque and Oriental styles.

*Stavropoleos Church*

◐ **The Monastery is dedicated to the Archangels Michael and Gabriel, St Justin Martyr and Philosopher, St Athanasios, and St Charalambos Martyr.**
**The collection of artefacts can be viewed by appointment.**

- *4 Stavropoleos St*
- *021 313 47 47*
- *www.stavropoleos.ro*

## Highlights

1. A Zealous Monk
2. Stavropoleos Ensemble
3. Porch
4. Restoration by Architect Mincu
5. The Interior Murals
6. Chiostro
7. Art Collection
8. Library
9. Choir
10. Archaeological Finds

**A Zealous Monk**
**1** The foundation of the church is linked to the name of a Greek monk from Epirus, Ioannikos Stratonikeas. In April 1722, he built an inn and then a church, which was financed by the inn, a common practice in those days. In time, the monastery amassed great wealth: country estates, vineyards, houses, cattle, and Gypsy slaves.

**Stavropoleos Ensemble**
**2** Of the original complex, only the Brâncoveanu-style church has survived. The other buildings were designed by Ion Mincu during restoration work carried out in the early 20th century.

**Restoration by Architect Mincu**
**4** Restoration, needy after the earthquakes of 1802 and 1832, was begun in 1900 and completed after the death of Ion Mincu (1912), thanks to his student, architect Alexandru Zagoritz. A belfry, monastic wing, and chiostro were added on that occasion. The most recent restoration work took place between 2003 and 2005.

## The Interior Murals

**5** The murals are remarkable for their sweeping scope. In the nave, at the base of the spire, the Angelic Liturgy is depicted. On the west wall of the church there are portraits of the founders: Archimandrite Ioannikos and his brothers; and Prince Nicolae Mavrocordat and his family.

## Chiostro

**6** Next to the church, architect Mincu built a chiostro, a courtyard, where the columns, slabs and tombstones of the old monastery can be viewed *(above, central photograph)*.

## Art Collection

**7** Among the antique objects in the monastery's collection are the censer donated to the church by its founder in 1734, a throne with the coat of arms of the Mavrocordat family, a Brâncoveanu-period candelabra, and fragments of murals salvaged from churches demolished under communism. The collection can be visited by appointment.

## Library

**8** Stavropoleos Church has a collection of almost 10,000 volumes, including, besides patristic and biblical texts, an important collection of old manuscripts and books in Greek, Slavonic and Romanian (more than 80 manuscripts and 400 printed books). The library can be visited by appointment (telephone or e-mail).

## Choir

**9** The church choir has a repertoire of Neo-Byzantine music (a single voice accompanied by an ison, a prolonged vocal drone), rare in Romanian churches today.

## Archaeological Finds

**10** During municipal work carried out in 1998, the ruins of walls from different periods of the old Stavropoleos inn were unearthed.

## Deacon Arghezi

(1880 –1967)

Few know that poet Tudor Arghezi (real name: Ion N. Theodorescu) was a priest in his youth. He seems to have had a mystical awakening and became a monk, following the example of an uncle, who was a bishop. In 1900, he was appointed deacon of Stavropoleos Monastery, where he officiated for a time. Aged 19, he entered Cernica Monastery. A few years later, he renounced the monastic life, subsequently oscillating between faith and atheism.

Left **The entrance to Cotroceni Palace**   Center **The Central University Library**   Right **Al.I. Cuza (statue)**

# Moments in History

### 20 September 1459
**1** Legend has it that Bucharest was founded by the shepherd Bucur. But the true founder was probably Mircea the Elder, in the late 14th century. The first written mention of the city is in a khrysoboulion issued by Vlad the Impaler, whereby he granted an estate to some boyars. The Dâmbovița Fortress was of strategic importance. In 1465, Radu the Fair transformed it into a princely residence.

### 1659
**2** In the summer of 1595, the grand vizier Sinan Pasha occupied Bucharest during the war against Michael the Brave. The city was burnt to the ground and rebuilt a year later. In 1659, during the reign of Gheorghe Ghika, Bucharest became the capital of Wallachia by order of the Ottoman Empire.

### 1689
**3** Bucharest was occupied by Austrian troops for the first time, during a war against the Ottomans.

### 21 March/ 2 April 1821
**4** Between 1711/1716 and 1821, Wallachia and Moldavia were ruled by the Phanariots and began to develop and flourish. Paved streets and the first schools appeared. The Phanariot period came to an end with the revolt led by Tudor Vladimirescu in 1821. On 21 March he entered Bucharest in triumph. The district where he pitched his tents ("tabere") was later named Taberei Road.

### 19 October 1829
**5** Following the Russo-Turkish War of 1828-29, Wallachia and Moldavia were occupied by the Russians. General Pavel Kiseleff headed the Russian administration of Wallachia until 1834. Kiseleff established the Organic Regulation (Romania's first constitution) and commenced modernisation of the city.

### 11 June 1848
**6** The revolutions sweeping Europe reached Bucharest, where a public demonstration led to the abdication of ruler Gheorghe Bibescu.

**The statue of Carol I in Revolution Square**

### 7 24 January 1859
In the lobby of the Concordia Hotel, it was decided to elect Al.I. Cuza ruler of Wallachia (on 5 January 1859 he had been elected ruler of Moldavia). There followed an economic and demographic explosion. Bucharest had 120,000 inhabitants. On 24 January it became the country's capital.

### 8 10 May 1866
Karl of Hohenzollern Sigmaringen, later Carol I, enters the capital and is greeted with enthusiasm. The city is gradually transformed, and in the inter-war period it comes to be known as "the Little Paris".

### 9 23 August 1944
Romania joins the Allied side in the World War II. Marshal Antonescu is arrested following a coup planned by King Michael I.

### 10 22 December 1989
The revolution spreads from Timişoara to Bucharest. Nicolae and Elena Ceauşescu flee to Târgovişte by helicopter, and are captured and executed.

## City Modernisation

### 1 1661
The first cobbled streets appear in Bucharest.

### 2 1779
The first public drinking fountains are established.

### 3 1869
The Bucharest-Giurgiu railway line and Bucharest's first station, Filaret, are opened.

### 4 13 September 1872
The Northern Station and the Bucharest-Ploieşti railway line are inaugurated.

### 5 1871
The first trams: horsedrawn covered wagons for up to ten passengers.

### 6 9 December 1894
Bucharest's first electric tram line, running along the boulevard between Obor and Cotroceni.

### 7 1882
Electricity is introduced. The first generator was by the Royal Palace (on the site of what is now the Central University Library) and also supplied the Cotroceni Palace.

### 8 1883
The first telephone line links the Socec Bookshop (on the site of what is now the Victoria Department Store) with its printing press. By 1898, there were around 700 telephone subscribers.

### 9 1930–1935
A marshy area is drained to make way for Herăstrău Park in 1936.

### 10 16 November 1979
The first Metro line is opened, running for 8.1 km between Semănătoarea and Timpuri Noi.

Left **The National Museum of Art**   Center **Peasant Museum**   Right **The Geology Museum**

# Museums

### 1 Grigore Antipa National Museum of Natural History

Founded in 1834, this was one of the world's first natural history museums. It has more than 30,000 unique exhibits. It was recently reopened after a lengthy restoration.
⊛ *1 Kiseleff Chaussée • 021 312 88 26 •*
*Tue.–Sun., 10–18 • www.antipa.ro*

### 2 The Romanian National Museum of Art

The museum is housed in the former Royal Palace and has a valuable collection of European art, as well as numerous Romanian and foreign masterpieces *(p. 20–23)*.

### 3 Village Museum

One of the most valuable ethnographic museums, it was created by Romanian sociologist Dimitrie Gusti in 1936 *(p. 30–33)*.

### 4 The Romanian National Museum of History

Housed in a building with an interesting past, the museum covers 8,000 m² and features significant exhibits for the history of Romania *(pag. 26–27)*.

### 5 Cotroceni National Museum

The museum recreates the atmosphere of the mediaeval Cotroceni Church and also the former royal court of Ferdinand. The building

is a remarkable historic and architectural monument. ⊛ *1 Geniului Boulevard •*
*021 221 12 00 • Mon.–Sun., 9–17.30 • Entrance fee*
*• www.muzeulcotroceni.ro*

### 6 The Romanian Peasant Museum

With a rich collection of icons, wayside crosses, ceramics, folk costumes, etc., the museum is housed in a Neo-Romanian historic monument. It was founded in 1906 by Al. Tzigara-Samurcaş. The Museum on the

**The Antipa Museum**

Chaussée, as it was known, has undergone many transformations over the years, but its present style was defined under the inspired directorship of Horia Bernea from 1990 to 2000. The museum's originality and vision were recognised in 1996, when it was declared European Museum of the Year.
🕾 *3 Chaussée Kiseleff • 021 317 96 61 •*
*Mon.–Sun., 10–18 •*
*www.muzeultaranuluiroman.ro*

### 7 The Theodor Pallady Museum (Melik House)

Built in 1760, this is the oldest civil building in Bucharest to have been preserved in its original form. After 1820, it belonged to the family of Iacob Melik. Bequeathed to the Armenian community, it was a home for poor widows between 1921 and 1947. It has been a museum since 1994. The museum exhibits the collection of Serafina and Gheorghe Răut, which includes works by Pallady and European paintings and drawings from the 16th to 19th centuries.
🕾 *22 Spătarului St • 021 211 49 79 •*
*Wed.–Sun., 11–19 (May–Sep.), 10–18 (Oct.–Apr.);*
*closed Mon., Tue., 1 Jan., Easter Sunday, 25 Dec.*

### 8 The Museum of Art Collections

The museum is housed in the historic Romanit Palace, built in the early 19th century during the reign of Alexandru Ghika (1834–1842), which was originally the Chancellery and later the Administrative Court of Wallachia. Temporarily closed

**Muzeul Theodor Pallady**

for renovation. 🕾 *111 Calea Victoriei • 021 211 17 49 • Wed.–Sun., 11–19 (May–Sep.), 10–18 (Oct.– Apr.); closed Thur., Fri., 1 Jan., Easter Sunday, 25 Dec.*

### 9 The Museum of the Municipality of Bucharest

The museum is housed in the former residence of Grigore Suțu the High Postelnik. Founded in 1921, the museum has more than 400,000 items. 🕾 *2 Brătianu Boulevard (University Square) • 021 315 68 58 • Wed.–Sun., 10–18 • www.muzeulbucurestiului.ro*

### 10 The National Museum of Geology

Founded in 1990, the museum is dedicated to mineralogy, earth dynamics, mineral substances, crystals, etc.
🕾 *2 Chaussée Kiseleff • 021 212 89 52 •*
*Open daily 10–18 • Entrance fee*
*• www.geology.ro*

Left **Alexandru Ioan Cuza Park**   Center **Herăstrău Park**   Right **Carol Park (fomerly Liberty Park)**

# Parks and Gardens

### 1 Herăstrău Park (Carol II National Park)

The park was laid out in 1936 and is the largest in Bucharest, with a surface area of 110 hectares. Before 1930, the area was a marsh, which was drained between 1930 and 1935. The park's attractions include a summer theatre, exhibition pavilions, and sports clubs. *See also p. 104.*

### 2 Cişmigiu Garden

Cişmigiu *(above)* is the oldest public garden in Bucharest, and was first laid out in 1847. It is located in the centre of the city and covers around 16 hectares. *(p. 28–29).*

### 3 Carol I Park (Liberty Park)

Located on Filaret Hill, the park was designed by French landscape architect Edouard Redont and laid out between 1900 and 1906. The park is home to the Roman Arenas, for open-air performances, the National Technical Museum, the Astronomic Institute of the Romanian Academy, and the Heroes' Monument (Mausoleum), built in 1962 *(right).*

### 4 Tineretului Park

Situated in the southern part of Bucharest, the park covers around 80 hectares. Work on the park, directed by architect Valentin Donose, commenced in 1965 and was finished in 1974. The Ioan Kunst Ghermănescu Hall (formerly Sala Polivalentă) is a venue for sporting and cultural activities.

### 5 Kiseleff Park

Situated on both sides of the boulevard of the same name, this small but elegant park was first laid out in 1832. Covering just 31,690 m², it is home to the Monument to the Romanian Infantry *(opposite, top right)*, cast in bronze by sculptor Ioan Bolborea.

### 6 The National Park

Also known by its older name of 23 August, the park is home to the National Sports Complex. The National Arena

(formerly Lia Manoliu) Stadium, which reopened in 2011 after massive renovation work, is nearby. The summer theatre hosts concerts and shows, and there are open-air restaurants on the shore of the lake.

### 7 Alexandru Ioan Cuza Park (Titan or IOR Park)

The park covers around 85 hectares and is located in the eastern part of the city. Its attractions include a fountain sixteen metres in diameter, a small wooden church in the Maramureş style, and a lake with an island that is home to exotic birds. The acronym IOR comes from the nearby Întreprinderea Optică Română (Romanian Optics Factory). The park, very popular in the Titan district, is packed with roller skaters and families with children during weekends.

### 8 The State Circus Park

Opened in 1961, the park covers 26 hectares around the State Circus. Egyptian lotuses grow on the banks of its Natural Springs Lake. The park features carvings made from tree trunks by artist C. Teodorescu.

### 9 The Dimitrie Brândză Botanical Garden

Named after its founder, the garden is one of Bucharest's attractions. It has been located on its current site since 1884. More information on p. 114. ✆ *32 Chaussée Cotroceni • 021 318 15 59 • Mon.–Sun., 8–20*

### 10 The Zoo

It was founded in 1955, initially as "zoological corners" in the capital's main parks and in Băneasa Forest. Covering an area of six hectares in Băneasa Forest, the Zoo (left) has been in its present location since 1959. More information on p. 60 ✆ *4 Aleea Vadul Moldovei • 021 269 06 00 • Mon.–Fri. 9–19; Sat.–Sun 9–17*

Left **Mihail Sadoveanu**   Center **Haimanale village, birthplace of I.L. Caragiale**   Right **Memorial plaque, Lipscani**

# Writers and Artists

### 1 Theodor Aman
(1831–1891)

Although born in Câmpulung-Muscel, the artist spent the greater part of his life in Bucharest. He founded the first Romanian school of fine arts in Bucharest. The city commemorates him in the museum named after him, on C.A. Rosetti St. The sculptures on the façade and the furniture were made by Aman himself.

### 2 Tudor Arghezi
(1880–1967)

Arghezi's name is strongly linked to Bucharest. Born in the capital, he left his mark on it when, in 1926, he bought a 15,000 $m^2$ plot of land on Mărțișorului Hill, where he planted an orchard and vines and built himself a manor house, which is now a museum (26 Mărțișorului St).

### 3 Maria Tănase
(1913–1963)

Born into a poor family in the brick makers' quarter, Maria Tănase became a symbol of Romanian folk music. She was discovered and promoted by Constantin Tănase, performing at his variety theatre. She led a tumultuous life, full of affairs with famous men of the time (Armand Călinescu) and was involved in espionage.

### 4 Ion Luca Caragiale
(1852–1912)

The greatest Romanian playwright was born in Haimanale village (now I.L. Caragiale) in Dâmbovița County and made Bucharest his adopted home. A regular customer at the Gambrinus and other beer halls, Caragiale created characters that have not dated. The National Theatre is now named after him.

### 5 Mircea Eliade
(1907–1986)

A philosopher, historian of religions and writer, one of the most important thinkers of the 20th century. The streets around Rosetti Square, where Eliade *(below)* spent his youth, still preserve something of the fascinating atmosphere of his fantastic novellas. He studied at the primary school on Mântuleasa St and then at the Spiru Haret Lycée, where he was a classmate of Constantin Noica, one of the greatest thinkers of late 20th century.

## Mihai Eminescu
(1850–1889)

Although born in Botoşani, in the north of the country, the poet arrived in the capital while a young man, taking a job as a prompter and copyist at the National Theatre. Between 1877 and 1879, he was a journalist for *Timpul*, one of the most famous newspapers of the day. He lived by Cişmigiu Park and local legend tells that he used to quench his thirst at the drinking fountain that nowbears his name.

## George Enescu
(1881–1955)

A composer, violinist, professor, pianist and conductor, Enescu is regarded as Romania's most important musician. Born in Liveni, Botoşani County, he divided his time between Bucharest and living abroad. The National Philharmonic, Bucharest's most important music festival, and the national museum *(right)* housed in the

building where Enescu lived for a few years are all named after him today.

## Nicolae Grigorescu
(1838–1907)

The great painter was born in the village of Pitaru, Dâmboviţa County. After the death of his father, the family moved to Bucharest. In 1861, he was awarded a scholarship to study in Paris.

## Liviu Rebreanu
(1885–1944)

A novelist, playwright and Academy member, Rebreanu was the indisputable father of the modern Romanian novel. Born in Târlişua, Bistriţa-Năsăud County, the writer spent many years in Bucharest. The Liviu Rebreanu Memorial Museum is housed in the flat the writer bought for his daughter, next to that of his friend, the poet Ion Minulescu, at 19 Gh. Marinescu Boulevard, near Cotroceni Palace and the Botanical Garden.

## Lucia Sturdza Bulandra
(1873–1961)

A descendent of the aristocratic Sturdza family (who forbade her to use the surname on the stage), the actress founded the prestigious Municipal Theatre, which was renamed the Bulandra Theatre after her death.

**George Enescu Museum**

Left **Stavropoleos Church**   Center and right **The Romanian Patriarchate, details**

# Churches and Monasteries

**1 Mihai Vodă Monastery**
One of the city's oldest monasteries, Mihai Vodă was founded by Michael the Brave in 1594. It was a princely residence, military hospital, medical school, and deposit for the state archives. Today, only the church and belfry remain. 🔍 *35 Sapienţei St*

**2 Radu Vodă Monastery**
Situated near Union Square and Patriarchate Hill, the Radu Vodă ensemble is a historic monument and centre of Romanian spirituality. It comprises a church *(below)*, bell tower (the city's highest, at 25 m), Theological Seminary, and the ruins of a princely palace. The monastery has a long and intricate history: it was founded by Voievode Alexandru II (reigned 1568–1577), destroyed by the Turkish invaders led by Sinan Pasha, and rebuilt by Voievode Radu Mihnea at the beginning of the 17th century. 🔍 *24A Radu Vodă St*

**3 Stavropoleos Church**
The small but exquisite church, behind the Romanian National Museum of History, is one of the most representative buildings of the post-Brâncoveanu style. It is described in detail on pp. 36–37. 🔍 *4 Stavropoleos St*

**4 Plumbuita Monastery**
The monastery was founded in 1560, but the present buildings date from 1647, in the reign of Matei Basarab. Its name comes from the fact that for a long time its roof was leaded ("plumbuit"). 🔍 *58 Plumbuita St*

**5 The Church of Ss Peter and Paul the Apostles**
A wooden church was documented on the site in 1585–1586, and this was replaced by a stone church in 1636 in the reign of Matei Basarab. The beautiful stone inscription and door setting dates from the time of Ştefan Cantacuzino. 🔍 *33A Sf. Apostoli St*

**6 Domnească Church**
Also known as the Church of the Old Court, the Church of St Anthony was built in the reign of Mircea Ciobanul in the mid-16th century and is considered to be the oldest

in Bucharest. It has been rebuilt, enlarged and altered many times, particularly in the reigns of Bibescu-Vodă and Barbu Știrbei. Worthy of note is the decoration of the façades, consisting of alternating bands of brick and plaster.

🕭 *33 Franceză St*

### Antim Monastery

The beautiful monastery *(below)* was founded by Bishop Antim Ivireanul, who was born in Iviria (the old name for Georgia) and came to Wallachia in the reign of Constantin Brâncoveanu, around the year 1690. Built between 1713 and 1715, the monastery was affected by the systematisation carried out in the area under communism in the

1980s. The church was moved 25 m and rotated 13 degrees. Unfortunately, it is hidden now behind the massive buildings on Unirii Boulevard.

🕭 *29 Antim Ivireanul St*

### Colțea Church

The Colțea Complex, near University Square, is a Bucharest landmark. Founded by Mihai Cantacuzino the Spatharius in 1702,

it has been rebuilt and renovated, regaining its original beauty. The church was founded by Udrea the Court Victualler in the mid-17th century.

🕭 *1 Brătianu Boulevard*

### Kretzulescu Church

Built in 1720–1722, the Church of the Dormition of the Theotokos *(above)* is one of the most valuable architectural monuments in Bucharest. It was built at the behest of Iordache Kretzulescu the High Logothete and his wife, one of the daughters of Constantin Brâncoveanu. It originally had an inn, which was demolished to make way for the Royal Palace. Next to the church a bust of Corneliu Coposu (a symbol of anti-communist resistance) was erected after 1989. 🕭 *47 Calea Victoriei*

### Cașin Monastery

The foundation stone of the church was laid in 1937, on a site provided by the City Hall. The building combines the Wallachian Brâncoveanu style (the entrance columns) with the Byzantine style (the mosaics, the Greek Cross plan, the lofty, spacious architecture).

🕭 *16 Mărăști St*

Left **Radu Vodä Monastery**    Center **Bucur the Shepherd Church**    Right **St Joseph's Cathedral, detail**

# Other Places of Worship

### 1 Bucur the Shepherd Church
It is not known exactly when the church was built, but legend tells that it was erected by Bucur, the founder of the city. The historical evidence reveals that it dates from the 17th century, however. The church stood on the same hill as the Negru Vodä Monastery and was used as a chapel. Hidden among communist-era blocks, the small church has particularly rich icons.
🜚 *33 Radu Vodä St*

### 2 The Russian Church
Located near the University, the Russian Church was built in 1905–1909 at the behest of Tsar Nicholas. The seven Russian-style cupolas were originally covered in gold leaf. The church served the Russian Embassy. It is currently undergoing restoration. Read more on pp 87–88.
🜚 *3 Ion Ghica St*

### 3 Church of St Spiridon the New
The largest Orthodox church in Bucharest stands not far from Union Square. The original church, built by Scarlat Ghika in 1767–1768, stood here until 1852, when it was replaced by the present Gothic structure. The murals are by Gh. Tattarescu.
🜚 *29–31 Calea Şerban Vodä*

### 4 St Joseph's Cathedral
The Cathedral of the Roman-Catholic Archbishopric of Bucharest, it was designed by Viennese architect Friedrich Schmidt and built in the Romanic style with Gothic features between 1873 and 1884. The Cathedral was severely damaged in the World War II. 🜚 *19 General Berthelot St*

### 5 Domniţa Bălaşa Church
Hidden behind the communist-era blocks of Union Square, the church is remarkable for its size and beauty. The original church was built in 1743-1744 at the behest of Domniţa Bălaşa (daughter of Constantin Brâncoveanu). The present church dates from 1881–1885 in the reign of Carol I and is in the Neo-Romanian style. 🜚 *60 Sfinţii Apostoli Petru şi Pavel St*

## 6 The Anglican Church of the Resurrection

Situated near Icoanei Garden, the Anglican Church *(above)* was built in 1913-14, under the patronage of Queen Maria, and was consecrated in 1922. The English-style redbrick building was designed by architect Victor Gh. Ştefănescu. Sunday services are held in English. ❂ *2 Alexandru D. Xenopol St*

## 7 The Italian Church

Many people pass the church without noticing it, because of the tall blocks that flank it *(right)*. Consecrated in 1916, the church served the Italian community. It is impressive for its solemnity and its beautiful interior murals. Services are in Italian and Polish. The church hosts concerts of baroque organ music. ❂ *28 Bălcescu Boulevard*

## 8 The Lutheran Evangelical Church

The church dates from 1853, when it was one of the city's tallest buildings, at 36 m. The architecture combines Romanic and Renaissance elements. In the church can be found the tomb of William Prince of Albania, the nephew of Queen Elisabeta of Romania. The church hosts frequent concerts of organ and violin music. ❂ *2 Luterană St, near Sala Palatului*

## 9 The Choral Temple

This is the synagogue of the Jewish community of Bucharest and the largest Jewish place of worship in the city. A historic monument, the synagogue was built in the neo-Moorish style in 1864-1866 and has been restored many times. In front of the choral temple there is a monument to the victims of the Holocaust. ❂ *9 Sf. Vineri St, near Union Square*

## 10 Church of St Eleftherios the New

One of the capital's largest churches, whose building work began in 1935, but was not completed until 1971, because of World War II and the communist period. Read more on p. 114.
❂ *1 Sf. Elefterie St*

*Following pages – Old door, detail*

Left and right **Gravestones**   Centre **The tomb of Mihai Eminescu, detail**

# Bellu Cemetery

Up until the 19th century, the people of Bucharest buried their dead in their churchyards, but there were also cemeteries outside the city, mainly for paupers. In 1850, it was decided to create new cemeteries, one of which was to be sited on Şerban Vodă Lane, where Baron Barbu Bellu (1825–1900), the Minister of Religions and Justice, owned a large garden, which he donated to the Town Council. In 1852, under the direction of C.A. Rosetti (1816–1885), work commenced on the new cemetery, which was completed in 1858. Following a government decision to abolish churchyard cemeteries, wealthy families moved their ancestral remains to Bellu. Over the years, the most illustrious members of Bucharest society were buried here, and the cemetery became a true open-air museum, stretching over 28 hectares. Many of the tombs are works of art, created by famous sculptors such as D. Paciurea, K. Storck, and M. Pătraşcu. The lanes are marked with plaques, enabling visitors to locate famous graves easily. Since 2011, the cemetery can be visited on Museums Night.

## 1 The Chapel

The first chapel, designed by Alexandru Orescu and built in 1853, had murals by Constantin Lecca. After it fell into disrepair, it was replaced by a structure in the style of the Karlsbad Cathedral, in 1890. The first murals were by Mihail Popp, and later murals by Dimitrie Belizarie and Arthur Verona.

## 2 Writers' Lane

Along with Actors' Lane, this is the most visited place in the cemetery. Major Romanian writers Mihai Eminescu, Ion Luca Caragiale, George Coşbuc, Mihail Sadoveanu, Nicolae Labiş and Marin Preda are buried here. Other famous writers including George Bacovia, Nichita Stănescu, and Titu Maiorescu are buried elsewhere in the cemetery.

## 3 Actors' Lane

Situated symmetrically to Writers' Lane, on the left side of the cemetery, Actors' Lane is the last resting place of Maria Filotti, Grigore Vasiliu Birlic, George Calboreanu, Constantin Tănase, Toma Caragiu, and Anda Călugăreanu. The late Amza Pellea is also buried in Bellu Cemetery.

## 4 The Tomb of Aurel Vlaicu

An engineer, inventor and aviation pioneer, Aurel Vlaicu (1882–1913) died on 13 September 1913, while attempting to cross the Carpathians. His tomb (located in Figure 1, Bellu Military Cemetery) is flanked by a monument representing an eagle, sculpted by Ion Georgescu. Two other famous Romanian aviators, Traian Vuia and Henri Coandă, are buried in Figures 83 and 49 respectively.

### The Alexandru Costescu Chapel
**5** The Gothic chapel (Figure 62) erected in honour of Alexandru Costescu (1848–1910), Secretary General of the Ministry of Justice, was designed by German sculptor Karl Storck, who founded a dynasty of artists. Nearby stands the Mavrocordat family chapel, also designed by Storck.

### The Tomb of the Poroineanus
**6** Located in Figure 18 bis, the tomb of the Poroineanus is visited by many people, moved by the couple's tragic story. They met in Paris and fell in love, but on returning to Romania they discovered by chance that they were siblings. Unable to endure the shame and the agony, they committed suicide. Their tomb was created by sculptor Rafaello Romanelli in 1902.

### The Tomb of Iulia Hasdeu
**7** The daughter of scholar Bogdan Petriceicu Hasdeu, Iulia Hasdeu, a child prodigy of Romanian culture, died of phthisis aged just nineteen. Her tomb, like her castle in Câmpina, was built by Ion Georgescu to the specifications of her father, who, in his turn, was guided by his daughter's spirit. The tomb is in Figure 25, Plot 19.

### The Tomb of Nicolae Paulescu
**8** Dr Nicolae Paulescu, a Romanian professor of physiology at the University of Medicine and Pharmacy in Bucharest, was the first to isolate insulin, in 1916. Unfortunately, his discovery was recognized decades later. He is buried near the main entrance (Figure 15, Plot 10). The sculpture on the tomb, by Dimitrie Paciurea, depicts the agony of Christ.

### The Gheorghieff Mausoleum
**9** The crypt of the Gheorghieff brothers, who were 19th-century bankers, was

designed by Ion Mincu and has four life-size sculptures of the Evangelists by Frederick Storck. The crypt, located in Figure 47, is a historic monument.

### The Lady with the Umbrella
**10** Legend tells that "the lady in white" or "the lady with the umbrella" was the mistress of a rich man from Bucharest. A teacher of foreign languages and governess, Katalina Boschott had a passionate affair in Herculane before dying as a result of a botched peritonitis operation. On her deathbed she is supposed to have said, "Cet animal de médécin m'a tué!" The words were originally written in gold letters on her tombstone. The statue is by Rafaello Romanelli.

Left **Street concert of classical music**   Centre **Bookfest**   Right **Palace of Parliament**

# Festivals and Events

**1 The George Enescu International Festival**

The George Enescu International Festival and Competition was founded in 1958 by conductor George Georgescu, in homage to Enescu's musical genius. Over the years, major figures such as Yehudi Menuhin, David Oistrach, and Herbert von Karajan have been guests of the Festival.
The twenty first Festival was held in September 2013 in Bucharest, Timişoara, Arad, Cluj, Sibiu, and Iaşi.
✆ *www.festivalenescu.ro*

**2 Bookfest – the Bucharest Book Salon**

At the end of May or beginning of June, the pavilions of the RomExpo Complex bring together Romania's leading publishers and press trusts. Besides literary events, Bookfest also hosts concerts, film showings, and other cultural events.
✆ *www.bookfest.ro*

**4 The European Film Festival**

The event is held at the beginning of May and is organised by the Romanian Cultural Institute. The films are selected with the help of European embassies and cultural institutes. The 17th European Film Festival took place in 2013, in Bucharest, Braşov, Timişoara, Iaşi, and Târgu Mureş. ✆ *www.festivalulfilmuluieuropean.ro*

**4 Museums Night**

An event initiated by the French Ministry of Culture and Communications and in its seventh year, Museums Night has been drawing increasing numbers of visitors in all the countries. In 2013, at about 3,000 European museums celebrated the event, opening their doors free of charge to visitors on the night of 18 May. More than 20 museums in Bucharest and 30 in the rest of the country were open all night long and drew record numbers of visitors.
✆ *www.noapteamuzeelor.ro*

**5 EUROPAfest**

An event held since 1993, featuring concerts, competitions, and musicians from all over the world. From 9 to 25 May 2013,

EUROPAfest brought 300 international musicians to Bucharest. Audiences were treated to concerts of jazz, blues, and pop, in both traditional and unconventional concert spaces. The three main sections of the competition were: Bucharest International Jazz Competition, Jam Sessions and Workshops, and Jeunesses International.
🔗 www.jmevents.ro

### 6 B'ESTFEST

Since 2007, Romania's first major pop festival has been held in the north of the city at the beginning of each July. B'ESTFEST has brought dozens of international stars to Bucharest, and young people now plan their summer holidays around the festival. During the event, the capital fills with fans from all over the country. Among the stars who have performed at the festival are Santana, Pink, Alice Cooper, Marilyn Manson, Judas Priest, and Moby.
🔗 www.bestfest.ro

### 7 Bucharest Days

Every September, Bucharest City Hall and the ArCuB Cultural Projects Centre invite the city's inhabitants to a series of free events and concerts held in public spaces. Over the course of one week, the public can watch free theatre performances, while museums and cultural institutions open their doors until 3 a.m. Open-air concerts in the city's parks draw large crowds.

### 8 The I. L. Caragiale National Theatre Festival

Now in its twenty third year, the festival, organised by UNITER with the support of Bucharest City Hall, in the most important annual theatre event.

In November, a selection of Romania's best theatre shows are presented, as well as a shortlist of debuts. Theatre companies from abroad are also invited.
🔗 www.fnt.ro

### 9 Bucharest Masters of Jazz

Having now a tradition of several years, Romania's most important jazz festival brings together the world's most famous jazz musicians in late October and early November.
Past guests have included Jan Garbarek, Chick Corea, Stanley Clarke, Lenny White, the Branford Marsalis Quartet, and the Mike Stern Band.
🔗 www.mastersofjazz.ro

### 10 The DaKino International Film Festival

The oldest film festival in Romania is organised by DaKino, also the sponsor of Advertising Devourers' Night. The festival draws professionals from cinema and related fields and is held in November. The prestigious jury members and guests have included Christopher Lambert, Giuliano Gemma, Charlotte Rampling, Nikita Mikhalkov, Costa Gavras, Emir Kusturica, and Anthony Minghella.
🔗 www.dakino.ro

**The Palace Hall**

Left **Poster for the Animation Theatre Festival**    Centre **Small Theatre**    Right **Odeon Theatre**

# Theatres

### 1 Bucharest National Theatre
The capital's most important theatre was founded in 1852 and the first performance was held on 31 December. Initially, the theatre was located on Calea Victoriei (Victory Avenue), on the site of the present Novotel Hotel. It was destroyed by German bombs in the World War II. The present National Theatre, located in University Square, near the Intercontinental Hotel, dates from 1973. Renovation work started in 2010 and is due to be completed in 2015.
◈ *2 Bălcescu Boulevard • 021 314 71 71 • www.tnb.ro • Map E6*

### 2 Bulandra Theatre
The theatre was founded in 1947 in honour of actress Lucia Sturdza Bulandra. Remarkable productions by directors Liviu Ciulei, Lucian Pintilie, Alexandru Tocilescu and Cătălina Buzoianu have transformed it into an elite theatre. It is the only Romanian member of the Union of the Theatres of Europe.
◈ *Izvor Auditorium – 1 Schitu Măgureanu Boulevard • 021 314 75 46, Map E4; Toma Caragiu Auditorium – 76A J.L. Calderon St • 021 212 05 27, Map C7 • www.bulandra.ro*

### 3 Nottara Theatre
Named after great actor Constantin Nottara (1859–1935), the theatre was founded as the Army Theatre in 1947. Its directors have included prestigious names such as George Vraca and Horia Lovinescu. Its Magheru and Studio auditoriums put on plays by Romanian and foreign authors.
◈ *20 Magheru Boulevard • 021 318 89 02 • www.nottara.ro • Map D4*

### 4 Odeon Theatre
Founded in 1946, it was originally called the Giuleşti Railway Workers' Theatre. The Majestic Auditorium was opened in 1974 and is one of the most elegant in Bucharest, and the only one in Europe with a sliding ceiling. It was renamed the Odeon in 1990. It currently organises weekly theatre visits and activities for children and young people.
◈ *40–42 Calea Victoriei • 021 314 72 34 • www.teatrul-odeon.ro • Map D6*

### 5 Comedy Theatre
Radu Beligan founded the theatre in 1960. With a comedy repertoire, ranging from

**Bucharest National Theatre, before renovation**

**Novotel Hotel reconstructs the façade of the former National Theatre**

Chekhov to Eugene Ionesco, the Comedy Theatre is one of the best-loved in Bucharest. In 2002, it launched the Romanian Comedy Festival (festCO), which went international in its fifth year.
🔊 *2 Sf. Dumitru St • 021 315 91 37 • www.comedie.ro • Map D7*

### Small Theatre
One of the best-loved theatres in Bucharest, thanks to the actors who have trodden its boards: Octavian Cotescu, Olga Tudorache, Leopoldina Bălănuţă, Mitică Popescu, Ştefan Iordache, Valeria Seciu. It was founded in 1914, and has been called the Small Theatre since 1964. In 1979, a second auditorium, the Very Small Theatre, was inaugurated. 🔊 *Teatrul Mic – 16 Constantin Mille St • 021 312 36 63 • 21 Carol Boulevard • 021 314 09 05 • www.teatrulmic.ro • Maps D6*

### Metropolis Theatre
An innovative theatre, founded on 1 January 2007, where contemporary drama meets classic texts, in remarkable productions. The modern theatre building also organises courses in the dramatic arts, exhibitions, and concerts. There is a first-floor café. 🔊 *89 M. Eminescu St • 021 210 51 08, 0728 138 265 • www.teatrulmetropolis.ro • Map F3*

### Jewish State Theatre
The theatre's long tradition began in Iaşi, when artist and writer Adam Goldfaden founded the world's first professional Jewish theatre in 1876. After a series of performances, Goldfaden and his company moved to Bucharest. In the World War II, Jewish actors were forbidden from performing. It was thus the Romanian-language Barasheum Theatre came into being. Today, Yiddish performances can be watched with headphone translation.
🔊 *15 Dr. Iuliu Barasch St • 021 323 45 30 • www.teatrul-evreiesc.ro • Map F8*

### Ion Dacian National Operetta Theatre
Founded in 1950, this is Romania's only theatre dedicated to the much-loved musical genre. The original theatre was demolished in 1986, and since then performances have been held in the Small Auditorium of the National Theatre.
🔊 *2 N. Bălcescu St • 021 314 11 87 • www.opereta.ro • Map E6*

### Constantin Tănase Variety Theatre
The origins of the theatre are linked to Constantin Tănase and his Company, founded in 1919. The theatre has been named after the famous actor since 1990. The Savoy Auditorium was recently renovated.
🔊 *33 Calea Victoriei • 021 312 10 29 • www.teatrultanase.ro • Map D6*

*The Ion Creangă and Ţăndărică theatres are described on pp. 60–61.*

Left **Ţăndărică Theatre**   Centre **Globus Circus & Varieté**   Right **The Botanical Garden**

# Places for Children

### 1 The Zoo

It was founded in 1955, when small contingents of animals were established in Cişmigiu, Carol I, and Herăstrău parks, and in the Băneasa Forest. In 1959, the animals were all brought to the current zoo in Băneasa. Covering an area of 5.85 hectares, the zoo has deer, wolves, mouflons, kangaroos, parrots, and tigers. You can watch the animals live at www.digitalzoo.kappa.ro. 🕹 *4 Aleea Vadul Moldovei (bus 301–Roman Square) • 021 269 06 00 • www.zoobucuresti.ro • Mon.–Fri. 9–19; Sat.–Sun. 9–17 • Entrance fee: children 6.5 lei, adults 13 lei*

### 2 Ţăndărică Theatre

The puppet and marionette theatre was created in 1945, and is one of Bucharest's most loved theatres. In 2004, the Lahovari Auditorium was completely renovated, and a second auditorium, the Anima, opened in 2003, as an experimental theatre space. Since 2008, the official name has been the Ţăndărică Animation Theatre. 🕹 *24 Eremia Grigorescu St • 021 315 23 77 • www.teatrultandarica.ro*

### 3 The Grigore Antipa Natural History Museum

Created on 3 November 1834 by Mihalache Ghika the Great Ban. The museum is named after Grigore Antipa, the director of the zoology section from 1893 to 1944. He was responsible for the building of the current museum, inaugurated in 1908. The fascinating collections of fauna, minerals, rocks etc. include 2 million items. In September 2011 the museum reopened after a two-year-long renovation. More information on p. 103. 🕹 *1 Chaussée Kiseleff • 021 312 88 63 • www.antipa.ro • Entrance fee: children and students 5 lei, adults 20 lei*

### 4 Children's Island, Herăstrău Park

A space for children aged between 3 and 12, featuring puppet and marionette shows, games, competitions, and karaoke. There are also slides and inflatables and a recreation space for parents and grandparents. 🕹 *Herăstrău Complex, road access at 7–9 Chaussée Nordului • 0721 223 272, 0721 261 632 • Tue.–Sun. 10–20 • Entrance fee (valid all day): children Mon.–Fri. 15 lei, Sat.–Sun. 20 lei, adults free*

### 5 Globus Circus & Varieté

Magic, juggling, mounted acrobatics, lion- and tiger-taming – children will be enchanted by the shows here. In 2011, the circus celebrates its fiftieth anniversary with the "Destiny of the Dacians" show. 🕹 *15 Aleea Circului • 021 210 49 98 • Ticket office Wed.–Sun. 10–18 • Tickets 30–65 lei • www.circulglobus.ro*

### 6 Ion Creangă Theatre

A favourite children's theatre, which opened in December 1964 with a performance directed by Ion Lucian. Performances are currently held in the Rapsodia Auditorium while consolidation work on the theatre in Piaţa Amzei is carried out. 🕹 *Rapsodia Auditorium, 53 Lipscani St • 021 317 85 90 • Tickets: children 10.60 lei (category 2),*

*13.78 lei (category 1), adults 14.84 lei (category 2), 18.02 lei (category 1)* • *www.teatrulioncreanga.ro*

## Otopeni Water Park

The largest water park in Romania, open in summer, has 27 slides and 9 swimming pools. There are children's play areas, football pitches, and sand volleyball courts. Performances and competitions are also held here. *255A Calea Bucureşti, Otopeni, opposite the Henri Coandă International Airport • Bus 783, ICSIM stop • 0731 111 131 • L–V 9:30–20, S, D 9–20 • Mon.–Fri. 9:30–20, Sat–Sun. 9–20 • Entrance fee: adults Mon.–Fri. 30 lei, Sat.–Sun. 50 lei; children under 1.40m in height Mon.–Fri. 15 lei, Sat.–Sun. 25 lei • www.waterpark.ro*

## The Dimitrie Brândză Botanical Garden

The best place for children to learn about plants. Founded in 1860, in the reign of Al.I. Cuza, at the initiative of Dr Carol Davila, the garden covers 17.5 hectares. There are hundreds of plant species, from exotic ferns to water lilies.
The Nature School programme organises ecological education activities. The garden is described on p. 114. *32 Chaussée Cotroceni • 021 318 15 59 • 8–18 daily,*

*Botanical Museum Thur., Sat., Sun. 9–13* • *Entrance fee* • *www.gradina-botanica.ro*

## Lucianca Adventure Park

Opened in 2006, the adventure park is just 18 km from Bucharest, in Lucianca Forest. It is aimed at children of all ages, and offers various activities including rock climbing, archery, mini golf, and swimming. *Comuna Butimanu, Dâmboviţa County, after Crevedia • 0742 062 182, 0736 940 546 • Mon.–Sun. 9–18 • Entrance fee: children under 1m – 30 lei, over 1m – 40 lei; adults 50 lei • www.aventuraparc.ro*

## Cişmigiu Park

Located in the centre of the capital, close to University Square, Cişmigiu Garden is one of the most beautiful parks in Bucharest. There are children's play areas and rowing boats and water bicycles on the lake for children accompanied by adults. In winter, the lake becomes a skating rink. One special attraction is the exotic birds. More about the park on pp. 28–29.

Left **Crama Domnească**    Right **Liver with forest fruits, Burebista Game Restaurant**

# Traditional Romanian Restaurants

## Burebista Game Restaurant

Located near the National Theatre, Burebista Vânătoresc is one of the few restaurants in Bucharest to specialise in game dishes. Try pork on the bone with beans or grilled carp for lunch, or spend an evening with friends dining on venison or wild boar. There is always live music. You can also try the other Burebista restaurant at no. 195 Calea Moșilor. ⊗ *14 Batiștei St • 021 211 89 29 • www.restaurantvanatoresc.ro • Map E6 • ♣♣–♣♣♣*

## Caru' cu Bere

In the last few years, the historic Caru' cu Bere (The Beer Dray) has regained its place as one of Bucharest's favourite restaurants. In the evenings, there is live music and dancing. The Beer Dray is always full, as befits a true beer hall. ⊗ *More details on pp. 34–35 • Map D7 • ♣-♣♣*

## La mama

Founded in 1999, La Mama is Bucharest's most popular chain of restaurants, with good food at reasonable prices. The chain has a number of locations, but the best known is behind the Athenaeum, with a large terrace and spacious interior. Reservations are recommended. ⊗ *9 Episcopiei St • 021 312 97 97 • www.lamama.ro • Map D5 • ♣-♣♣*

## Crama Domnească

Self-titled a "voievodal restaurant," Crama Domnească is part of the Princely Court and boasts a 400-year-old vaulted cellar. The dishes, prepared according

to old Romanian recipes, are served in ceramic or clay dishes. The wine list is extensive. ⊗ *13–15 Șelari St (next to the Glassmakers' Court) • 0722 291 195, 0726 322 004 • www.cramadomneasca.com • Map E7 • ♣♣*

## Locanta Jariștea

For an evening at the Jariștea, you should dress elegantly, because the patroness has a spectacular 1930s show in store for you. You will be pleasantly surprised by the theatrical atmosphere and sumptuous dishes. A place to invite your friends from other cities (be careful at the price list though).

🕲 *50–52 G. Georgescu St (next to Antim Monastery)* • *021 335 33 38, 0744 240 126* • *www.jaristea.ro* • *Off the map* • 👥👥👥 👥👥👥👥

### 6 Hanu' Berarilor Interbelic

Located in a beautiful, century-old building with a spacious terrace, Hanu' Berarilor (the Brewers' Inn) is five minutes' walk from Lipscani. The restaurant opened in 2009 and combines traditional Romanian cooking with that typical of German beer halls. Try the cockerel borsht with noodles or Romanian sausages drizzled with home-brewed beer. It is part of the same chain as Caru' cu bere.

🕲 *2 Poenaru Bordea St (in the former Casă Bucur, United Nations Square)* • *021 336 80 09* • *www.citygrill.ro* • *Map D8* • 👥 👥👥

### 7 Vatra

A restaurant famous among foreign visitors to Bucharest, thanks to its wonderful home-style cooking. The mici can compete even with those from Cocoşatu (which are said to be the best in town), and the sarmale and tochitura are excellent. Given the reasonable prices, you will end up eating more than you set out to.

🕲 *19 Brezoianu St (near Cişmigiu Garden)* • *021 315 83 75* • *www.vatra.ro* • *Map D6* • 👥👥

### 8 Casa Doina

When it comes to Casa Doina, everybody praises the architecture, white façades, the flowers on the veranda,

and the summer garden. An authentic Romanian-style building from the 18th century, the beautiful manor house on the Chaussée is now a high-class restaurant, with a luxury dining room, traditional Romanian salon, cocktail bar, and heated garden in winter.

🕲 *4 Chaussée Kiseleff* • *021 222 67 17* • *www.casadoina.ro* • *Map A1* • 👥👥👥

### 9 Nicoreşti

Centrally located, in an old and tranquil quarter, the Nicoreşti has good food and reasonable prices. The kitschy décor and live music might be stressful to some, but most people go with the mood. Nicoreşti is not pretentious: the menu

is based on grilled dishes, the waiters are prompt, and your fellow diners are friendly.

🕲 *13 Toamnei St (on the corner with Maria Rosetti)* • *021 211 24 80* • *www.restaurantnicoresti.ro* • *Map F4* • 👥👥

### 10 Casa Jienilor

Located near Iancului Square, this restaurant is well liked, as it is always full. The food is tasty and the prices neither high nor low. The spacious interior seats 200, and there is also a very nice terrace and even a play area for children. The restaurant recently opened a second location on Făinari Street.

🕲 *12 Agricultori St* • *021 252 03 08* • *www.casajienilor.ro* • *Off the map* • 👥👥

Left **Taj Restaurant** Right **Sangria Restaurant**

# International Cuisine

### 1 Heritage
Juan Amador, a Michelin 3-star chef, is the guarantee of quality and good taste. Opened in April 2011, in a building with a long history, Heritage is considered to be the best and most sophisticated restaurant in Bucharest. The three types of menu combine Spanish, German, and French cuisine.
⊗ *19, Polonă St • 021 210 88 50 • www.heritage-restaurant.eu • Map E3* • ♨♨♨♨

### 2 Benihana
Bucharest's top Japanese restaurant is located on the first floor of the Howard Johnson Grand Plaza Hotel. At teppan tables, the Asian chefs put on a real show, preparing food in front of the diners. The prices are high, but it is well worth a visit.
⊗ *5–7 Calea Dorobanților • 021 201 50 30 • www.benihana.ro • Map D3* • ♨♨♨–♨♨♨♨

### 3 La Cantine de Nicolai
Often said to be the best French restaurant in Bucharest. Located between Roman Square and Victory Square, near Lascăr Catargiu Boulevard, La Cantine de Nicolai will spoil you with authentic haute cuisine. The house specialty is foie gras with fig jam.
⊗ *15–17 Povernei St • 0725 210 608 • www.lacantinedenicolai.ro • Map C3* • ♨♨♨♨

### 4 Orașul interzis
One of the capital's best-known Chinese restaurants. The menu covers all the regions of China, and the chefs are Chinese masters. In 2010, *Time-Out Bucharest* named it the best Chinese restaurant in the city.
⊗ *3 Silvestru St (on the corner with Armenească St) • 031 425 47 48 • www.orasul-interzis.ro • Off the map* • ♨♨

### 5 Villa Rodizio
One of the best-known Mediterranean restaurants in Bucharest, located in an elegant 18th-century building. The Italian chef will delight you with specific dishes such as fish carpaccio with salsa sauce. On the first floor, the Villa Rodizio

**Villa Rodizio Social Club**

Social Club has live music and karaoke in weekends.
🔖 32 I.L. Caragiale St • 0755 041 480 •
www.villarodizio.ro • Map F5 • ♦♦–♦♦♦

### The Serb's Tavern
6 An authentic tavern, not far from Herăstrău Park, popular with locals thanks to its ambience and delicious Serbian food. The interior and the terrace are very large, with seating for 500. There are regular concerts of music by famous artists such as Goran Bregovic and Romanian folk singers.
🔖 31 Tipografilor St • 021 490 60 50 •
www.tavernasarbului.ro • Off the map
• ♦♦–♦♦♦

### Sangria
7 If you feel like seafood paella and a glass of sangria, this is the place to go. One of the most beautiful restaurants in Bucharest, with lots of greenery and a retractable roof. The terrace is very elegant.
🔖 78 Căderea Bastiliei (near the Gr. Alexandrescu Children's Hospital) • 021 211 22 76 • Map D2 • ♦♦♦

### Taj
8 Aapka Swagat hai! – This is the welcome waiting for you at what is regarded as one of the capital's best Indian restaurants, which opened eight years ago. Try the delicacies cooked in the tandoori oven, but be careful with the hot sauces: when ordering tell the waiter how hot

you would like them to be.
🔖 127–131 Calea 13 Septembrie (near the Marriott)
• 021 410 18 20 • www.tajrestaurant.ro •
Map B8 • ♦♦♦

### Mesogios
9 All that swims in the Mediterranean Sea can be found here, from sea bream to squid. You can choose your fish and seafood from the refrigerated display case. The prices are high, but the food is delicious and always fresh.
🔖 49 Jean Calderon St (near the Hotel Intercontinental) • 0727 239 239 •
www.mesogios.ro • Map F6
• ♦♦♦–♦♦♦♦

### Piccolo Mondo
10 Probably the best-known Lebanese restaurant in Bucharest (and one of the oldest, having opened in 2003), a serious competitor with the Four Seasons, El Bacha, Chez Toni, and Habibi. The food is always good and the prices reasonable. The spacious interior and pleasant terrace are another reason to come back.
🔖 9 Clucerului St (behind Piaţa 1 Mai) •
021 222 57 55 • www.piccolomondo.ro •
Map A1 • ♦♦–♦♦♦

Left **Verona Garden, sign**   Centre **Peasant Museum Terrace**   Right **Chocolat, confectionary**

# Cafés, Tearooms and Bars

### 1 Grand Café Van Gogh

Lipscani is becoming a cosmopolitan area and the Dutch café is proof of this. The friendly exterior attracts you from the first. Then you enter a magnificently restored colonnaded room, full of light and life. In the cellar, there is a wine bar, which periodically hosts photography exhibitions. As you will see from the massive metal door, the building was once the Swiss-Romanian Bank.
- 9 Smârdan St • 0311 076 371
- www.vangogh.ro • Map E7

### 2 Chocolat

*Chocolat, createur de gout* is an unusual concept for Bucharest, and was inspired by 1930s France: a combination of confectionary shop, bistro, café, and bakery. At weekends, families with children come here to eat brunch topped off with a generous dessert. There are two other locations, at 217 Calea Moșilor and 13 Radu Beller St.
- 12A Calea Victoriei • 021 314 92 45
- www.chocolat.com.ro • Map D7

### 3 Atelier mecanic

One of the most original bars in Lipscani, with a décor of old machine parts from factories: motors, files, welding gear, etc. Even the word "mecanic" on the sign is made of tools once wielded by craftsmen and labourers. Friendly waiters and reasonable prices.
- 12 Covaci St • 0726 767 611 •
- Map E7

### 4 Verona Garden

First there was the Cărturești Bookshop, then the cellar café, and since 2009 the bright, leafy Verona Garden. It is the ideal place for meeting friends or a romantic tryst. The menu has numerous kinds of tea, coffee, lemonade, beer, and wine, as well as light dishes. There are occasionally concerts and book

**Grand Café Van Gogh**

launches. ✎ *15 Pictor Verona St • 0732 003 060
• www.carturesti.ro • Map E4*

### Cafepedia Romană

The third Cafepedia to open in Bucharest, after the one in Alba Iulia Square and the one at the University, this is the most spectacular. The wallpaper, candelabras and wood panelling create a sophisticated setting for good music, cognac and cigars. There are occasionally concerts and theatre performances.
✎ *2 Pictor Verona St • 0721 102 101 • www.cafepedia.eu • Map D5*

### Green Tea

Located near Hala Traian, a twenty minutes walk from Union Square, the tearoom is a magical spot, where the din and dust of Bucharest are left at the gate. An elegant house and rose garden provide the relaxing ambience for tea, cakes and hookahs. Every room is decorated differently – you can sit in the Japanese Room or in the Indian one.
✎ *24 Dr Burghelea St • 021 320 93 96 • Mon.–Fri. 15–23, Sat., Sun., 12–23 • www.greentea.ro • Off the map*

### Peasant Museum Terrace

The club and terrace fit perfectly into the cultural space created by the Peasant Museum – a lively, dynamic place for artists and intellectuals. The terrace is heated, allowing you to linger late over a glass of wine and a cheese platter.
✎ *Chaussée Kiseleff (Monetăriei St entrance)*

• *Mon.–Sun. 11–1 • 021 310 80 48 • www.muzeultaranuluiroman.ro • Map B2*

### Godot Café-Teatru

An interesting space in the Lipscani quarter, which hosts plays and concerts in the pleasant setting of a café. Opened a few months ago, the Godot is already famous for its quality performances. ✎ *14 Blănari St • 021 316 16 82 • www.godotcafeteatru.ro • Map E7*

### Lente & cafea

A small café in the University area, a favourite spot for people looking to tell or listen to stories, surrounded by friends and books. In the three rooms and on the terrace you can play chess, go, and rummy. In the evenings, there are sometimes jazz concerts.
✎ *31 General Praporgescu St • 021 310 74 24 • www.lente.ro • Map E5*

### Bruno

If you are looking for a place to enjoy a glass of good wine, this is the right spot. Located in Lipscani area, Bruno has wines from all over the world, from Chile to South Africa. Call before you go – the small bar is always crowded.
✎ *3 Covaci St • 021 317 17 41, 0757 557 291 • Mon.–Sun. 16–24 • www.brunowine.ro • Map E7*

**Verona Garden**

The Ark Underground Club

# Clubs

### 1 Club A

The veteran of Bucharest clubs, founded by architecture students some forty years ago: the history of Romanian rock is inseparable from 12 Blănari Street.
The children of the students who once came here to listen to rock bands now pack the club for rock and jazz concerts, film showings, and theatre performances. Club A is a lively, non-conformist venue for Bucharest's students.
✆ 14 Blănari St • 021 316 16 67 •
www.cluba.ro • Map E7

### 2 Green Hours 22 Jazz Café

The miniature Green Hours garden, tucked away behind Calea Victoriei and sharing a courtyard with the Humanitas Bookshop and 22 magazine, is a refuge on hot summer days.
The jazz club was founded in 1994 and is located in a historic building. The regular jazz concerts and "underground" Monday Theatre performances have become famous for their non-conformism.
✆ 120 Calea Victoriei
• 0722 23 43 56,
0788 45 24 85
• www.greenhours.ro •
Maps C4

### 3 Silver Church

One of the coolest clubs in Bucharest, on the site of the former Preoteasa Club. The Silver Church organises concerts by Romanian and foreign bands, from Urma to ROA and The Amsterdams. The interior is spacious, the décor original, and the atmosphere hot. ✆ 61 Calea Plevnei
• 0723 37 90 26 • www.tscarena.ro •
Map A6

### 4 Fabrica (Club and Pub)

An alternative urban culture zone in the Bucharest landscape, for fans of rock, indie, jazz, and drum and bass. With weekend concerts, documentary and short film showings, and stand-up comedy, it is no wonder it is one of the capital's most popular clubs.
In 2010, Romania's first indoor skatepark opened here.
✆ 50 11 Iunie St (next to Carol Park)
• 021 335 0323 • www.fabrica-club.ro •
Off the map

### 5 Control

If you feel drawn to underground culture or listen to indie/alternative music, this is the club for you.
Control is the place for the in-crowd, who come to see live music and theatre.

Club A

The space has a number of rooms, each with different genres of music.
🕭 4 Constantin Mille St • 0733 927 861 • www.control-club.ro • Map D6

### Art Jazz Club
Located in the heart of the city, in the basement of the Orizont Art Gallery, the club has played host to the best of Romanian jazz. The live concerts are the main attraction, and on Sundays (after 7 p.m.) there are films projections, dance and theatre performances.
🕭 23A Nicolae Bălcescu Boulevard • 0731 645 918 • www.artjazzclub.ro • Map E5

### El Grande Comandante
The club truly is "grande", with two floors, five bars, and lots of space, always packed with people dancing to oldies but goldies. In addition, there are concerts, plays, karaoke, and themed parties. Student prices. 🕭 26 Viitorului St (Gemeni Square) • 0728 556 043 • www.elcomandante.ro • Map F4

### Music Club
Founded in 2003, a landmark for good music, behind the Cocor Department Store (Union Square). On Thursdays, Fridays and Saturdays there are rock/pop concerts by bands Publika and Cortez. The atmosphere is lively, especially when there is a party.
🕭 31 Bărăției St • 0720 88 71 15 • www.music-club.ro • Map E7

### Fratelli Social Club
This is where the in-crowd comes to see and be seen. The music is good, the atmosphere friendly, and the décor cool. It is a venue for live music and famous foreign DJs, as well as fashion shows and other high-society events.
🕭 1–3 Glodeni St (Lake Tei area) • 0731 036 222 • www.fratelli.ro • Off the map

### The Ark Underground Club
An original venue, opened in 2009, after restoration work on the historic Stock Exchange, dating from 1898. On the first floor there is a restaurant, lounge area and silent cinema space. In the basement there are concerts of alternative music, featuring top Romanian and foreign bands of the moment.
🕭 150 Uranus St (next to the Coșbuc Flower Market) • 0724 588 534 • www.theark.ro • Off the map

Left **Young people playing ping-pong on Kiseleff Boulevard**   Centre **Skating**   Centre and right **Cycling**

# Sports and Recreation

**1 Horse-riding**
There are a number of equestrian clubs in Bucharest, including the Piccadilly Club at 542 Chaussée Bucureşti–Ploieşti (between Sãftica and Tâncãbeşti) and the Corbeanca Hipocan Club. A learner's session costs between 50 and 70 lei. Children can ride ponies and take horse-riding lessons. Find out more at the following websites: www.piccadillyhorses.ro; www.hipocan.ro; www.batesaua.ro

**2 Fishing**
The outskirts of the capital provide interesting opportunities for amateur and professional anglers. There is angling at Tâncãbeşti, Sãruleşti, Fundulea, etc. Bucharest and the surrounding area are famous above all for carp fishing. In 2012, the World Carp Fishing Championship will be held at Hobaia Lake, 40 km from the capital, in the village of the same name in Giurgiu County.

**3 Cycling**
Although it is still an adventure to cycle in Bucharest, more and more people are chosing bicycles instead of cars or public transportation. The best-known places for cycle hire are Cicloteque (www.cicloteque.ro),

Biciclop (www.biciclop.ro) and Raitabike (www.raitabike.ro). Prices are usually 10 lei per 12 hours. The Green Revolution Association and Sector 1 City Hall have opened free cycle centres in Kiseleff and Bazilescu parks, where you can take a bike for two hours after showing your identity card.

**4 Bowling**
Most of the malls have bowling alleys: Play Planet (Plaza România), Rock & Roll Bowling (Bucharest Mall), Split Club (City Mall). You can also bowl at the IDM Club and Good Time Texas in the Regie student complex, and at Club Champion (no. 32, Chaussée Kiseleff). The price per hour is around 75 lei.

**Kiseleff Boulevard, the Via Sport event**

## Pool

The best pool tables can be found at IDM Club (319B Splaiul Independenţei), Club Underworld (Bucur Obor underpass), King's Club (8A Iuliu Maniu Boulevard), London Club (36–42 George Enescu St), Club Texas (290 Splaiul Independenţei). The price per hour ranges from 15 to 20 lei.

## Swimming

In recent years, more and more top-class swimming pools have opened. Among the best are those at the Floreasca Club Complex (1 Mircea Eliade Boulevard), the Radisson Blu Hotel (63–81 Calea Victoriei),

Berry Fitness Spa (66 Elev Ştefănescu Ştefan St), Daimon Sport Club (10 Piscului St, Tineretului Park), and the National Arena Stadium. The entrance fee is around 50 lei and usually include sauna.

## Skating

This is a popularly sport in Bucharest in winter. There are skating rinks in Herăstrău Park (by the entrance near the Chinese Embassy), Cişmigiu Park, Floreasca (16 Mircea Eliade St), and Drumul Taberei (Moghioroş Park). One of the most popular, thanks to its central location, is Ice Park Unirii (opposite Unirea Shopping Centre), although it is packed with people during the weekend. At the AFI Palace Cotroceni you can take skating lessons and take part in hurling contests and hockey matches. Access costs usually between 10 and 15 lei, and skate hire – 10 lei.

## Paintball

Since its invention in the 80s, paintball has become an international phenomenon.

It is a dynamic sport, in which players try to eliminate each other by hitting them with paint pellets. In Romania, the first paintball pitches appeared after the year 2000, and the best are Paintballas, by the Zoo in Băneasa (www.paintballas.ro), Citypaintball, behind the House of the Free Press (www.citypaintball.ro), and Academia de Paintball, in Petricani (www.academiade-paintball.ro). An alternative to paintball is laser tag, using infrared guns.

## Go-carting

The best tracks are at Amckart, on the Bucharest Ring Road (no. 5A, Şoseaua de Centură). A 6.5 hp cart costs 45 lei/10 min., and a 13hp cart 60 lei/10 min. More details at amckart.ro. There are other tracks at AFI Palace Cotroceni, in the car park (www.megacarting.ro), and Carrefour Militari, on the Bucharest-Ploieşti Highway (C&C Karting).

## Rock-climbing

There is indoor rock-climbing near the University (46, Tudor Arghezi St, in the sports hall of School No. 19), near the Obor Station (80 Baicului St, in the Electronica complex), in Crângaşi (Galactic Gym, 16A Constructorilor Boulevard), and in Grozăveşti (Ecran Club, 82 Chaussée Grozăveşti). There are beginners' courses for children and adults. A beginner's session, with equipment included, costs between 50 and 60 lei. Details at: www.verticalspirit.ro, www.sala-escalada.ro, www.carpatic.ro

Left and right **Snagov Monastery and Lake**   Centre and below **Mogoșoaia Palace**

# Day Trips from Bucharest

### 1 Snagov Monastery and Lake

Snagov is the capital's largest recreational lake. Fed by the Ialomița River, it is 16 km long and has a maximum depth of 9 m. Snagov Monastery stands on an island and dates from 1408. Vlad the Impaler is said to be buried here. ✎ *Head north from Bucharest on the DN1 and turn right on to the 101b or 101C.* www.fundatiasnagov.ro

### 2 Mogoșoaia Palace

Situated just 13 km from the capital, the palace was built in 1698–1702 by Constantin Brâncoveanu. At the beginning of the 19th century it belonged to the Bibescu family. The architecture combines Wallachian, Byzantine and Italian Renaissance features. You can visit the Museum of Courtly Traditions, the Refectory, Gate Tower, Ice Room, English Park, the Bibescu Greenhouses, the Bibescu Chapel, and the Church of St George, built by Constantin Brâncoveanu in 1688. ✎ *www.palatebrancovenesti.ro*

### 3 Stirbey Palace

The palace is one of the most eloquent examples of Romantic architecture in Romania. In 1850, Barbu Dimitrie Știrbey, ruler of Wallachia (1849–1853, 1854–1856) ordered construction of a palace at Buftea. The palace is surrounded by a large park with centuries-old trees. The park and palace are open to the public. ✎ *Head north from*

*Bucharest on the DN1A in the direction of Târgoviște. The palace is in the town of Buftea, on the shore of the lake, near the film studios.* ✎ *www.domeniulstirbey.ro*

### 4 Comana Natural Park and Comana Monastery

On the road to Giurgiu, the Comana park is the second-largest protected area in Romania after the Danube Delta. There is a reserve for flora such as the peonies of Padina Tătarului Woods and the lilies of the valley of Fântânele Woods. Comana Monastery is one of the oldest in Wallachia and was founded by Vlad the Impaler. It is said that Vlad was slain here in 1476, the victim of a plot. ✎ *www.comanaparc.ro*

### Căldărușani Monastery

 Situated on the shore of a lake, the monastery founded by Matei Basarab was built in 1637-38. You can visit the church and museum of religious art, which has icons painted by Nicolae Grigorescu.

❧ *Head out of Bucharest on the DN1 and immediately after the entrance to Baloteşti, turn right on to the road to Moara Vlăsiei. The monastery is at the end of Căldărușani village.* • *www.manastirea-caldarusani.go.ro*

### Cernica Monastery

 Surrounded by the waters of Lake Cernica, the monastery was founded by Cernica Ştirbey and his wife, Chiajna, and is recorded from 1608. The monastery has two churches and a museum of old books and ecclesiastical art.

❧ *Head east out of the city on the DN3 as far as Pantelimon village, and then turn right on to the road to Cernica. www.cernica.go.ro*

### Scrovistea special conservation area

30 km north of the capital, near Ţigăneşti Lake, Bălteni village, the Scrovistea Forest covers 3,000 hectares. This special conservation area includes a habitat of lakes, ponds, with oak and hornbeam forests. The perfect spot for country walks.

### Peleş Castle

Built in 1873-1883 and 1896-1914, by order of King Carol I (reigned 1866-1914), in the German Renaissance style. The castle (right) situated in Sinaia, 150 kilometres from Bucharest, has 160 rooms and a 66-metre-high central tower. It was the royal summer residence until 1947 and is now a museum, with collections of paintings, sculptures, armour, furniture, etc. The nearby Pelişor Castle was built later as a residence for Prince Ferdinand.

❧ *0244 310 918* • *www.peles.ro*

### Ţigăneşti Monastery

Half way between Bucharest and Ploieşti, the monastery is located outside the village of the same name and is surrounded by a forest and the so-called Nuns' Lake. Recorded since the 17th century, it was built by Romanian monks from Mount Athos. It became a convent at the beginning of the 18th century. It is renowned for its weaving workshops, and it was here that the embroidery for the Moorish Room of Peleş Castle was made.

❧ *Head north on the DN1 towards Ploieşti as far as Ciolpani. 35 km from Bucharest there is a signpost on the left. Follow the secondary road to the end of the village.*

### Pasărea Monastery

29 km from Bucharest, the monastery was founded in the 19th century by Archimandrite Timotei, who also built Cernica Monastery. Legend tells that a bird (pasăre) guided him to the spot where he built the monastery, whence the name.

❧ *Head east out of the city on the DN3 as far as Pantelimon village, then turn left near the woods* • *www.manastireapasarea.ro*

# AROUND TOWN

BUCHAREST

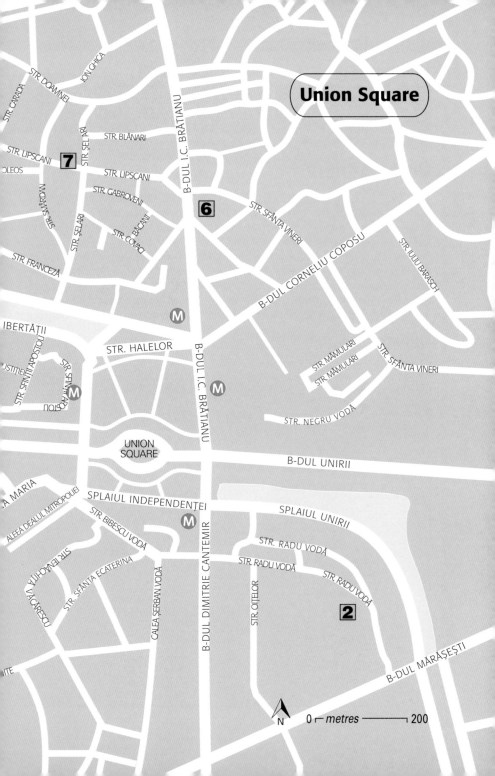

Left **Manuc's Inn**    Centre **The Patriarchate, architectural detail**    Right **Bucur Church**

# Union Square

ON THE SITE OF THE PRESENT UNION SQUARE (PIAŢA UNIRII), *one of the capital's largest, the Union Market, later called the Ghika Market, once stood. The large covered butchers' market dated from the reign of Alexandru Ioan Cuza and was modelled on the one in Paris. The former square looked nothing like it does today, as it was a much more open space. The Domniţa Bălaşa Church once dominated the square, as it was not obscured by tall buildings as it is today. From the edge of the square the Jewish quarter stretched along what is now Calea Călăraşilor. The Brâncoveanu Hospital, built in 1835–1838 also once stood here, but it was demolished in 1984–1985, along with a number of other historic monuments, to make way for the present boulevard. Only Manuc's Inn survives as a reminder of the old Bucharest.*

## Highlights

| | | | |
|---|---|---|---|
| 1 | The Patriarchate | 6 | Bărăţia Church |
| 2 | Radu Vodă Monastery | 7 | Lipscani |
| 3 | Mihai Vodă Church | 8 | Macca-Villacrosse Passage |
| 4 | Palace of Parliament | 9 | Vama Poştei Palace |
| 5 | The Romanian National Museum of History | 10 | Victoria Department Store |

**Victoria Department Store**

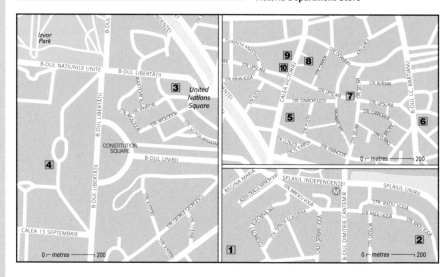

# The Patriarchate

In the 16th–18th centuries, there was a monastery among the vines of what was then called Metropolia Hill. It was here, on the morning of 24 January 1859, that it was decided to unify Wallachia and Moldavia. A few years later, in 1862, beneath the walls of the belfry founded by Constantin Brâncoveanu, prime minister Barbu Catargiu was assassinated. The Church of the Patriarchate was built by Prince Constantin Șerban in 1654–1658, and after consecration it became the Metropolia of Wallachia. At the end of the World War I it became the Patriarchate of the Romanian Orthodox Church. The church houses the relics of St Demetrios the New (Basarabov) in a silver casket, brought from Bulgaria in 1774. The Palace of the Patriarchate (1907) was originally the Chamber of Deputies. The oldest building in the Patriarchate complex is the 17th-century chapel, rebuilt in 1723.

## Radu Vodă Monastery

The original monastery was used as a munitions dump by Sinan Pasha and was blown up by the retreating Turks when they were driven out by

Christ Pantocrator, Patriarchate

Michael the Brave. It was rebuilt in the reign of Radu Mihnea (1613–1614). After the earthquakes of 1860 and 1878, the monastery was rebuilt and the murals repainted by Constantin Lecca. There is another series of murals by Gheorghe Tattarescu. The monastery is described on p. 48.

## Mihai Vodă Church

The church, a monument of 16th-century Romanian architecture with an intricately decorated façade, was founded by Michael the Brave in 1591. Legend tells that between 1589 and 1591, Michael was captured and accused of plotting to seize the throne. On his way to

The Patriarchate

St Anthony Square, where he was to be beheaded, Michael asked permission from his guards to attend the liturgy at the Alba Postăvari Church, below Spirii Hill. Kneeling before the icon of St Nicholas, he made an oath to build a monastery.
֍ 4 Sapienţei St

### Palace of Parliament
Even today the Palace of Parliament, formerly the House of the People, is a symbol of the transformations to which Union Square was subjected during the final years of the communist period. It is described on pp. 12–13.

### The Romanian National Museum of History
Under renovation and modernisation for the last few years, two of the museum's permanent exhibitions can still be visited (the Historic Treasury and the Lapidarium, where

there is a copy of Trajan's Column). The museum is described on pp. 26–27.

### Unirea Department Store
A symbol of the communist "Golden Age", the Unirea was destined to be the capital's most modern department store. It was designed by architect Gh. Leahu and built in 1976–1977. It was extended in 1980, when Union Square was systematised. Unfortunately, dozens of surrounding historic buildings were demolished in the process. The department store covers 84,000 m².

### Bărăţia Church
Known as the Bărăţia, the Church of Sancta Maria Gratiarum is the oldest Catholic place of worship in Bucharest. A wooden church was built on the same site in 1321 by Franciscan friars. Destroyed by fire, it was rebuilt in 1629. The present church (above) dates from 1848. The large bell was cast in 1855, at the expense of Emperor Franz Joseph.

### Lipscani
Locals and tourists crowd the cobbled streets of this quarter, fascinated by the surreal juxtaposition of elegant cafés, historic buildings, and ruins overrun with weeds, all of which has a distinctly Balkan flavour. More details on pp. 10–11.

### Macca-Villacrosse Passage
Very beautiful and practical at the same time, covered arcades were fashionable in 19th-century western cities. Bucharest's most beautiful arcade stretches between Eugen Carada St and Calea Victoriei (opposite). It was built in 1891 and is named after Macca, a Greek merchant, and Xavier Villacrosse, the Catalan chief architect of the capital, from 1790 to 1855. The passage was home to Bucharest's first stock exchange. In the communist period it was called Pasajul Bijuteria (the Jewel Passage), after the shop of the same name on Calea Victoriei. Today, there are cafés and restaurants on the ground floor, bathed in the yellowish light reflected by the glass roof.

### Vama Poștei Palace

**9** Situated at the intersection of Lipscani and Mihai Vodă streets, this Neo-Romanian building is the pair of the nearby Palace of the Ministry of Public Works (now the City Hall). Designed by Statie Ciortan, the palace was built between 1914 and 1926. It is now the headquarters of the General Inspectorate of the Romanian Police.

### Victoria Department Store

**10** On Calea Victoriei, at the intersection with Lipscani St, the building preserves the atmosphere of the early 20th century. It was formerly known as the Lafayette Galleries, and was built by architect Herman Clejan in 1928. In their day, the Galleries introduced a new way of shopping to Bucharest, very different to the small shops of Lipscani. The department store has spacious interiors, large windows, and excellent metalwork.

⊗ *19 Calea Victoriei*

**Macca-Villacrosse Passage**

## A day in Union Square

**Morning**

Begin the day in the Izvor area. If you arrive by Metro, turn right as you leave Izvor station and follow the river toward Union Square. Sapienței St, the site of the beautiful **Mihai Vodă Church**, built by Michael the Brave in 1591, is on the way. Then, take a detour along Libertății Boulevard and spend two hours visiting the **Palace of Parliament**. The full tour takes in the terraces and underground levels. After working up an appetite in the museum, head along Splaiul Dâmboviței as far as United Nations Square (Piața Națiunile Unite) and thence along Calea Victoriei until you reach **The Romanian National Museum of History** and the **CEC Palace.** Turn right down Stavropoleos St and you will see **Caru' cu bere**, the perfect spot for lunch.

**Afternoon**

After recharging your batteries, set off to explore Lipscani. The exquisite **Stavropoleos Church**, is a few paces away from Caru' cu bere. Then head into the bustle of Lipscani, making your way toward Smârdan St. Walk downhill past the pavement cafés until you reach Franceză St. At 27–31 you will find the **Old Court**, the historic core of old Bucharest. Visit the **Voievodal Palace** and **Church of the Annunciation**, where princes were crowned of old. Have dinner in the atmospheric Crama Domnească at 13–15 Șelari St. Finish your day with a drink at one of the lively outdoor cafés.

Left and centre **Interbellic Cocktail Bar**    Right **Bordello's**

# Cafés and Bars

### 1 French Bakery
An ideal spot for a coffee and Paris-style *croissant au beurre*.
🔊 *13 Smârdan St • 021 316 10 27 • www.frenchbakery.ro • Map E7*

### 2 Interbelic Cocktail Bar
A bar with a relaxed atmosphere and excellent cocktails, tucked away down the passage linking Lipscani and Blănari streets.
🔊 *1 Intrarea Şelari • 0722 100 193 • www.interbelic.ro • Map E7*

### 3 Les Bourgeois
A café for les bourgeois, as its name suggests, located in a beautifully restored old building.
🔊 *Intersection of Smârdan and Sf. Dumitru streets • 021 310 60 52 • www.lesbourgeois.ro • Map E7*

### 4 La Historia 1
A bistro-pub in a house dating from 1850, it has numerous regulars thanks to its large terrace, pleasant music, and good food.
🔊 *3 Sf. Dumitru St • 0722 626 043 • www.lahistoria-restaurant.ro • Map E7*

### 5 La Comedie
An unassuming café next to the Comedy Theatre, where you can have coffee or cocktails. Inside there are photographs of famous Romanian actors and theatre productions.
🔊 *2 Sf. Dumitru St • 021 315 91 37 • barlacomedie@yahoo.ro • Map E7*

### 6 Bordello's
A pub in a house with a colourful history, which was first a noble's residence, then a brothel, then a hotel. The walls have naughty photographs of inter-war ladies.
🔊 *9-11 Şelari St • 0748 881 085 • www.bordellos.ro • Map E7*

### 7 Arcade Café
Long popular with locals, the café has an interesting décor consisting of wrought iron and brick.
🔊 *30 Smârdan St • 021 314 50 66 • www.arcadecafe.ro • Map E7*

### 8 Old City – Lipscani Beer Garden
A huge bar with two entrances and an inner courtyard, where you can watch theatre performances.
🔊 *45 Lipscani St • 0729 37 77 74 • www.oldcity-lipscani.ro • Map E7*

### 9 St. Patrick
A pub remarkable for its solid wood façade. It serves the whole range of Irish drinks, from Guinness to Irish coffee.
🔊 *20-25 Smârdan St • 021 313 03 36 • www. bucharest-irishpub.ro • Map E7*

### 10 La Scena
Located not far from Union Square, this particularly charming building houses a café, a restaurant, and a theatre.
🔊 *55 Calea Călăraşi • 021 320 35 67 • www.lascena.ro • Map E7*

**Price categories**

| | |
|---|---|
| ▲ | cheap |
| ▲▲ | middling |
| ▲▲▲ | not cheap |
| ▲▲▲▲ | expensive |

Left **Red Angus Steakhouse**   Centre **Sushi Ko**   Right **Manuc's Inn**

# Restaurants

**1 Caru' cu bere**
No matter how many days you are staying in Bucharest, having lunch or dinner at Caru' cu bere is a must. Read more about the historic building at pp. 34–35.

**2 La Bonne Bouche**
A likeable, pleasingly furbished bistro with an impressive list of French and New World wines.
⊗ 30 Franceză St • 0731 247 876 • www.bistrovin.ro • ▲▲▲–▲▲▲▲

**3 Divan**
With its original oriental décor and Turkish dishes, Divan is one of the most popular restaurants in Lipscani. Book in advance.
⊗ 46–48 Franceză St • 021 312 30 34 • www.thedivan.ro • ▲▲–▲▲▲

**4 Red Angus Steakhouse**
The best quality beef is brought from the US, Europe and New Zealand. The name comes from one of the oldest breeds of cattle, renowned for its meat: the Red Angus. ⊗ 56 Franceză St • 021 312 03 83 • www.redangus.ro • ▲▲▲

**5 Levantin**
After a long wait, Manuc's Inn (see p. 8) has reopened its doors and is now home to Levantin, a Lebanese restaurant. The chef, Mohammed, was brought specially from Egypt. ⊗ 62-64 Franceză St • 021 313 14 11 • www.hanulluimanuc.ro • ▲▲

**6 City Grill**
One of Lipscani's older restaurants, which has seen off the competition with brio. The menu features Romanian dishes, cooked well, but unpretentiously.
⊗ 12 Lipscani St • 021 314 24 89 • www.citygrill.ro • ▲

**7 Malagamba**
This Italian restaurant opened in 2010 brings a western air to the Bucharest scene. It is named after Sergiu Malagamba, percussionist of genius and consummate dandy famous in the 1930s and 1940s.
⊗ 2 Sf. Dumitru St • 021 313 33 89 • www.malagamba.ro • ▲▲–▲▲▲

**8 St. George**
A Hungarian restaurant that opened before Lipscani became the capital's busiest area. The décor is rustic, and folk musicians enliven the atmosphere. ⊗ 44 Franceză St • 021 317 10 87 • www.stgeorge.ro • ▲▲–▲▲▲

**9 Tuscany**
Recently opened in Lipscani, Tuscany is tastefully furnished and the Tuscan dishes are delicious.
⊗ 1-3 Gabroveni St (on the corner with Șelari St) • 0720 990 110 • ▲▲

**9 Sushi Ko**
A Japanese restaurant, furbished in an understated way, with a terrace overlooking the CEC Palace. Try the miso and sashimi soup. ⊗ 8 Stavropoleos St • 0758 088 400 • www.sushiko.ro • ▲▲▲

*Other restaurants in this area: Locanta Jariștea (pp. 62) and Crama Domnească (p. 62).*

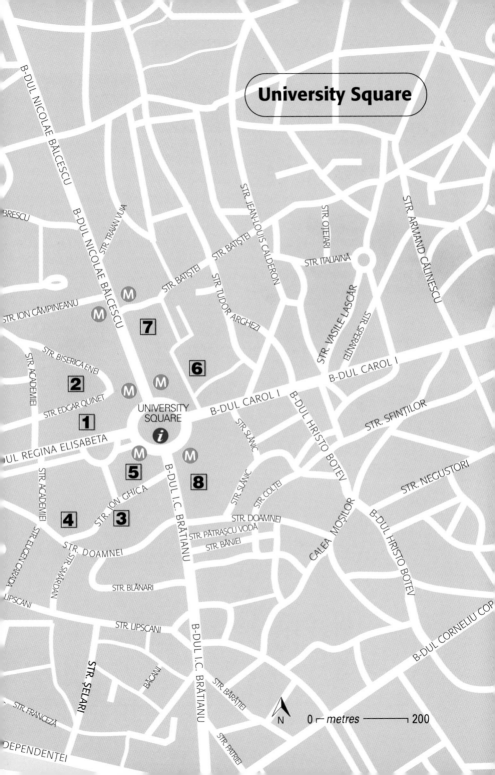

Left **Bucharest University**   Centre **Colțea Hospital and Church**   Right **Second-hand books**

# University Square

A S A SPACE, UNIVERSITY SQUARE (PIAȚA UNIVERSITĂȚII) *is a model of stylistic and urbanistic cohesion, and is regarded as Kilometre 0 of the capital. The area began to take shape between 1857 and 1869, when Bucharest University was built. In 1874, one of the city's first public monuments was erected here: the statue of Michael the Brave on horseback by sculptor Carrier Belleuse, the teacher of Auguste Rodin. The history of the square has been marked by the events of recent decades. It is a symbol of both the Revolution of 1989 and the miners' rampages. It was here between 22 April and 15 June 1990 that the largest anti-communist demonstrations in Romania's history took place.*

## Highlights

1. Bucharest University
2. The Ion Mincu University of Architecture and Urbanism
3. The Russian Church
4. The National Library of Romania
5. Suțu Palace (History Museum of Bucharest Municipality)
6. The Ion Luca Caragiale National Theatre
7. The Intercontinental Hotel
8. Colțea Hospital and Church
9. The National Military Club Palace
10. Universul

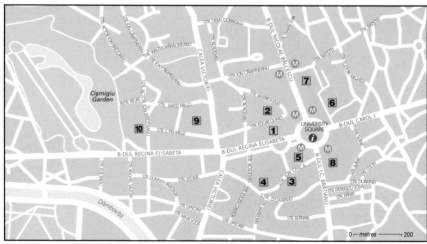

*There is an information point in the Pasajul Universității (University underground passage)*

# Bucharest University

The University building is striking even to the hurried passer-by. The imposing edifice was built on the site of the former St Sava Monastery, which was home to the celebrated Princely Academy founded by Constantin Brâncoveanu. The foundation stone was laid on 10 October 1857, and building work was completed in 1869. In 1864, Prince Alexandru Ioan Cuza created Bucharest University, with the faculties of Law, Science and Literature housed in a single corpus. At present, the university has 19 faculties and more than 30,000 students.

⊛ www.unibuc.ro

# The Ion Mincu University of Architecture and Urbanism

Architectural education was established by decree of Alexandru Ioan Cuza on 1 October 1864. The first department soon disappeared, due to lack of funds and students, but, in 1891, the Society of Romanian Architects founded a private architectural school, which became an official state institution in 1897. The present building, near the Bucharest University, houses the Faculty of Architecture, the Faculty of Urbanism, and the Faculty of Interior Design, the last two having

**The Russian Church**

been founded after 1990. ⊛ 18–20 Academiei St • 021 307 71 12 • www.uauim.ro

# The Russian Church

The Church of St Nicholas (the Russian Church) was built in 1905-09 at the behest of the Russian Ambassador to serve

**The Ion Mincu University of Architecture and Urbanism**

as the embassy's chapel. In 1934, at the request of Minister Nicolae Titulescu, the Soviet Union donated the church to Bucharest University. It was restored to the Russian state after the World War II, and was donated to the Romanian Orthodox Church ten years later. Since 1992, it has been the Students' Church.

⊗ *3 Ion Ghika St • www.paraclisuluniversitar.ro*

### 4 The National Library of Romania

Formerly the Stock Exchange Palace, built in 1906–1912, it has housed the Romanian National Library since 1955. The building is home to priceless treasures, such as the Codex Aureus, an illuminated gold-letter copy of the Gospels on parchment dating from 810.

⊗ *4 Ion Ghika St • Mon.–Fri. 9–16:45 • www.bibnat.ro*

### 5 Suţu Palace (History Museum of Bucharest Municipality)

This is one of the most elegant buildings in central Bucharest. The residence of Grigore Şuţu the High Postelnik, it was built in 1833 and is striking even today thanks to its Neo-Gothic architecture. The museum was inaugurated in 1959, and its collections present the tumultuous history of Bucharest, from the Neolithic to the present day. See also p. 41.

### 6 The Ion Luca Caragiale National Theatre

The old theatre, which stood on the site of the present Novotel on Calea Victoriei, was destroyed by bombs in 1944. After being housed in "borrowed" buildings, the National Theatre was

---

#### The Suţu Palace Balls

Built in 1833 by two Viennese architects, by 1875 the Suţu Palace was the centre of Bucharest high-society life. The balls and soirées were celebrated for their elegance. King Carol I himself used to attend the New Year's Eve Ball. The guests arrived in sumptuous carriages and left at dawn. In the palace grounds there were many exotic birds.

---

given a new building in 1973, designed by architects H. Maicu, R. Belea and N. Cucu. At the time, it had a hat-shaped roof, inspired by Caragiale's famous headwear. The theatre is currently undergoing renovation. More details on p. 57.

⊗ *Ticket office: 2 Bălcescu Boulevard • 021 314 71 71 • Mon. 10–16, Tue.–Sun. 10–19 • www.tnb.ro*

### 7 The Intercontinental Hotel

A symbol of Bucharest for the last few decades, the Intercontinental Hotel stands in the immediate vicinity of the National Theatre. Now a five-star hotel, it was built in 1968–1970. With 22 storeys and standing 90 metres tall, it is one of the capital's tallest buildings.

⊗ *4 Bălcescu Boulevard • 021 407 47 33 • www.ichotelsgroup.com*

### 8 Colţea Hospital and Church

After lengthy renovation work, Colţea Church has regained its former beauty. The church inn, monastic cells, and fire watchtower no longer survive. The church

**The Intercontinental Hotel**

# A day in University Square

## Morning

🕐 Begin your day by visiting the **Bucharest History and Art Museum** in the beautiful Suțu Palace. It is the ideal place to learn about the city's history. You can also see here the khrysoboulion issued by Vlad the Impaler in 1459, the earliest document to mention Bucharest, as well as the sword of Constantin Brâncoveanu.

🍴 For lunch, visit the **Bellini**, an Italian restaurant on the nearby Ion Ghika St, where you can refresh yourself with a prosciutto salad and an espresso. Opposite the restaurant is the Russian Church, with its coloured domes.

## Afternoon

After lunch, head back towards the Suțu Palace, cross the square through the Metro underpass, and visit the **Colțea Church**, which has been carefully restored. Alongside the church, on Carol I Boulevard, stands the magnificent **Ministry of Agriculture**. Go through the underpass to see the **National Theatre** and **Intercontinental Hotel** opposite the Ministry, and then to the other side of the square, to the **University and Architecture University**, with their fountain, a popular meeting place. Proceed down Regina Elisabeta Boulevard, admiring the **National Military Club Palace** and **Universul** building on the way. At the end of your walk, you can dine in the historic setting of the **Casa Capșa**. Afterwards, the nearby Cișmigiu Garden awaits you for a stroll.

---

was built by Mihail Cantacuzino in 1701–1702, and the murals are by Tattarescu. Originally, the church had a 24-bed hospital. The current hospital dates from 1887, and due to the renovation, became one of the most modern in the capital.
🔑 1 Brătianu Boulevard • 021 387 43 00
🌐 www.coltea.ro

### 9 The National Military Club Palace

Built in 1911, on the site of the former Sărindar Monastery, the building houses the Romanian Army's main cultural institution. The building was designed by D. Maimarolu, V. Ștefănescu and E. Doneaud. It was officially inaugurated in February 1923, in the presence of King Ferdinand I and Queen Maria.
🔑 1-3 Constantin Mille St • 021 314 37 35

### 10 Universul

In the olden days, Sărindar St (now Constantin Mille St) was home to the city's newspaper offices. The inter-war Universul building was the offices of the newspaper with the same name. The palace was built in 1926, at the initiative of famous journalist Stelian Popescu.

Left **Rendez-Vous tearoom**   Right **Jos pălăria**

# Cafés and Bars

### 1 Cafeneaua Actorilor
A café and club with a large terrace, located next to the Operetta Theatre. Bohemian atmosphere and excellent pizza, made in a wood-burning oven. ⓢ *2 Bălcescu Boulevard • 0721 900 842 • www.cafeneauaactorilor.ro • Map E6*

### 2 Gio Café
You can find it opposite the Russian Church. In the hot Bucharest summers, Gio Café has a terrace sprinkled with artificial mist. ⓢ *3 Toma Caragiu St • 021 313 97 40 • www.giocafe.ro • Map E7*

### 3 French Bakery
If you are looking for a quiet spot, a fresh croissant and a cappuccino, this small boulangerie is ideal. ⓢ *10 Câmpineanu St • 021 313 28 22 • www.frenchbakery.ro • Map E6*

### 4 Lente & Cafea
In a narrow courtyard shaded by vines, you can work on your laptop undisturbed. The bookshelf with comics for sale might be another reason to come back. ⓢ *31 General Praporgescu St • 031 102 06 61 • www.lente.ro • Map E5*

### 5 Rendez-Vous
A pleasant tearoom with an irresistible aroma, where it will be hard to choose between so many kinds of tea. There are also delicious cakes. ⓢ *8-10 Edgar Quinet St • 0723 541 998 • www.ceainarie.ro • Map D6*

### 6 Edgar's Pub
English-style pub, ideal for having a beer with friends. ⓢ *9 Edgar Quinet St • 021 314 18 43 • www.edgarspub.ro • Map D6*

### 7 Charlatans Irish Pub
On the corner opposite the Eminescu Bookshop, close to the University, Charlatans is the perfect place for a coffee and an Irish breakfast. ⓢ *11-13 Regina Elisabeta Boulevard • 0721 10 44 51 • www.charlatans.ro • Map D6*

### 8 Lăptăria lui Enache
On the 4th floor of the National Theatre, the Lăptărie and La Motoare rooftop terrace are famous. Due to renovation work on the theatre, the bar is seeking another location.

### 9 Jos Pălăria Café Club
Open almost non-stop, "Hats Off" is located near the Russian Church. The owner, famous actor George Mihăiță invites you to meet your friends and favourite actors. ⓢ *3 Toma Caragiu St • 021 311 34 56 • Map E6*

### 10 Turabo Café, University
Outstanding coffee, hot chocolate, and tea. Turabo is one of the best-known chains of cafés in the city. ⓢ *3 Ion Ghika St • 0722 73 21 41 • www.turabo-cafe.ro • Map E7*

**Price categories**

| | |
|---|---|
| ♣ | cheap |
| ♣♣ | middling |
| ♣♣♣ | not cheap |
| ♣♣♣♣ | expensive |

Left **Mesogios**   Right **Burebista Game Restaurant**

# Restaurants

### 1 Casa Capşa
In the late 19th century, Capşa was Bucharest's most famous restaurant. Admire the sumptuous interiors and lobby of the 5-star hotel. ✆ *36 Calea Victoriei • 021 313 40 38 • www.capsa.ro • Map D6 • ♣♣♣*

### 2 Burebista Game Restaurant
Located near the Intercontinental Hotel, the restaurant is a favourite with those looking for game dishes and traditional Romanian food. The terrace was recently enlarged. Closed for the moment.
✆ *14 Batiştei St • 021 210 97 04 • www.restaurantvanatoresc.ro • Map E6 • ♣♣–♣♣♣*

### 3 Mesogios
A Mediterranean restaurant where you can choose your own fresh fish, squid, and seafood. Arguably the best fish restaurant in Bucharest. ✆ *49 Jean Louis Calderon St • 0727 239 239 • www.mesogios.ro • Map F6 • ♣♣♣ ♣♣♣♣*

### 4 Bellini
Italian restaurant from whose terrace you can admire the Russian Church. The pizza is baked in a wood-burning oven, and the pasta and lasagna will convince you to come back. ✆ *2 I. Ghika St • 021 310 29 78 • Map E7 • ♣♣*

### 5 Vatra
Near Cişmigiu can be found one of Bucharest's best Romanian restaurants. Try the smoked pork with beans. ✆ *19 Brezoianu St • 021 315 83 75 • www.vatra.ro • Map D6 • ♣♣*

### 6 Gallienus
If you have a hankering for grilled trout or beefsteak, Gallienus is the perfect choice. The menu has a wide selection and the atmosphere is pleasant. ✆ *21 Doamnei St • 0732 725 052 • www.gallienus.ro • Map E7 • ♣♣♣*

### 7 Da Vinci l'Inventore
The perfect place to get away from the city grind. Tucked away down a side street opposite Dalles bookshop, this Italian restaurant has an interesting interior. ✆ *11 I. Câmpineanu St • 021 312 21 57 • www.linventore.ro • Map E6 • ♣♣♣*

### 8 Boutique du pain
With its French atmosphere, this is an ideal place for breakfast or a light lunch. ✆ *28–30 Academiei St • 0723 607 732 • www.boutiquedupain.com • Map D6 • ♣♣ ♣♣♣*

### 9 Rossetya
A stone's throw from Rosetti Square, this elegant restaurant serves Balkan and other dishes. ✆ *9 D. Bolintineanu St • 0748 220 220 • www.rossetya.ro • Map F6 • ♣♣–♣♣♣*

### 10 Violeta's Vintage Kitchen
An intellectual turned chef is the owner of this bijou restaurant. Traditional home cooking is the daily fare. ✆ *23 Batiştei St • 021 310 06 81 • www.violetas.ro • Map E5 • ♣♣♣ ♣♣♣♣*

B-DUL IANCU DE HUNEDOARA
STR. GRIGORE ALEXANDRESCU
B-DUL LASCĂR CATARGIU
CALEA VICTORIEI
STR. V. ALECSANDRI
6
STR. POVERNEI
STR. CĂDEREA BASTILIEI
STR. SEVASTOPOL
STR. GINA PATRICHI
STR. VIȘOAREI
STR. C-TIN DANIEL
STR. GHEORGHE MANU
10
B-DUL LASCĂR CATARGIU
STR. FRUMOASĂ
STR. GHEORGHE MANU
CALEA VICTORIEI
STR. NICOLAE IORGA
STR. MIHAIL MOXA
B-DUL DACIA
7
STR. BISERICA AMZEI
STR. CHRISTIAN TELL
STR. D.I. MENDELEEV
B-DUL DACIA
CALEA GRIVIȚEI
8
INTR. AMZEI
CALEA VICTORIEI
STR. PIAȚA AMZEI
STR. TRANSILVANIEI
STR. GENERAL BERTHELOT
STR. LUTERANĂ
CALEA VICTORIEI
STR. ȘTIRBEI VODĂ
STR. ȘTIRBEI VODĂ

**Roman Square**

STR. DAVID EMANUEL

STR. ION BOGDAN

STR. POLONĂ

STR. POLONĂ

STR. AUREL VLAICU

STR. FECIOAREI

STR. TUNARI

STR. CARAGEA IOAN VODA

STR. ERNEST BROȘTEANU

STR. EROU ION CĂLIN

CALEA DOROBANȚILOR

STR. POLONĂ

STR. MIHAI EMINESCU

STR. MIHAI EMINESCU

STR. MIHAI EMINESCU

STR. AUREL VLAICU

STR. MIHAI EMINESCU

B-DUL DACIA

B-DUL DACIA

B-DUL DACIA

B-DUL

STR. URALI

**1** LAHOVARI SQUARE

Ion Voicu Park

STR. POLONĂ

STR. AUREL VLAICU

STR. AUREL VLAICU

STR. ICOANEI

B-DUL

GEORGE ENESCU

STR. G-RAL EREMIA GRIGORESCU

STR. DIONISIE LUPU

STR. JULES MICHELET

STR. COLUMB

STR. ALEXANDRU D. XENOPOL

STR. DIMITRIE GEROTA

STR. AUREL VLAICU

STR. ICOANEI

STR. VASILE LASCAR

STR. PITAR MOȘ

**3**

**2**

**4**

**5**

STR. AL DONICI

Deco Flora Park

Universitarilor Park

STR. C.A. ROSETTI

STR. VASILE LASCAR

B-DUL G-RAL GHEORGHE MAGHERU

STR. C.A. ROSETTI

STR. C.A. ROSETTI

STR. C.A. ROSETTI

N

0 — metres — 200

Left **Grafitti**   Centre **Balcony with flowers** and **Architectural detail**   Right **Icoanei Park**

# Roman Square

SITUATED BETWEEN THE TWO SQUARES THAT DEFINE *central Bucharest (University Square and Victory Square), Roman Square is a dynamic and eclectic space from the architectural point of view, featuring very different types of building: small old-fashioned bourgeois residences, decorated large buildings, communist-era blocks, and, dominating the square, the imposing Academy of Economic Sciences. In the middle of the square there was originally a statue of Prime Minister Lascăr Catargiu, destroyed in the communist period. The current name comes from the famous nearby Romană Street, now renamed after Mihai Eminescu.*

## Highlights

| | |
|---|---|
| **1** The Assan House | Cuțescu Storck Museum |
| **2** Icoanei Garden | **7** The National Museum |
| **3** Bulandra Theatre | of Romanian Literature |
| (Toma Caragiu Auditorium) | **8** Amzei Church |
| **4** The Central School for Girls | **9** The Academy of Economic Studies |
| **5** Darvari Hermitage | **10** The Admiral Vasile Urseanu |
| **6** The Frederick and Cecilia | Astronomic Observatory |

**The Anglican Church, statue**

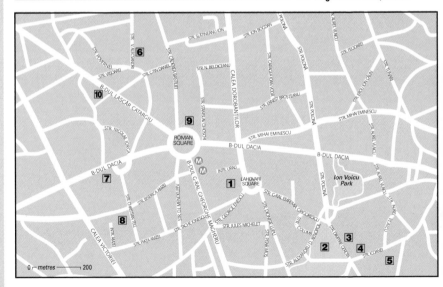

*Two nearby attractions, the Anglican Church and the Italian Church, are described on page 51.*

### The Assan House

Located in Lahovary Square, the building was designed by architect I.D. Berindei in the French Neoclassical style and was finished in 1914. The first owner was Bazil George Assan, an engineer and explorer, and the first Romanian to circumnavigate the globe, in 1899. He was also the owner of the first motorcar in Bucharest, with a No. 1 licence plate. In 1945, the building became the Scientists' House. It now has a small restaurant and terrace.

*9 Piaţa Lahovary*

### Icoanei Garden

This is a small park near Roman Square, laid out by horticulturist Louis Leyvras in the 1870s on the site of a marsh drained by the town hall. At the entrance there is a statue of Alexandru Lahovary (1841–1897), an illustrious diplomat during the reign of Carol I. Nearby, on the site of a wooden church built in 1680, stands the Icoanei Church, thus named after an icon of the Theotokos donated by Constantin Brâncoveanu.

### Bulandra Theatre (Toma Caragiu Auditorium)

The building, situated next to Icoanei Garden, was designed by architect

**The Anglican Church, window**

Ion Mincu in 1890 as a ceremonial hall for the Central School for Girls. Badly damaged in the earthquake of 1940, the building was subsequently altered in the style of the Helsingborg Concert Hall in Sweden. In 1956, it was taken over by the theatre run by Lucia Sturdza Bulandra and is now the prestigious Toma Caragiu Auditorium. *76A J.L. Calderon St • 021 212 05 27 • www.bulandra.ro*

### The Central School for Girls

The school was founded by Prince Barbu

**The Assan House**

Ştirbey on 19 March 1851, but not officially inaugurated until 1852. It was originally the best school in town for noble and wealthy girls. The present building was designed by Ion Mincu. ◈ *3–5 Icoanei St*

### 5 Darvari Hermitage

Near Icoanei Garden can be found one of Bucharest's most beautiful hidden corners, an oasis of tranquillity and spirituality: the Darvari Hermitage. It was founded in 1834 by Mihail Darvari and his wife Elena. Originally it was a small wooden church with cells for nuns. In 1894 a spire was added to the church, and in 1933–1934 the hermitage acquired its present form. ◈ *3 Schitu Darvari St • 021 212 32 47 • www.schituldarvari.ro*

### 6 The Frederick and Cecilia Cuţescu Storck Museum

Founded in 1951, the museum is housed in the family home of the Storcks, built by architect A. Clavel at the beginning of the 20th century. Karl Storck settled in Romania in 1849, and was the first professor of sculpture at the Bucharest School of Fine Arts. His two sons, Carol and Frederick, continued the family artistic tradition. Frederick married artist Cecilia Cuţescu. The museum houses paintings and sculptures that belonged to the family. ◈ *16 Vasile Alecsandri St • 021 211 38 89 • Wed.–Sun. 9–17, closed Mon., Tue., national holidays • www.muzeulbucurestiului.ro*

### 7 The National Museum of Romanian Literature

Since 1967, the museum has been housed in the Scarlat Kretzulescu Palace, built by

rich Wallachian boyar Alecu Villara as a dowry for his daughter Elena. The building has gone down in history thanks to Elena's husband, Scarlat Kretzulescu, a man of exquisite taste who renovated and refurbished it according to the fashion of the day. Celebrated for its balls, the palace was a centre of attraction for Bucharest's rich and powerful.

Over the years, the building has also housed the Bucharest University electrical laboratory, a girls' school, the library of the German Embassy, and the Romanian-Russian Museum. The Literature Museum has more than 300,000 exhibits, including old books and priceless manuscripts. ◈ *12 Dacia Boulevard • 021 212 96 54 • Tue.–Sun. 9–17, closed Mon., national holidays • www.mnlr.ro*

### 8 Amzei Church

With its impressive eclectic architecture, Amzei Church is one of the capital's most important churches. The small original church was built in 1807-10, destroyed in a fire, and rebuilt in 1875. In 1898, it was demolished to make way for the present church. ◈ *12 Biserica Amzei St (near Piaţa Amzei)*

MUZEUL LITERATURII ROMÂNE

---

### Miţa Biciclista

An urban legend, Miţa the Bicyclist (1885–1968) was a real person. Maria Mihăescu, her real name, was a famous socialite in the inter-war period. She was the first person to ride a bicycle in Bucharest, in 1898, and was nicknamed "Miţa Biciclista" by a journalist who saw her cycling down Calea Victoriei. Her house is opposite Amzei Church.

## 9 The Academy of Economic Studies

Formerly the Palace of the Commercial Academy, the building has been an emblem of Roman Square for almost a century. Built in 1916–1926, it was designed by architects Grigore Cerchez, Arghir Culina and Edmond van Saanen. The murals in the reading room are by Sabin Bălaşa.

## 10 The Admiral Vasile Urseanu Astronomic Observatory

The century-old house was built by Admiral Vasile Urseanu as a museum to popularise astronomy. Shaped like a ship, it was inaugurated on 1 November 1910. On clear days you can watch the heavens through the telescope, and on Fridays and Saturdays you can travel through the universe virtually with the help of a special programme.

◈ 21 Lascăr Catargiu St • 021 212 96 44
• Stargazing Tue., Fri., Sat., after nightfall, last visitor admitted at 21:45 • Tickets 5 lei •
www.astro-urseanu.ro

The House of Miţa Biciclista, detail

## A day in Roman Square

### Morning

Start the day with a visit to the **National Museum of Romanian Literature**, where you can view manuscripts of famous Romanian writers, and old, rare books. Then return to Roman Square, turn right onto Mendeleev St, and then right again, as far as **Amzei Church**, which is striking for its mixture of architectural styles. Opposite, on the corner, you will see the house where **Miţa Biciclista** lived. On the other side of Amzei Market, you can take lunch at the Harbour Restaurant, described on p. 99.

### Afternoon

After lunch, cross Magheru Boulevard and head to Lahovary Square, from where it is a short distance to **Icoanei Garden**. In the park you can watch groups of pétanque players. Nearby you will see the **Anglican Church**, **Bulandra Theatre** and **Central School for Girls**. Further along from the Central School for Girls, on a small street to the right, you will find the **Darvari Hermitage**. After a short visit, return to Roman Square and head down L. Catargiu Boulevard towards Victory Square. Halfway down the boulevard, on the right, you will come to the **Storck Museum**, which is well worth a visit (note that it closes at 5 pm). If you are feeling hungry, the Mamma Leone seafood restaurant is located nearby. To round off a perfect day, visit the **Astronomic Observatory** to gaze at the stars.

Left **Grădina Verona**   Centre **Cafepedia**   Right **Green Hours**

# Cafés and Bars

### 1 Grand Café Galleron
A sumptuous building behind the Athenaeum is home to one of the capital's poshest cafés.
*18A Nicolae Golescu St • 021 312 45 65 • www.grandcafegalleron.ro • Map D5*

### 2 Cafepedia
Coffee of every variety and from every continent in a sophisticated décor with the sounds of jazz.
*2 Pictor Arthur Verona St • 0721 102 101 • www.cafepedia.eu • Map D5*

### 3 Grădina Verona
Coffee, lemonade, beer, sandwiches and salads in a beautiful garden laid out in a minimalist-ecological style.
*13-15 Pictor Arthur Verona St (behind the Cărtureşti Bookshop) • 0732 003 060 • Map E4*

### 4 Shift Pub
Located in an old house with a mansard roof between Lahovary Square and Icoanei Garden and with a small terrace. The menu combines French and Italian influences.
*17 Eremia Grigorescu St • 021 211 22 72 • www.shiftpub.ro • Map E4*

### 5 Café Boheme
If you're looking for a good coffee or a light lunch, this is an ideal spot, a few steps from the Academy of Economic Sciences.
*11 Căderea Bastiliei St • 021 317 25 08 • www.cafeboheme.ro • Map D3*

### 6 Green Hours
An ideal place for working lunches during the day, or concerts and theatre in the evening.
*120 Calea Victoriei • 0722 23 43 56 • www.greenhours.ro • Map C4*

### 7 Sala de Lectură
On the second floor of the ACT Theatre, discover a tearoom with a library, musical evenings, and drawing lessons for children.
*126 Calea Victoriei, 2nd floor • 021 312 00 42 • www.saladelectura-act.ro • Map C4*

### 8 Uniter Terrace
A garden bursting with greenery where you can meet friends for a coffee or cold beer. You may also catch a theatre performance. The Terrace is owned by the Romanian Theatre Union.
*2-4 George Enescu St • 021 311 32 14 • www.uniter.ro • Map D4*

### 9 OAR Garden
In the garden of the house of architect Ion Mincu, there are tables in the cool shade of the trees, the ideal place for a coffee or a cold beer.
*19 Pictor Arthur Verona St • 0743 027 981 • Map E4*

### 10 The Embassy
A club and large terrace, with an original, highly modern design. The tree-shaded garden is the perfect place to meet friends.
*8 Piaţa Lahovary • 0733 500 300 • www.embassy-club.ro • Map E4*

### Price categories

| | |
|---|---|
| ▲ | cheap |
| ▲▲ | middling |
| ▲▲▲ | not cheap |
| ▲▲▲▲ | expensive |

Left **Villa Rodizio**   Right **The Harbour**

# Restaurants

**1 Villa Rodizio**
Elegance, taste, refinement, 18th-century allure, and the best Mediterranean food in the city. At weekends, the restaurant is a venue for book launches and other events.
◈ *32 I.L. Caragiale St • 0755 041 480 • www.villarodizio.ro • Map F5 • ▲▲–▲▲▲*

**2 La Mama, Athenaeum**
Very popular, especially in summer, when the terrace is open.
◈ *9 Episcopiei St • 021 312 97 97 • www.lamama.ro • Map D5 • ▲–▲▲*

**3 Trattoria Il Calcio (Amzei Market)**
A restaurant whose quality has been consistent for many years. There is another Il Calcio close by, near the Athenaeum. ◈ *14 Mendeleev St • 0722 134 299 • www.trattoriailcalcio.ro • Map D4 • ▲▲–▲▲▲*

**4 The Harbour**
The terrace and interior are decorated in sea tavern style. The menu is international, with Mediterranean accents.
◈ *10 Piața Amzei • 021 319 72 57 • www.harbour.ro • Map D4 • ▲▲–▲▲▲*

**5 Mamma Leone**
Sturgeon, mullet, mackerel – you can find here any fish you want. Located in a beautiful building, this is one of city's best seafood restaurants.
◈ *22 Povernei St • 021 311 46 06 • www.mammaleone.ro • Map C3 • ▲▲–▲▲▲*

**6 Chez Marie**
A restaurant with a pleasant atmosphere and good food, near the Anglican Church. International menu.
◈ *48 Dionisie Lupu St • 0730 344 810 • www.chezmarie.ro • Map E5 • ▲▲–▲▲▲*

**7 La Taifas Bistro**
Located behind the Enescu Museum, the bistro is remarkable for its Levantine décor and tasty food.
◈ *16 Gheorghe Manu St • 021 212 77 88 • Map B3 • ▲▲*

**8 Balthazar**
To understand what fusion cooking means, try the Franco-Asian menu at Balthazar. The restaurant is located near Icoanei Garden.
◈ *2 Dumbrava Roșie St • 021 212 14 60 • www.balthazar.ro • Map E4 • ▲▲▲*

**9 La Mandragora**
Even the sophisticated interior design pales in comparison with the delicacies prepared by Paul *the chef*. Painter Ștefan Luchian once lived and worked in this house.
◈ *29 Mendeleev St • 021 319 75 92 • www.lamandragora.ro • Map D4 • ▲▲▲▲*

**10 Papa la Șoni**
If you've never been to the Șoni at Vama Veche, you can sample the smoked pork broth here.
◈ *13 Sfinții Voievozi St (Moxa area) • 0755 659 653 • www.papalasoni.ro • Map B3 • ▲–▲▲*

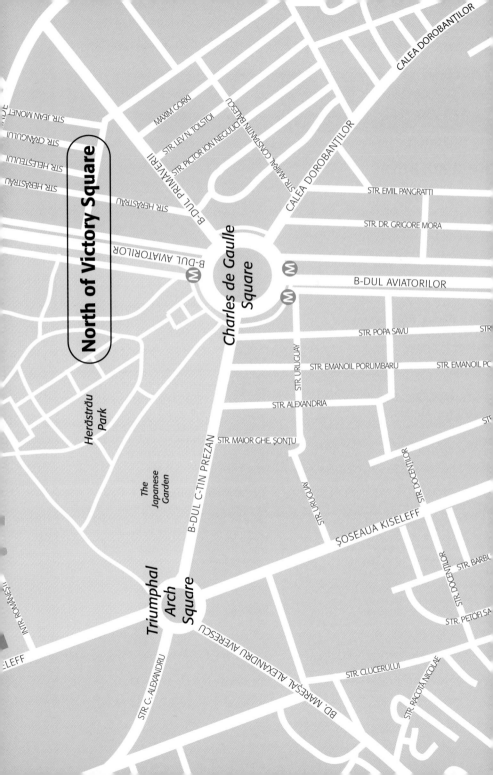

# North of Victory Square

Charles de Gaulle Square

Triumphal Arch Square

Herăstrău Park

The Japanese Garden

CALEA DOROBANȚILOR

STR. EMIL PANGRATTI

STR. DR. GRIGORE MORA

B-DUL AVIATORILOR

STR. POPA SAVU

STR. EMANOIL PORUMBARU

STR. EMANOIL PO

STR. ALEXANDRIA

STR. MAIOR GHE. ȘONȚU

ȘOSEAUA KISELEFF

STR. DOCENȚILOR

STR. URUGUAY

STR. URUGUAY

B-DUL C-TIN PREZAN

B-DUL AVIATORILOR

CALEA DOROBANȚILOR

STR. AMIRAL CONSTANTIN BĂLESCU

STR. PICTOR ION NEGULICI

STR. LEV N. TOLSTOI

MAXIM GORKI

B-DUL PRIMĂVERII

STR. HERĂSTRĂU

STR. HERĂSTRĂU

STR. HELEȘTEULUI

STR. GRĂNUȚEI

STR. JEAN MONET

B-DUL AVIATORILOR

STR. C. ALEXANDRU

BD. MAREȘAL ALEXANDRU AVERESCU

STR. CLUCERULUI

STR. RACOTĂ NICOLAE

STR. DOCENȚILOR

STR. BARBU

STR. PETŐFI SA

STR. ROMÂNEȘTI

ELEFF

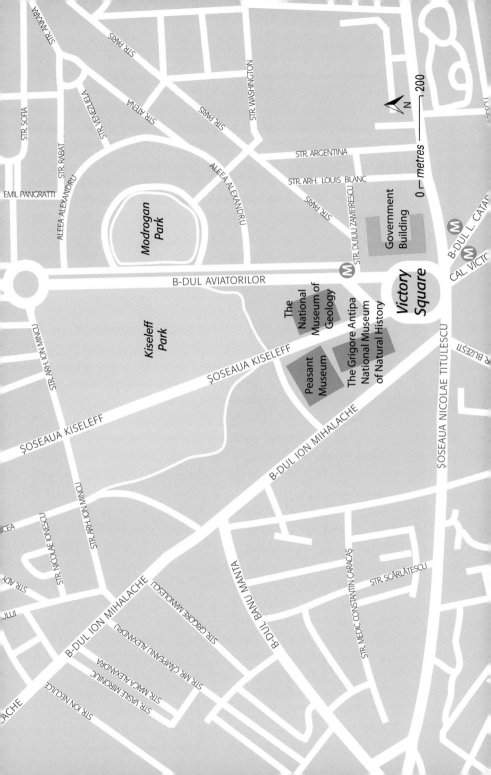

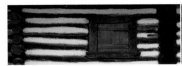  

Left **House from the Village Museum**   Centre **Tulips in Kiseleff Park**   Right **Traditional plate**

Bucharest

# North of Victory Square

THE CAPITAL'S MOST DEVELOPED AREA *is elegant and very green, with lots of beautiful parks and houses from the inter-war period. A historical figure emblematic of the district, Russian General Pavel Kiseleff had this part of the city redesigned in the modern spirit in the 1830s. The boulevard named after him witnessed the first "flower fights" (formerly a popular pastime) and velocipedes, and more recently the first Chinese restaurant: the famous Fu Chang night bar of the inter-war years (on the site of what is now the Doina Restaurant). The area conceals many hidden treasures.*

## Highlights

1. Grigore Antipa National Museum of Natural History
2. Peasant Museum
3. The National Museum of Geology
4. Kiseleff Park
5. The Monument to the Aviators
6. The K.H. Zambaccian Museum
7. Herăstrău Park
8. The Triumphal Arch
9. Village Museum
10. The House of the Free Press

**Peacock, Bordei Park**

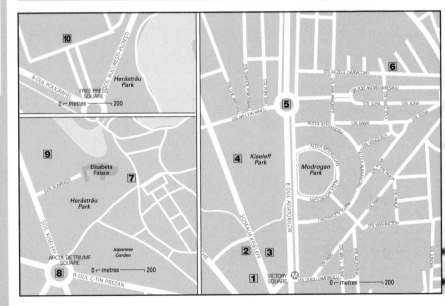

# Grigore Antipa National Museum of Natural History

The museum houses more than two million items from the fields of zoology, palaeontology, mineralogy, and ethnography. The building was the first to be constructed specially as a museum, at the beginning of the 20th century, under the direction of Grigore Antipa, who was head of the institution for 51 years. Sculptor Dimitrie Paciurea created a frieze of statues depicting the science of geology for the fronton, but it was destroyed in the earthquake of 1940. The most valuable exhibit in the museum is the skeleton of a *Deinotherium gigantissimum*, a mammal extinct for around 2.5 million years. The skeleton is 4.5 m tall and 3.5 m long and was discovered in a village in Moldavia at the end of the 19th century. After extensive renovation and modernisation work, the museum reopened in the autumn of 2011. See also p. 40.

# Peasant Museum

The 90,000 items recreating the atmosphere of the rural community of former times include 18,000 ceramic exhibits (the oldest dating from 1746), 20,000 items of folk costume, some donated by Queen Maria herself, 10,000 woven items, 8,000 wooden items, and around

**Exhibit, Peasant Museum**

4,000 icons on wood and glass, religious woodcuts, priestly vestments, and wayside crosses. In 1996, the institution was named European Museum of the Year. See also pp. 40–41.

# The National Museum of Geology

The idea of founding a "collection of rocks and minerals from around country" that could be "visited and consulted by the public" goes back to 1834. The building, typical of the so-called Neo-Brâncoveanu style, was finished in 1908. The permanent exhibition is made up of 14 collections with a total of 7,700 exhibits. See also p. 41.

**The House of the Free Press**

### Kiseleff Park

**4** Laid out after 1832 (when the avenue of the same name was cut) and incorporating part of a forest in the area, the park was designed by landscape architect W. Mayer. It is named after the Russian general who administered the Romanian Principalities during the time of the Organic Regulations and who was in part responsible for the modernisation of the city. In 2001, a statue of Persian poet and astronomer Omar Khayyam was erected on the plinth on which a statue of King Ferdinand once stood. See also pp. 44.

### The Monument to the Aviators

**5** Also known as the Monument to the Heroes of the Air, it is a symbol of the district of the same name. The group of statues was created in 1935 by sculptor Lidia Kotzebue and Iosif Fekete in honour of the aviators of the World War I. It has a total height of 20 m. The plinth and obelisk are made of stone from the Apuseni Mountains and the 5 m-high winged figure was cast from bronze and weighs 5 tonnes.

**The Monument to the Aviators**

### The K. H. Zambaccian Museum

**6** The Zambaccian Museum opened in 1947 and exhibits works by major Romanian painters (Aman, Baba, Grigorescu, Andreescu, Luchian), as well as valuable works by the French school (Delacroix, Renoir, Matisse, Picasso, Cézanne). The collection was donated to the Romanian state by Krikor H. Zambaccian (1889–1962),

an Armenian merchant and patron of the arts.
◈ *21A Muzeul Zambaccian St (near Piața Dorobanți)* • *021 230 19 20* • *Open Sat.–Wed. 11–19, May–Sep., 10–18, Oct.–Apr., closed Thu., Fri., national holidays* • *Entrance fee 7 lei* • *www.mnar.ro*

### Herăstrău Park

**7** Laid out in 1936 after the draining of a marsh on the shores of the lake of the same name, Herăstrău is Bucharest's largest park. Visit the Island of Roses, Japanese Garden, Avenue of Caryatids, the complex of 12 statues representing the "parents of Europe," the statue of Charles de Gaulle, and the Village Museum. You can hire a bicycle or take a boat trip on the lake. See also p. 44.

### The Triumphal Arch

**8** The Triumphal Arch, a monument commemorating Romania's victory in the World War I, is still standing after almost 100 years. Designed by architect Petre Antonescu, the monument was built in 1921–1922 to mark the coronation of King

---

## Romanian Television

The Romanian public television (TVR) building is a landmark on Calea Dorobanți. The television station was inaugurated in 1956 and moved to its current location in 1968. From 1985, the broadcasting program was cut to two hours per day, dedicated to the Ceaușescu family personality cult. In December 1989, demonstrators occupied the television building and the revolution was broadcasted live. TVR thus played a crucial role in the events of 1989.

Ferdinand and Queen Maria and renovated a few years later. It wasmodelled on the Arc de Triomphe in Paris. 27 m tall, the Arch is decorated with inscriptions and bas-reliefs. It also houses a small museum, open only on special occasions.

### 9 Village Museum

After the crowded big boulevard, the Village Museum, one of the first open-air ethnographic museums in the world, offers an escape into the tranquil atmosphere of the traditional Romanian village. See also pp. 30–33.

### 10 The House of the Free Press

Casa Scânteii (House of the Spark), now the House of the Free Press, is an example of communist-era architecture. Built in only five years (1952–1957), the building was intended to house the main newspaper of the time, Scânteia (The Spark). Inspired by the buildings of Stalinist Moscow, it was the first structure in Bucharest to be earthquake-proofed.

## A day north of Victory Square

### Morning

🕐 Don't linger too long over your coffee. Set out from the **House of the Free Press** and **Herăstrău Park**, part of which is the **Village Museum**. Regardless of the season, it is worth spending two or three hours among the beautiful traditional houses from Romanian villages. You can buy souvenirs from the museum shop. Then head to the **Triumphal Arch** and Charles de Gaulle Square.

🍴 Here you can have lunch at the City Grill, at 3 Primăverii Boulevard.

### Afternoon

Refreshed, set off down Aviatorilor Boulevard, past the tall building with the glass façade, and after five minutes' walk turn left down **Muzeul Zambaccian** St. The charming museum, founded by an Armenian merchant, has an astonishingly varied collection. After visiting the museum, return to the boulevard. At the **Monument to the Aviators**, cut across **Kiseleff Park** to see the sculptures by George Apostu. Near Victory Square, which is dominated by the government building, cross Kiseleff Boulevard and visit the **Peasant Museum**, which is neighbours with the **Antipa Museum** and the **Geology Museum**.

🍴 Have dinner on the Peasant Museum terrace, or if you fancy something more elegant, try Casa Doina, a little up the road, at 4 Chaussée Kiseleff.

*Following pages – **Traditional plates, Peasant Museum***

# CreArT
## The Bucharest Centre for Creation, Art and Tradition

**"Holiday Traditions and Flowers"** is a cultural event now at the fifth edition, organised around the Easter time, in Cişmigiu Park. It features an Easter fair, a rabbit exhibition, carriage and ponies rides and a flower market and also an exhibition. Every participant in this fair has the chance to present a vast array of traditional objects and products, manually crafted decorations, flower arrangements and other goodies specific for this holiday. The audience is also presented with a show which takes place in the park.

**The International Folk Festival "Music and Traditions in Cismigiu"** is the oldest event organised by CreArT. It takes place in the second to last weekend of June and brings the authentic tradition into the urban environment, through folk music, dance and art. The programme includes folk shows, an arts and crafts fair, cooking shows, carriage and ponies rides, workshops and many other activities for all kind of audience. The three stages host over 1 200 artists from all over the world, and another 500 people participate in the traditional costumes parade, representing national and international ensembles, communities and minorities and also brass bands. The young audience is dedicated an entire section of the festival – Fân Zone (Hay Zone)– a nonconventional space, both for entertainment and relaxation, where everybody can sit on the grass, next to a hay stack. The authentic folk music is reinterpreted by well known Djs and bands. For those who are willing to carry on the torch of old crafts, we organise workshopd, where one can learn various traditional arts, like weaving, sewing, paiting, sculpture or pottery making.

**Bucharest Days** marks the first mentioning of Bucharest in an official document (September 20, 1459). It is an event that transforms the capital city in a giant stage and actors, singers, circus artists, brass bands and craftmen are occupying the squares and the streets. For a few days CreArT tries to re-enact the old times of Bucharest in a craftmen's fair, through carriage rides and a costume parade, and also through shows bringing together folk music and dance, brass bands, communities and national minorities, old music and entertainers dressed in old costumes. We organise also a flower battle which, with the other special events, manage to turn Bucharest, for a few days, at least, in a Capital of Entertainment.

**Bucharest Christmas Market** is the official Christmas fair organised by the City Hall and CreArT and dedicated to all those living in or just visiting Bucharest. The event is part of the Christmas Fairs Circuit in Europe and aims to become a national and European touristic atraction during winter holidays. The fair takes place in the middle of University Square, in a location already traditional, and extends in the historical centre. Bucharest Christmas Market includes not only traditional art and food, but also shows with carol singers and folk groups from all around the country, and also concerts by artists performing different musical genres, from etno, pop and indie, to rock and reggae. And, as there is no Christmas without gifts, Father Christmas comes every year from his workshop in the North Pole and stops at the Bucharest Christmas Market to tell stories and make surprises to children.

**Teatrelli – Theatre, Music & More –** in the middle of Bucharest, just around the corner from the Roman Square, CreArT awaits you in a trendy location, where every show is turned into a unique experience dedicated to all those who want to let themselves be enchanted by the sounds of music, to live to the fullest every theatre play and to be able to notice even the slightest change of rithm in the dancers' steps. Having more than 70 places, Teatrelli – Theatre, Music & More wants to offer you a quality cultural alternative, in a welcoming and refined space.

For more details about the programme and tickets, go to www.creart.ro or to the teatrelli facebook page.

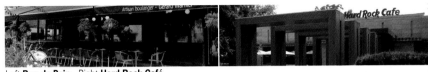

Left **Rue de Pain**   Right **Hard Rock Café**

# Cafés and Bars

### 1 Clubul Ţăranului
An excursion to the Chaussée, taking in a museum or a film, can be combined with a beer on the terrace of the Peasant Museum. *3 Chaussée Kiseleff • 021 310 80 48 • www.muzeultaranuluiroman.ro • Map B2*

### 2 Hard Rock Café
The same as Dublin, Paris and New York, Bucharest has a Hard Rock Café with Tex-Mex food and gigantic cocktails. *32 Chaussée Kiseleff • 021 206 62 61 • www.hardrock.com • Off the map*

### 3 Rue de Pain
First thing in the morning, have a coffee and a (authentic) croissant at the beautiful boulangerie next to Floreasca Market. *111–113 Calea Floreasca • 021 312 00 60 • Map D1*

### 4 White Horse
One of the first pubs in Bucharest, still famous for its relaxed atmosphere and excellent beer. *4A George Călinescu St (near Piaţa Dorobanţi) • 021 231 27 95 • www.whitehorse.ro • Map D1*

### 5 Afternoons and Coffeespoons
Located close to Victory Square, Afternoons and Coffeespoons is a good spot for a lunch break or business meeting. *63–69 Iacob Felix St • 0731 343 095 • www.afternoons-coffeespoons.com • Map A3*

### 6 Rouge Café
The iced lemonade and inimitable cheesecake are on the summer menu at this elegant café. *7 Ankara St • 021 230 31 47 • www.rouge.ro • Map C1*

### 7 Rendez-Vous
Four oak-furnished rooms are the setting for a cup of Indian tea and lemon cake. *102 Calea Floreasca • 0720 070 286 • www.ceainarie.ro • Map E1*

### 8 MonKaff Roasting House
The coffee is brought straight from India, Salvador, Indonesia, Nicaragua, and Brazil and roasted right here. *111–113 Calea Floreasca • 0771 795 281 • www.monkaff.ro • Map E1*

### 9 Juice Zone
A Canadian concept promoting health food and drinks: freshly squeezed fruit juice, salads, and delicious sandwiches. *67 Ion Mihalache Boulevard • 0741 133 029 • www.juicezoneromania.ro • Map A1*

### 10 Veda Lounge
From outside you would never suspect the silk, velvet, gleaming hookahs, and sandalwood scents within: a place for hedonists, with aromatic teas, Brazilian coffee, and fine wines. *45 Cpt. Octav Cocărăscu St (near Piaţa 1 Mai) • 0721 065 402 • www.vedalounge.ro • Off the map*

**Price categories**

| | |
|---|---|
| ♨ | cheap |
| ♨♨ | middling |
| ♨♨♨ | not cheap |
| ♨♨♨♨ | expensive |

Left **La Cocoşatu**   Right **Taverna Sârbului**

# Restaurants

### 1 Taverna Sârbului
Located behind the House of the Free Press, the tavern serves Serbian specialties in a generous space.
◈ *31 Tipografilor St • 021 490 60 50 • www.tavernasarbului.ro • Off the map*
• ♨♨–♨♨♨

### 2 La Cocoşatu
One of the capital's legendary gastronomic landmarks, frequented by VIPs and ordinary locals, who come for the best *mici* in Bucharest. ◈ *52 Neagoe Vodă St (near Băneasa Airport) • 021 232 87 96 • www.lacocosatu.ro • Off the map* • ♨–♨♨

### 3 Uptown
Located in the Dorobanţi area, Uptown is an agreeable restaurant for businessmen and tourists. International menu. ◈ *9 Rabat St • 021 231 40 77 • www.uptown.ro • Map C1*
• ♨♨♨–♨♨♨♨

### 4 Casa di David
Luxury cars in the parking lot, a beautiful view from the shore of Herăstrău Lake, and good food.
◈ *6–9 Chaussée Nordului • 021 232 47 15 • www.casadidavid.ro • Off the map*
• ♨♨♨–♨♨♨♨

### 5 La Belle Époque
A lively, unpretentious Belgian restaurant, where you can have Leffe and a steak after work. ◈ *6 Radu Beller St (near Piaţa Dorobanţi) • 021 230 07 70 • www.labelleepoque.ro • Map D1* • ♨♨–♨♨♨

### 6 Trattoria Il Calcio
A restaurant next to Herăstrău Park, with a large terrace. The same Italian menu as in other Il Calcio locations.
◈ *7–9 Chaussée Nordului • 0724 706 665 • www.trattoriailcalcio.ro • Off the map*
• ♨♨–♨♨♨

### 7 City Grill
Good Romanian food a stone's throw from Charles de Gaulle Square. The shady terrace is perfect in the dog days of summer. ◈ *3 Primăverii Boulevard • 021 314 24 89 • www.citygrill.ro • Off the map • ♨♨–♨♨♨*

### 8 Isoletta
An elegant restaurant on the shore of Herăstrău Lake. The fish and seafood are brought directly from Italy!
◈ *7–9 Chaussée Nordului (by the BTT tennis courts) • 021 232 32 23 • www.isoletta.ro • Off the map*
• ♨♨♨♨

### 9 Mica Elveţie
A friendly, secluded restaurant with Swiss specialties, grills, salads, and sophisticated desserts.
◈ *64 Sandu Aldea St • 021 224 50 17 • Off the map • ♨♨♨*

### 10 Osho
The name comes from the initials of the four brothers who founded the brand in Chicago in 1939: Oskar, Sam, Harry, and Oliver. American menu.
◈ *19 Primăverii Boulevard • 021 568 30 31 • www.osho-restaurant.ro • Off the map • ♨♨♨*

*Other restaurants in the area: Casa Doina (p. 63), Piccolo Mondo (p. 65), Taverna Sârbului (p. 65).*

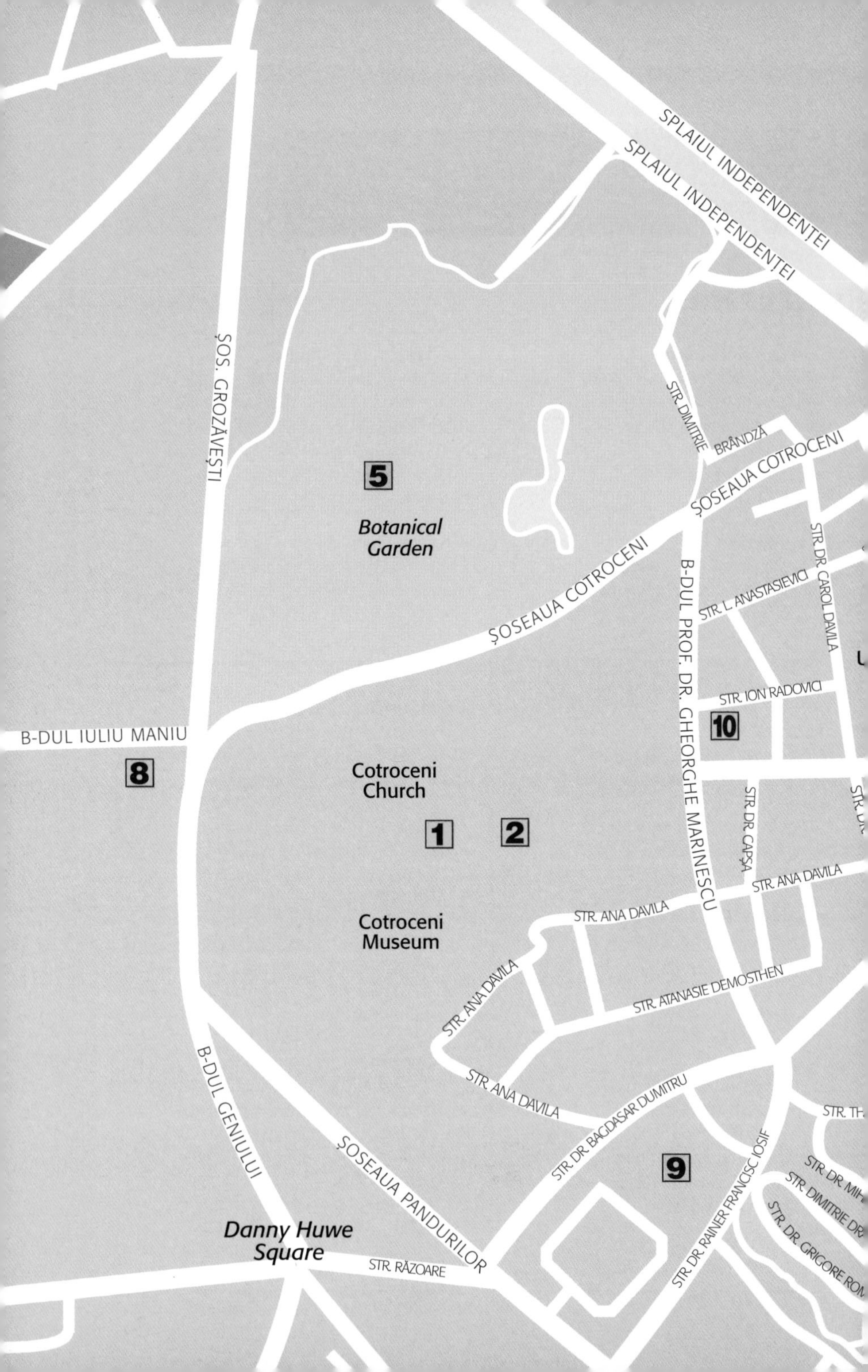

**SPLAIUL INDEPENDENTEI**

**SPLAIUL INDEPENDENTEI**

ȘOS. GROZĂVEȘTI

STR. DIMITRIE

BRÂNDZĂ

**ȘOSEAUA COTROCENI**

STR. DR. CAROL DAVILA

STR. L. ANASTASIEVICI

5

*Botanical
Garden*

**ȘOSEAUA COTROCENI**

B-DUL PROF. DR. GHEORGHE MARINESCU

STR. ION RADOVICI

10

B-DUL IULIU MANIU

8

*Cotroceni
Church*

STR. DR. CAPȘA

STR. DR.

1   2

STR. ANA DAVILA

*Cotroceni
Museum*

STR. ANA DAVILA

STR. ANA DAVILA

B-DUL GENIULUI

STR. ANA DAVILA

STR. ATANASIE DEMOSTHEN

STR. DR. BAGDASAR DUMITRU

STR. TH.

STR. DR. MIH

9

STR. DR. DIMITRIE DR.

STR. DR. RAINER FRANCISC IOSIF

ȘOSEAUA PANDURILOR

*Danny Huwe
Square*

STR. RĂZOARE

STR. DR. GRIGORE ROM

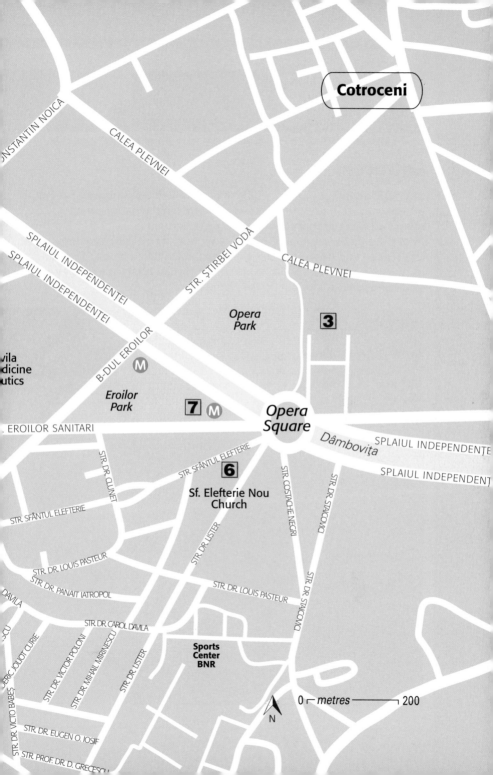

Left **The Romanian Opera**   Centre **The Botanical Garden**   Right **Monument to the Heroes of the Homeland**

# Cotroceni

COTROCENI IS ONE OF THE MOST SELECT *and the least altered neighbourhoods of Bucharest, with a tranquil atmosphere, winding streets, and very few tall or ultra-modern buildings. Here you can admire old ivy-clad buildings with ornate frontons.*

*The history of this area is linked to the Romanian Royal Family. The area began to develop after King Carol I built the Royal Palace around the monastery on Cotroceni Hill. His successor, King Ferdinand, added buildings to the palace for royal and military staff. Cotroceni Palace is now home to the Romanian Presidency.*

## Highlights

1. Cotroceni Palace
2. Cotroceni National Museum
3. The Romanian National Opera
4. The Carol Davila University
5. The Botanical Garden
6. The Church of St Eleftherios
7. The Monument to the Medical Corps Heroes
8. The Lion Monument
9. The Monument to the Heroes of the Homeland
10. The Liviu Rebreanu and Ion Minulescu–Claudia Millian Memorial Museums

**The Lion Monument, detail**

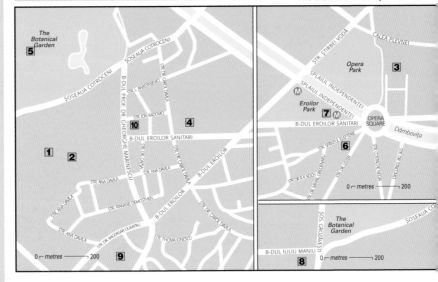

### Cotroceni Palace

The fame of Cotroceni dates back to 1679, when Şerban Cantacuzino built a monastery here. After 1893, it became the main residence of the Crown Prince of Romania. French architect Paul Gottereau built the present palace, to which a northern wing was added a few years later, in 1895–1900. The old Cotroceni Monastery was demolished in 1984, but the church has since been rebuilt. After the 1989 Revolution, the palace became the official residence of the Romanian President.
*1 Geniului St • www.presidency.ro*

### Cotroceni National Museum

Located in the grounds of Cotroceni Palace, the museum was inaugurated on 27 December 1991. It recreates the atmosphere of the Cantacuzino epoch and the period when the palace was home to members of the Royal Family. There is an exhibition of icons, manuscripts, and ornaments in the former monastic cells. *1 Geniului St • 021 317 31 07 • Tue.-Sun. 9:30–17:30 by telephone appointment and with an act of identity • Entrance fee 12 lei • www.muzeulcotroceni.ro*

**Statue of Enescu, Romanian National Opera**

### The Romanian National Opera

The first recorded mention of an opera performance in Bucharest dates from 1772. The first Romanian Opera Company was directed by George Stephănescu and founded on 8 May 1885. The Romanian Opera was not founded until 1921.

**The Carol Davila University of Medicine and Pharmaceutics**

The premiere performance was *Lohengrin*, conducted by George Enescu. The present opera house was designed by Octav Doicescu and built in 1953. The Romanian Opera seats 2,200. On the top floor there is a museum of the Romanian Opera. A bronze statue of Enescu, sculpted by Ion Jalea, stands in front of the opera house.

*70–72 Mihail Kogălniceanu Boulevard • 021 314 69 80 • www.operanb.ro*

### 4 The Carol Davila University

The imposing building of the Medicine University was designed by French architect Louis Blanc and built in 1899-1903. The statue *(right)* of the founder, Carol Davila, was created by sculptor Karl Storck. The famous figures who have studied here include George Emil Palade described as the most influential cell biologist ever. His innovations in electron microscopy and cell fractionations laid the foundations of modern molecular cell biology. He was rewarded the Nobel Prize in Physiology and Medicine in 1974. He is the only Romanian Nobel winner.

*8 Eroilor Sanitari Boulevard • www.umf.ro*

### 5 The Botanical Garden

Covering 17.5 hectares, the Botanical Garden was founded by Dr Carol Davila in 1860, during the reign of Alexandru Ioan Cuza. It is located near the University of Medicine and Pharmaceutics. The present gardens were laid out in 1884 by Prof. Dimitrie Brândză

and the Belgian landscape architect Fuchs. In 1891, the hothouses and the Botanical Institute (destroyed by bombs in 1944) were inaugurated.

*32 Chaussée Cotroceni • 021 318 15 59 • Garden 8–18 daily; entrance fee 5 lei, Botanical Museum Tue., Thu., Sat., Sun. 9–13 • Entrance 2 lei • www.gradina-botanica.ro*

### 6 The Church of St Eleftherios

The church was built in the Neo-Romanian style by architect Constantin Iotzu. Work began in 1935, was interrupted by the World War II, and was not completed until 1971. The murals include a troubling scene painted by Father Arsenie Boca (1910–1989): the Child Jesus in a prisoner's uniform, a courageous reference to the communist persecution of religion. Further down the street, on an island

**Carol Davila (1832–1884)**

Absolvent al Facultății de Medicină din Paris, Carol Davila a venit în 1853, la invitația domnului Barbu Știrbey, pentru a organiza serviciul sanitar. În următorii ani a pus bazele unui sistem medical riguros, înființând Școala Națională de Medicină și Farmacie. Este întemeietorul învățământului veterinar și a unor societăți științifice. Bustul său din bronz, executat de Constantin Brâncuși, este expus în curtea Muzeului Militar din București.

**Carol Davila**

n the middle of the road, stands the old
Church of St Eleftherios, built in 1744.
The church was famed in the
past for the healing power of its
cons and picturesque setting.

## 7 The Monument to the Medical Corps Heroes

On the west side of Opera Square
stands a monument to the medical
corps heroes of the World War I.
Unveiled in 1932, the work is by sculptor
R. Romanelli. The main figure, a woman
in a nurse's uniform, might depict Queen
Maria, whose devotion to tending
the wounded was famous.

## 8 The Lion Monument

On Cotroceni Hill, at the intersection
of Iuliu Maniu and Geniului boulevards,
stands the monument known as the Lion.
The work of sculptor Spiridon Georgescu,
the statue was unveiled in 1929.
The monument consists of a lion,
symbolising strength, and four soldiers.
The inscription reads: "Tell future
generations that we made the supreme
sacrifice on the battlefield for the sake
of national unification."

## 9 The Monument to the Heroes of the Homeland

The monument, which stands in front of the
National Defence University, was unveiled
on 17 August 1957. The three 9 m-high
bronze statues represent an aviator,
an infantryman, and a mariner.

## 10 The Liviu Rebreanu and Ion Minulescu-Claudia Millian Memorial Museums

Opposite Cotroceni Palace can be
found the flats where writer Liviu
Rebreanu (1885–1944) and poet Ion
Minulescu (1881–1944) lived and worked.
You can admire personal items,
manuscripts and books.

19 Gh. Marinescu Boulevard, flat 11 (Rebreanu),
at 12 (Minulescu), buzzer 5 and 6
021 317 90 42 (Rebreanu), 021 317 90 41
(Minulescu) • Tue.–Sun. 10–17 •
www.mlr.ro

## A day in Cotroceni

### Morning

The area's main attraction is the
**Cotroceni Palace and Museum**.
Telephone a day in advance to
make an appointment and don't
forget to bring your identity card.
Among other things, you will be
able to visit the kitchen of the
former monastery, the Grand
Reception Hall, and the bedroom
of Queen Maria. After spending
a few hours in the atmosphere
of bygone days, leave the museum
and head down Chaussée
Cotroceni, past the **Botanical
Garden**, which you can visit
in the afternoon. Follow Gh.
Marinescu Boulevard as far as
Piaţa Eroilor, then turn down Sf.
Elefterie St to view the beautiful
church. At 15 Dr. Clunet St, have
lunch at the **Museum** Restaurant.

### Afternoon

After lunch, pay a short visit
to the **Dimitrie and Aurelia
Ghiaţă Museum**, at no. 14,
next to the restaurant.
It is open Tue.–Sun. from 10
to 18. Continue along Sf.
Elefterie St towards the **Opera**,
visiting the **New St Eleftherios
Church** on the way to look
at the murals. Pass by the
**Monument to the Medical
Corps Heroes** and skirt the park
along Eroilor Sanitari Boulevard
as far as the **University
of Medicine**. Five minutes'
walk away you will find
the block where **Liviu Rebreanu**
and **Ion Minulescu** lived.
The **Botanical Garden**
is nearby, where you can
spend the rest of the
afternoon. For dinner,
go to the **Taverna Brădet**
at 60 Carol Davila St.

Left **The Dâmboviţa river**    Right **The AFI Palace Cotroceni**

# Cafés, Tearooms and Bars

### 1 Ceai la Cotroceni
A popular spot for tea opposite the presidential palace. The atmosphere is bohemian and intimate. You will find here sweets and dozens of blends of tea. *25 Gh. Marinescu Boulevard • 0721 66 95 35*

### 2 Starbucks
A name that requires no introduction. Starbucks cafés came to Romania a few years ago and have lived up to their reputation. *4 Vasile Milea Boulevard (inside the AFI Palace Cotroceni) • www.starbucksromania.ro*

### 3 French Bakery
Delicious cakes and confectionary made according to traditional French recipes. *Opera Center, 1–5 Costache Negri St • 021 410 26 58 • Harta A7 • www.frenchbakery.ro.*

### 4 Club-Seven
You won't be bored here: on Wednesdays there is stand-up comedy, on Tuesdays and Thursdays karaoke, and concerts and other events the rest of the time. *11 Chaussée Cotroceni • 0763 852 694 • www.club-seven.ro*

### 5 Café du Pont
Before a good film at the Glendale cinema or a walk in the Botanical Garden, treat yourself to coffee or hot chocolate and pancakes at the Café du Pont. *16 Chaussée Cotroceni • 0726 279 857 • www.cafedupont.ro*

### 6 Expert Caffé
This is the perfect spot for whiling away a chilly autumn afternoon, warmed by the pleasant aroma of freshly ground coffee. *12 Dr. Lister St • 0743 53 58 89*

### 7 Glendale Art Café
A tasteful cup of coffee is just the thing after a good film, while you chat with friends about the actors and scenes you liked best. The café is located in the Glendale Studio. Coffee is included in the price of your cinema ticket. *9 Chaussée Cotroceni • 021 316 32 86 • www.glendale.ro*

### 8 The Spot 50's Pub
A pub where you can go to watch football matches or just chat with friends over a drink. *9 Chaussée Cotroceni • 021 224 89 63*

### 9 Land of Tea
The perfect place for a chilly autumn afternoon, with all kinds of teas, from black and green to fruit. Warm, tasteful décor. *4 Vasile Milea Boulevard (in the AFI Palace Cotroceni) • 0728 168 085*

### 10 Rogge Café
A chic, elegantly furnished café with an extensive list of coffees, teas and other drinks. *4 Vasile Milea Boulevard (in the AFI Palace Cotroceni) • 021 448 18 25 • www.roggecafe.ro*

Left **Derby Bar & Restaurant**   Right **Museum**

**Price categories**

| | |
|---|---|
| 🔹 | cheap |
| 🔹🔹 | middling |
| 🔹🔹🔹 | not cheap |
| 🔹🔹🔹🔹 | expensive |

# Restaurants

### 1 Museum
Located in a beautiful villa near the Old St Eleftherios Church, Museum is ready to welcome you with duck's breast in blackberry sauce, grilled cockerel, apple tart with walnut ice cream, and other treats.
🔹 *15 Dr. Clunet St • 021 411 91 28 • www.museumrestaurant.ro • 🔹🔹-🔹🔹🔹*

### 2 Taverna Brădet
Originally Casa Brădet, then Bistro-Librăria Aries, now Taverna Brădet, the restaurant is famous with locals for its beautiful building, charming terrace, and good food.
🔹 *60 Carol Davila St • 0724 257 675 • www.tavernabradet.ro • 🔹🔹*

### 3 Valencia – Casa Spaniolă
Founded in 1994, this Spanish restaurant continues to be popular with locals and visitors alike. The décor is pleasant, dominated by warm colours, perfect for a romantic date.
🔹 *12 Leonte Anastasievici St (behind the Municipal Hospital) • 021 312 81 96 • www.valencia.ro • 🔹🔹-🔹🔹🔹*

### 4 Mythos
Kleftiko, taramosalata, saganaki feta, musaka... all kinds of Greek specialties whose mere names make you think of the Mediterranean sun and tasty food..
🔹 *28 Costache Negri St (near Opera Center) • 021 410 23 76 • www.restaurantmythos.ro • 🔹🔹-🔹🔹🔹*

### 5 Derby Bar & Restaurant
Located in a beautiful building, the Derby is a good choice for a meal with friends. There is a pub on the ground floor, and the restaurant is on the upper floor 🔹 *49A Eroii Sanitari Boulevard • 021 410 85 45 • www.derbypub.ro • 🔹🔹*

### 6 Trattoria Roma
With a beautiful view of the Opera, the trattoria is ideal for a business lunch or an evening with family.
🔹 *1 Dr. Lister St • 021 441 63 30 • www.trattoria-roma.ro • 🔹🔹-🔹🔹🔹*

### 7 Azzurro Il Venetiano
A restaurant impressive for its size and expensive décor. Some of the Sicilian recipes are 100 years old.
🔹 *4 Vasile Milea Boulevard (AFI Palace Cotroceni) • 0788 362 983 • www.azzurro.com.ro • 🔹🔹🔹*

### 8 Davila
International restaurant with a Thai chef.
🔹 *19 Cotroceni Boulevard • 021 212 67 65 • 🔹🔹-🔹🔹🔹*

### 9 The Left Hand
A tranquil spot, in a historic building. Good food, without *haute cuisine* pretensions.
🔹 *4 Dr. P. Iatropol • 0727 277 300 • www.thelefthand.ro • 🔹-🔹🔹*

### 10 Bistro Bella Notte Café
Romanian and international restaurant in a Brâncoveanu-style building behind the Opera Center.
🔹 *4 Dr. Staicovici St • 021 781 45 56 • 🔹🔹*

# STREETSMART

BUCHAREST

Left **Băneasa Airport**  Centre **Henri Coandă Airport**  Right **Bucharest by sectors**

# General Information

## 1 Administrative organisation

With a surface area of 228 km², Bucharest is the only city in Romania that is not part of a county. The city is divided into six sectors, 3 and 6 being the most populous, each with around 400,000 inhabitants.

## 2 The Metro

Construction work commenced in 1975, and the first Metro line, between Semănătoarea and Timpuri Noi, opened in 1979. The most recently added stations are Jiului and Parc Bazilescu, inaugurated on 1 June 2011. There are four lines with a total distance of 69.25 km. The Metro runs from 5.00 to 23.00 daily. *www.metrorex.ro*

## 3 RATB

Bucharest public transport (RATB) operates buses, trolleybuses, trams, and express lines. The timetable is from 5.00 to 24.00, but some night services have recently been introduced. *www.ratb.ro*.

## 4 Henri Coandă International Airport

Located in Otopeni on the București–Ploiești highway, 16.5 km from the centre of Bucharest. There are two express bus links: 783 (from Union Square) and 780 (from Gara de Nord), 5.30–23.00 daily.

The journey time is 45–60 min. There is also a train from Gara de Nord. ℡ *021 204 1000* • *www.aeroportul-otopeni.info, www.bucharestairports.ro*

## 5 Aurel Vlaicu International Airport

Located 8.5 km from the centre of Bucharest, this airport is a hub for domestic and low-cost flights. Buses: 131 (from Roman Square), 335, 148, 112, 301, 783. ℡ *021 9371* • *www.bucharestairports.ro*

## 6 Gara de Nord

Inaugurated in 1872, Gara de Nord (North Station) is Romania's main rail hub. Connexions: Metro, bus (105, 123, 133, 178, 182, 205, 282, 780 express, 785), trolleybus (62, 69, 71, 79, 85, 86, 93, 96), tram (34, 35, 37, 44, 46, 52). The only **Romanian Railways (CFR) ticket agency** in the city centre is at 10 Brezoianu St, tel. 021 313 26 42. ℡ *021 9521* • *www.cfrcalatori.ro, www.infofer.ro, www.mersultrenurilor.ro*

## 7 Coach stations

Coaches are a cheaper but usually not so comfortable alternative to trains. There are coach stations at: **Băneasa** – B-dul Ion Ionescu de la Brad nr. 10, 021 230 56 45 **Grivița** – Șos. Chitilei nr. 221-223, 021 667 59 70 **Militari** – B-dul Iuliu Maniu

nr. 141, 021 434 17 39 **Obor** – B-dul Gării de Est nr. 17, 021 252 76 46 **Ritmului** – Str. Ritmului nr. 35, 021 250 86 69 *www.autogari.ro*

## 8 Taxis

There are more than 40 taxi companies operating around the clock. The usual tariff is 1.39 lei/km, but always check before getting into a taxi.

## 9 Post offices

Open Mon.–Fri. 7.30–13.00, 13.30–20.00 (some are also open Sat. 8–14) for sending and receiving letters, postcards, parcels, money. They are marked on the folding map of Central Bucharest.

## 10 Money

Romania's currency is the *leu* (plural *lei*), divided into 100 *bani*. At the time of writing one leu was equal to € 0,23. Notes come in denominations of 500, 200, 100, 50, 10, 5 and 1. Credit and debit cards are accepted almost everywhere.

### Taxis

**Cobălcescu** 021 9451
**Confort** 021 9455
**Cristaxi** 021 9421
**Speed Taxi** 021 9477
**Meridian** 021 9444
**Occident** 021 9413
**Perozzi** 021 9631
**2000** 021 9494

*The capital has 1,883,425 inhabitants (according to the 2011 census), but it is estimated that the daytime population is 3 million.*

Left **Cocor department store**   Right **Newspaper kiosk with graffiti**

# Sources of Information

### 1 24 FUN
Weekly brochure providing information about cultural events, restaurants, cafés and shops. Distributed free in bars, hotel lobbies, bookshops, cinemas, and malls. An excellent source of information for locals and tourists alike.
✸ www.24fun.ro

### 2 Şapte Seri
Published weekly. Provides cultural, tourist and free-time listings. If you want to know what films are showing or what concerts are playing, you will find all the details in Şapte Seri.
✸ www.sapteseri.ro

### 3 Bucharest in Your Pocket
A friendly English-language guide that assuages whatever fears foreign first-time visitors to Bucharest might harbour. Aimed mainly at foreigners, it recommends hotels, restaurants, and historical and cultural attractions.
✸ www.inyourpocket.com/romania/bucharest

### 4 Zile şi nopţi
All you need to know about hotels, cafés and restaurants in Bucharest, plus weekly listings of cultural events. Zile şi nopţi is the largest network of free magazines in Romania, with 21 local editions covering 33 cities.
✸ www.zilesinopti.ro

### 5 Bucharest-Guide
As well as info on hotels and restaurants, you will also find sections on business, shopping, relaxation and beauty salons, car rental, city maps, and city tours.
✸ www.bucharest-guide.ro

### 6 Nine O'Clock
English-language daily, published for 17 years in Bucharest. Provides information for foreign businessmen and tourists and covers Romanian political and economic affairs and cultural events.
✸ www.nineoclock.ro

### 7 Bucharest Hebdo
The only independent French-language publication, founded in 1996 as Bucarest Matin. Up-to-date information on politics and Bucharest social and cultural life.
✸ www.bucarest-hebdo.ro

### 8 Sette Giorni
In its third year, a weekly aimed at the city's Italian community. The best source of information on Bucharest and beyond. Available in restaurants, hotels, and public institutions.
✸ www.sette-giorni.ro

### 9 Disabled access
Although the authorities have taken some measures, it is still very difficult for people with disabilities to get around Bucharest. Most public buildings have access ramps, as do museums, theatres, banks, and hotels. More information at the National Authority for Disabled Persons website – www.anph.ro.

### 10 Internet
It is no longer hard to get on the Internet in Bucharest. Public spaces are connected, and bars and restaurants offer free wireless. You can find internet cafés on all the main boulevards. There is a non-stop Internet café at 120 Calea Victoriei, near Green Hours, and another at 47–53, Lascăr Catargiu Boulevard, part of the Orange Studio in Piaţa Victoriei, open Mon.–Fri. 9–21, Sat. 9–16.

The telephone code for Bucharest is 021, inclusively for calls made within the city.

Left **Currency exchange**   Centre **Policemen**   Right **Cash machine**

# Things to Avoid

### 1 Pickpockets
Pickpockets are a problem in Bucharest: be vigilant when using public transport and in queues or areas with street vendors. Don't keep money in backpacks or coat pockets. Don't leave bags unattended in public places.

### 2 Stray dogs
One of the biggest problems confronting the capital. There are tens of thousands of man's "best friends", and they can sometimes be aggressive. Avoid parks at night, vacant lots, and places where dangerous packs of dogs might gather.

### 3 Taxis with special fares
At taxi ranks you will sometimes notice yellow cabs that look similar to those of regular companies, but which belong to individual operators who charge exorbitant fares. Before getting into a taxi, check that it has a company name and a telephone number on the door. Above all, check the tariff, which should be clearly displayed. Make sure the driver starts the meter before setting off.

### 4 Gara de Nord and outlying districts
The same as in many big cities, the station is home to dangerous fauna (glue sniffers, thieves, dodgy taxi drivers), especially after nightfall. Avoid the environs of Gara de Nord and above all the park opposite after dark. Similarly, it is not advisable to venture into outlying districts at night. The poorly lit parks near the main shopping centres provide ideal conditions for muggers.

### 5 Paying by credit card
You can pay by credit card in most shops and restaurants. Waiters are required to complete the transaction in front of you. If a waiter insists on taking away your card, you may accompany him to the till.

### 6 Currency exchange offices
You can exchange currency at any bank in Bucharest. We advise you opt for a bank, even if exchange offices are more convenient. Many of them do not display the correct exchange rate, and you might find yourself losing up to 25% of the real sum. Check that banknotes are genuine . Banks are usually open from 9.00 to 17.00, Mon–Fri. You can find Piraeus Bank and Raiffeisen Bank opened on Saturdays on the ground floor of Unirea Shopping Center (Union Square).

### 7 Fake policemen
This scam is still used, albeit not as successfully as in the 1990s. If policemen ask your identification papers check their badges and make sure they are real policemen. Crooks will try to demand money and IDs under various pretexts. Refuse categorically and avoid being drawn into arguments with them. Anyway, better have a copy of your passport, not the original.

### 8 Unlicensed street vendors
You may be approached on a street corner by people trying to sell you jewellery, perfumes, watches and suchlike at bargain prices. Do not stop – their intentions are usually completely different.

### 9 Street food
Avoid buying food on the street, especially in summer. Cakes, pies, sandwiches or other food kept in unhygienic conditions can turn into an unpleasant experience.

### 10 Cash machines on the street
At some point, you may need to look for a cash machine. When withdrawing money, make sure the cash machine is in a well-lit main thoroughfare and there are no loiterers nearby. Also make sure that the cash point has a video surveillance camera.

Left **Shop on Calea Victoriei**   Right **Naïve paintings on glass**

# Shopping

### 1 Returns
You can return any item that subsequently proves to be defective. Be sure to keep the receipt for any item you purchase. Consumer Protection Office: phone: 021 980.

### 2 Credit cards
Shops usually display the credit cards they accept on the door. Otherwise, if it is a small, specialized shop, don't hesitate to ask.

### 3 Traditional Romanian products
At weekends, locals go to buy traditional products at the peasant markets held in various locations in Bucharest. The best-known outdoor markets are held at the Peasant Museum, the ARK Cultural Centre (flower market), the Suțu Palace, the Ministry of Agriculture, and on Edgar Quinet Street. You will find ecological products from all over the country at fair prices.

### 4 Pottery
You can find traditional Romanian pottery at the shops of the Peasant Museum and the Village Museum. You can also find souvenir shops in malls, on the central boulevards, and in the historical centre. Shops are usually open from 9 to 20 Mon.–Fri., 9–14 Sat.

### 5 Glassware
There are traditional glass factories in many Romanian cities. Their products have become increasingly diversified and soughtafter abroad. In the old centre of Bucharest and the Glass Makers' Courtyard you can find shops selling Romanian glassware.

### 6 Carpets and other handicrafts
The Peasant Museum and the Village Museum have the widest range of carpets and traditional woven articles. There you can also find rustic furniture and icons on wood and glass.

### 7 Second-hand books
There are plenty of antiquarian book dealers in Bucharest, and prices are lower than in other countries. We recommend the second-hand bookshops on Magheru Boulevard, Calea Victoriei, and Academiei St, and in the old centre.

### 8 Antiques
In recent years, the antiques trade has flourished in Romania. In the old centre of Bucharest, especially around Lipscani, you will find numerous antiques galleries, some small and dusty, others spick-and-span. Prices are always negotiable.

### 9 Art galleries
In the last few years, Romanian art has become increasingly visible, thanks to a growing number of galleries: the owners, who are generally young, promote their favourite artists. Notable galleries include Anaid, H'Art, Galeria Posibila, 2020 Home Gallery, Contrapunct, and HT003.

### 10 Malls
Around 20 malls have sprung up in recent years, featuring international chain stores and restaurants to suit every taste, as well as cinemas, supermarkets, and children's play areas. They are usually open till 22.

## Malls

**București Mall**
55–59 Calea Vitan,
www.bucurestimall.com.ro

**Băneasa Shopping City**
42D Șos. București–Ploiești,
www.baneasa
shoppingcity.ro

**AFI Palace Cotroceni**
4 B-dul Vasile Milea,
www.cotroceni.ro

**Plaza România**
26 B-dul Timișoara,
www.plazaromania.ro

Left **Motorcyclist**   Centre **Tram**   Right **Locals**

# Health and security

### Emergencies
The local health service is adequate, even hospitals suffer from a lack of funds and the Romanian doctors are underpaid. You are recommended to take out decent health insurance. In case of emergency, dial **112** (police, ambulance, fire brigade), the same as in the other 27 EU states. More details at www.112.ro. Other medical emergency numbers:
**Floreasca Emergency Hospital** 0721 275 478, 021 962; www.urgentafloreasca.ro
**Puls private ambulance** 021 9733, 021 2431333; www.pulsmedica.ro
**Emergency Ophthalmalogical Clinic Hospital** 021 319 27 51, 021 319 27 53.

### Police
In case of need, you can approach any policeman on the street or ask directions to the nearest police station. You will have to present your identity card and give a clear explanation of the problem. Emergency number: 112.

### Hospitals
There are a number of emergency hospitals in Bucharest. The main ones are Floreasca Emergency Hospital (021 962), Grigore Alexandrescu Children's Emergency Hospital (021 316 93 66), Elias Emergency Hospital (021 316 16 00, 316 16 04 109), and the University Emergency Hospital (021 318 05 19, 021, 318 05 20). There are also numerous private clinics.

### Dental services
In case of emergency, call: 021 252 66 59, 021 241 45 84. There are numerous private dental clinics in Bucharest. Dental-Med has a non-stop emergency programme: 021 402 87 35/36 , www.dental-med.ro.

### Pharmacies
You will have no problem finding a pharmacy (farmacie). A few of the centrally located ones: Sensiblu, 10–22, Amzei Market, Sensiblu, 65 Calea Dorobanți, Sensiblu, 2 Gara de Nord Boulevard (inside the station), Help Net, 27 Unirii Boulevard. Staff will also be able to advise you on minor ailments.

### Fire
In the case of a fire, call 112, alerting both the fire brigade *(pompieri)* and the police *(poliție)*.

### Pickpockets
Pickpockets are rife on all public transport, but particularly on the no. 104 bus and on the no. 32 tram. Don't carry large sums of money and don't keep money and identification papers in the same wallet. It is a good idea to carry only a photocopy of your passport with you. Losing your identity card will cause no end of bother.

### Traffic
In Bucharest, the traffic is more chaotic than in other Romanian cities. Watch out for potholes, other drivers, and jaywalkers. If possible, avoid the centre and rush hours. The Metro is

a good alternative. Take care where you park: fines are steep.

### Food and water
Tap water is drinkable, but most people prefer bottled water. In summer, don't buy food on the street. Likewise, avoid meat products in hot weather.

### Mosquitoes
In Bucharest, mosquitoes are no longer as much of a problem in summer, as the authorities now use modern pest control methods. At pharmacies you can buy effective sprays and creams if you suffer insect bites.

Left and right **Hotel Capitol**    Centre **Graffiti**

# Budget Hotels and Hostels

### Hotel Ibis – Gara de Nord
Close to the station and 10 minutes' walk from Victory Square, the Ibis is a good choice if you are on a low budget. 250 rooms with air conditioning, satellite TV, and fridge. Double rooms from 39€ per night. Find special offers on the hotel website. The Metro station is just in front of the hotel, so you won't need a taxi to get to the centre. There is another Ibis by the Palace of Parliament, at 82–84 Izvor St.
⊗ *143 Calea Griviței • 021 300 91 10 • www.ibishotel.ro* • ★★★

### Hello Hotels
A comfortable 150-room hotel 5 minutes' walk from Gara de Nord, opposite Hotel Ibis. All rooms have TV and air conditioning. Double rooms from 30€ per night. Breakfast optional (5€).
⊗ *143 Calea Griviței • 0372 121 800 • www.continentalhotels.ro* • ★★

### Hotel Capitol
Next to the National Military Club and near Lipscani, the hotel is housed in a historic building dating from 1901. The 80 rooms offer all the comfort you need. You can have lunch and dinner in the hotel restaurant. Double rooms from 45€ per night. ⊗ *29 Calea Victoriei • 021 315 80 30 • www.hotelcapitol.ro* • ★★★

### Caro Horoscop Hotel
In a leafy area near Floreasca Lake, the hotel has modern, nicely furnished rooms from 45€. Two restaurants are available, with a large number of Romanian specialties. There is also a business center with 12 conference halls.
⊗ *164 Barbu Văcărescu St • 021 407 47 20* • ★★

### Hotel Răzvan
A small, 44-room hotel located between Hala Traian and Piața Muncii, 20 minutes' walk from the city centre. The rooms are tastefully furnished and offer all the facilities. Rooms are 45€ at weekends and 54€ during the week, breakfast included. ⊗ *159 Calea Călărașilor • 021 320 01 73 • www.hotelrazvan.com* • ★★★

### Hostel Formenerg
Decent, 57-room hostel opposite Tineretului Park. Facilities include air conditioning, cable TV, fridge, and Internet access. Rooms from 25€/night, breakfast included.
⊗ *3 Gh. Șincai St • 021 306 99 15 • www.hostel. formenerg.ro*

### Grand Ville
Small, nicely furnished 20-room hotel, 5 minutes' walk from Roman Square, near Dorobanți Boulevard. Double room: 40€. ⊗ *4 Dimitrie Giurescu St • 0721 217 780* • ★★★

### Hotel Sir Lujerului
The hotel can be found close to the Polytechnic University of Bucharest within a complex featuring a shopping centre, gym, and other facilities. Easy access to the city centre by metro. The 27 rooms have air conditioning and cable TV. Double room: 35€.
⊗ *1A Chaussée Virtuții • 021 430 57 06 • www.sirgroups.ro* • ★★

### Hotel Domino
Built in 2003 and completely renovated in 2009, the hotel has 36 spacious rooms. Although located far from the city centre, it offers good value for money. Double room: 25€.
⊗ *10 Basarabilor St • 021 685 45 04* • ★★

### Hostel Wonderland
Centrally located hostel, behind the Colțea Hospital, with spacious 2-, 4- and 6-bed rooms. A bed costs 10€ a night. There are also two double rooms at 25€ a night. Facilities: air conditioning, jacuzzi, wireless Internet. ⊗ *48 Colței St • 0729 199 393 • hostelwonderland@gmail.com*

*Prices are for 2 persons/1 double room/per night.*

Left **Hotel Ambasador**   Centre **Tourists, Gara de Nord**   Right **Hotel Duke**

# Medium-priced Hotels

### 1 Hotel Ambasador
Founded in 1937, the 12-storey, ultra central Ambassador is a monument of architecture. The hotel has 209 rooms and panoramic views of the city centre. Double rooms from 67€. All rooms have air-conditioning and Wi-Fi. The terrace of the restaurant boasts a charming view of the boulevard. ⊕ *8–10 Magheru Boulevard • 021 315 90 80 • www.ambasador.ro • ★★–★★★*

### 2 Hotel Golden Tulip Victoria Bucharest
Located in the middle of one of Bucharest's oldest boulevards, Calea Victoriei, the Golden Tulip is a modern building surrounded by early-20th century architecture. The 83 rooms offer international standards. Double rooms from 80€. ⊕ *166 Calea Victoriei • 021 212 55 58 • www.goldentulip.com • ★★★★*

### 3 Ramada Bucharest Majestic Hotel
Situated in the very centre of the city, behind the University of Bucharest and close to Lipscani area, the hotel has 111 rooms and luxury facilities. Conference rooms, health centre, and fitness club. Double rooms from 68€. ⊕ *38–40 Calea Victoriei • 021 310 27 72 • www.majestic.ro • ★★★*

### 4 Hotel K+K Hotel Elisabeta
Located between University Square and Rosetti Square, the hotel is an ideal base for exploring the city. Note the unusual avant-garde architecture and design. Rooms from 75€, breakfast included. ⊕ *26 Slănic St • 021 302 92 80 • www.kkhotels.com • ★★★★*

### 5 Hotel Marshal
The hotel is located behind the National Theatre, close to University Square. Pleasant, intimate atmosphere, with tastefully furnished rooms and a superb rose garden. Double room: 75€, breakfast included. ⊕ *2 Emanoil Bacaloglu St • 021 314 08 80 • www.hotelmarshal.ro • ★★★★*

### 6 Hotel Best Western Stil
Best Western Stil is located at the entrance to the most elegant residential neighbourhood in Bucharest with villas, parks, restaurants and sport fields. 30 rooms, from 70€. ⊕ *63 Nicolae Caramfil St • 021 407 47 47 • www.hotelstil.ro • ★★★★*

### 7 Hotel Duke
Located in Roman Square, the hotel opened in 2003 and has 38 rooms with all the facilities. Double rooms from 75€, breakfast included. ⊕ *33 Dacia Boulevard • 021 317 41 86 • www.hotelduke.ro • ★★★*

### 8 Hotel Reginetta
Intimate, comfortable hotel 5 minutes' walk from Icoanei Garden. It has 31 nicely furnished rooms with prices starting from 60€. There is another Reginetta near Izvorul Rece, on Sf. Ştefan St. ⊕ *38 Vasile Lascăr St • 031 805 41 00 • www.hotelreginetta.ro • ★★★*

### 9 Hotel Tania Frankfurt
Excellent location, in Lipscani area, close to both Union and University squares. 17 modern and nicely furnished rooms from 59€. ⊕ *5 Şelari St • 031 104 20 83 • www.taniahotel.ro • ★★★*

### 10 Hotel Minerva
Hotel Minerva enjoys a top location, 300 metres from Roman Square and Victory Square. The 151 rooms offer all the facilities and prices start from 75€, breakfast included. There is a very good Chinese restaurant on the ground floor. ⊕ *2-4 Gh. Manu St • 021 311 15 55 • www.minerva.ro • ★★★★*

*Prices are for 2 persons/1 double room/per night.*

Left **Hotel Rembrandt**   Right **Starlight Suiten Hotel**

# Boutique Hotels

### Hotel Epoque

Inaugurated in 2011, a very elegant hotel next to Cişmigiu Park. The 45 rooms offer all the comfort and luxury of a 5-star hotel. There is a sauna, spa, and indoor swimming pool. The restaurant menus are created by Guy Martin, a Michelin 3-star chef. The private balcony in each room offers panoramic garden views of Cişmigiu Park. Rooms from 160€.
◈ *17C Intrarea Aurora • 021 312 32 32 • www.epoque.ro • ★★★★★*

### Hotel Residence Arc de Triomphe

Located near the Triumphal Arch and Herăstrău Park, Residence is noted for its refinement and luxury, like the other nearby hotel from the same chain. 35 rooms from 107€, breakfast included. ◈ *19 Clucerului St • 021 223 19 78 • www.residencehotels.com • ★★★★*

### Starlight Suiten Hotel

Located in the modern Metropolis Center, 10 minutes' walk from Roman Square, this boutique hotel has 78 spacious, comfortable rooms. One-bedroom apartments from 82€.
◈ *89–97 Grigore Alexandrescu St • 021 211 34 13 • www.starlighthotels.com • ★★★★*

### Carol Parc Hotel

Considered one of the best in Bucharest, the hotel is located in a superb villa near Carol Park, not far from the city centre. The 20 rooms are decorated by Italian designers and offer spectacular views of the area. Rooms from 140€, breakfast included. ◈ *23–25 Aleea Suter • 021 336 33 77 • www.carolparchotel.ro • ★★★★★*

### Hotel Rembrandt

Located in a recently restored building from 1925, the hotel is on Lipscani St, next to the Van Gogh Café. The interior design of the 16 rooms is remarkable for its good taste and quality materials. Rooms from 90€, breakfast included. The breakfast is served in the inviting Café Klein on the mezzanine floor, providing for an optimal start of the day. ◈ *11 Smârdan St • 021 313 93 15 • www.rembrandt.ro • ★★★*

### Z Executive Boutique Hotel

Located in the historic centre next to the Suţu Palace, the hotel was inaugurated in 2010 and has 21 rooms, some with a panoramic view. The airconditioned rooms include comfortable seating areas and work desks. Prices from 59€.

◈ *4 I. Nistor St • 031 1400 200 • www.zhotel.ro • ★★★*

### Boutique Hotel Monaco

A romantic and luxurious hotel in the French style, with views over Icoanei Garden. The 8 rooms offer excellent value. Double room: 54€. ◈ *74 Jean Louis Calderon St • 021 310 56 68 • www.hotelmonaco.ro • ★★★★*

### Le Boutique Hotel Moxa

Combining ultra-modern services and inter-war atmosphere, the hotel is located on Calea Victoriei, close to Roman Square. Rooms from 55€, breakfast included. ◈ *4 Mihail Moxa St • 021 650 55 55 • www.hotelmoxa.ro • ★★★★*

### Hotel Christina

A very modern hotel with original high-tech design and an eco-friendly attitude. 5 minutes' walk from Roman Square. 24 rooms, with prices starting from 79€. ◈ *13 Ion Slătineanu St • 021 210 73 03 • www.hotelchristina.ro • ★★★★*

### Scala Boutique Hotel

A luxury hotel near Magheru Boulevard and other major urban attractions, with 11 elegant, classically furnished rooms. Prices from 95€.
◈ *19 C.A. Rosetti St • 021 316 67 08 • www.hotelscala bucuresti.ro • ★★★★*

*Prices are for 2 persons/1 double room/per night.*

Left **Athénée Palace Hilton**   Centre **English Bar (Hilton)**   Right **Radisson Blu Hotel**

# Luxury Hotels

### 1 Hotel JW Marriott Grand
Located near the Palace of Parliament, the Bucharest Marriott is a miniature city in its own right, with restaurants, cafés, conference halls, and a casino. The hotel has 402 rooms, with prices from 145€.
◈ *90 Calea 13 Septembrie • 021 4030 000 • www.jwmamarriott.ro* • ★ ★ ★ ★ ★

### 2 Athénée Palace Hilton
Located next to the Romanian Athenaeum, the historic hotel was built in 1914 and has 272 rooms, 11 conference rooms, and 4 restaurants. Prices from 120€, breakfast included.
◈ *1–3 Episcopiei St • 021 303 37 77 • www.hilton.co.uk/bucharest* • ★ ★ ★ ★ ★

### 3 Radisson Blu Hotel
With a pleasingly original design, the hotel has 420 luxury rooms and 4 restaurants. Guests can pamper themselves in the swimming pools, exotic Bali Spa, and World Class Health Academy. Rooms from 110€. ◈ *63–81 Calea Victoriei • 021 311 9000 • www.radissonblu.com/hotel-bucharest* • ★ ★ ★ ★ ★

### 4 Hotel Intercontinental
A hotel symbolic of Bucharest, it was the tallest building in Romania for 30 years, at more than 90 m.

The fitness centre on the 22nd floor provides luxury services and a superb view. Rooms from 130€. ◈ *4 Bălcescu Boulevard • 021 310 20 20 • www.ichotelsgroup.com/intercontinental* • ★ ★ ★ ★ ★

### 5 Hotel Crowne Plaza
The hotel is an ideal location, between the Henri Coandă International Airport and the city centre. Guests can use the swimming pool, gym, jacuzzis, and tennis courts. Standard room: 75€, breakfast included.
◈ *1 Poligrafiei Boulevard • 021 224 00 34 • www.crowneplaza.com* • ★ ★ ★ ★ ★

### 6 Hotel Howard Johnson Grand Plaza
Located opposite the Academy of Economic Sciences, the hotel (below) is popular with Romanian and foreign businessmen. The 285 rooms have French-made furnishings. Prices start at 140€. ◈ *5–7 Calea Dorobanților • 021 201 50 00 • www.hojoplaza.ro* • ★ ★ ★ ★

### 7 Hotel Casa Capșa
Painstakingly renovated, Casa Capșa has regained

its former elegance. The 61 rooms offer guests all the facilities. 115€, breakfast included. ◈ *36 Calea Victoriei • 021 313 40 38 • www.capsa.ro* • ★ ★ ★ ★ ★

### 8 Continental Grand Hotel
Located in a recently renovated historic building in the city centre, the hotel provides exceptional services. The 59 rooms are classically furnished. Prices from 120€, breakfast included.
◈ *56 Calea Victoriei • 372 010 300 • www.continentalhotels.ro* • ★ ★ ★ ★ ★

### 9 Novotel
Centrally located, the hotel façade recreates that of the National Theatre, which was destroyed by bombs in 1944. Double room: 70€, swimming pool and sauna access included.
◈ *37B Calea Victoriei • 021 308 85 00 • www.novotel.com* • ★ ★ ★ ★

### 10 Phoenicia Grand Hotel
Located in the north of the city, near Băneasa Airport, the hotel has 348 luxury rooms, a casino, spa, and various business facilities. Double rooms from 80€, breakfast included.
◈ *87 Al. Șerbănescu Boulevard • 021 300 08 88 • www.phoenicia.ro* • ★ ★ ★ ★

*Prices are for 2 persons/1 double room/per night.*

Left and right **Buildings on Lipscani**   Centre **Old door, detail**

# Flat Rental

## 1 Bucharest Serviced Apartments

Completely furnished centrally located flats for tourists and businessmen. They have free Wi-Fi internet acces and a fully equiped kitchen. Prices start from 45€ per night.
Ⓢ *0720 906 725, 0745 500 676*
• *www.in-bucharest.com*

## 2 Bucharest Confort Suites

Flats in the heart of the city, next to Intercontinental Hotel and the National Theatre, just a few minutes' walk from shops and museums. Each flat is supplied with all the necessary comforts, combining the facilities of a hotel with the privacy of an apartment. Prices start from 45€ per night.
Ⓢ *16 Bălcescu Boulevard*
• *0746 167 216* •
*www.comfort-suites.ro*

## 3 Corporate Apartments Bucharest

Luxury flats for corporate clients at excellent value or money. You can choose short or long term rental. A centrally located flat with all the facilities costs between 30 and 50€ per night. All the apartments feature a complete kitchen, and have separate dining, living, and sleeping areas. Ⓢ *0751 066 876* •
*www.regimhotelierbucuresti.com*

## 4 Bucharest Comfort Apartments

All flats are fully furnished and equipped. Most are in the city centre, but some are in the north of the city, near Romexpo and on the way to the airport. Prices are from 30€ per night, with reductions the longer the stay.
Ⓢ *0735 812 576* •
*www.bucharest-apartments.ro*

## 5 Luxury Accommodation

Flats are located in ultra-central buildings, with all the facilities (airconditioning, TV cable, central heating). Airport pickups, flight booking, and car rental are also available upon request. 35€ per night.
Ⓢ *15 Tudor Ștefan St* •
*0744 55 13 13, 021 231 35 93*
• *www.bucharest-accommodations.ro*

## 6 Stil Suites Residence

Hotel-style accommodation in two buildings (Aparthotels), one located in Union Square, the other in Victory Square. 3- and 4-star standards. Guests have the option of airport pickup and drop-off services. Prices from 50€ per night for a one-room flat. Breakfast is served after 7:30 in room or in joined restaurant Sailors's after 9:30! It is optional and not included in room rate.

Ⓢ *0720 08 08 08, 0720 533355*
• *www.stilsuites.ro*

## 7 EastComfort Bucharest

Fully equipped one- to four-room flats are available. All are conveniently located and tastefully furnished. Prices from 30€ per night for 1–2 persons.
Ⓢ *0728 070007* •
*www.eastcomfort.com*

## 8 CazareLux.ro

Short- and long-term flat rental in centrally located buildings with parking access. A oneroom flat costs 39€ per night for a period of 1 to 10 days, and a larger flat 49€. Prices for longer periods are negotiable.
Ⓢ *0765 512 304, 0723524341*
• *www.cazarelux.ro*

## 9 RoSuites Accommodation

Flats in central Bucharest. Transport and car rental services available on request. A one-room flat costs from 30€ per night, larger flats from 45€.
Ⓢ *0722 229 274, 031 104 9431*
• *www.rosuites.com*

## 10 Expertcasa

Completely renovated and furnished flats with all the facilities, located in central Bucharest, close to main touristic attractions. A flat near the University or on Calea Victoriei costs 40–45€ per night. Also available long term rental.
Ⓢ *0722 209 880* •
*www.bucuresticazare.ro*

# USEFUL ADDRESSES

BUCHAREST

# Embassies and consulates

### Albania
7 Duiliu Zamfirescu St
Phone 021 211 98 29;
021 312 22 10
Monday–Friday 8.00–16.00

### Argentina
11 Ion Câmpineanu St
Phone 021 312 26 26;
021 312 30 44;
021 312 17 39
Monday–Friday 9.00–14.00

### Armenia
27 Intr. Poiana St
Phone 021 233 24 52;
021 319 76 04
Monday–Friday 10.00–13.00

### Austria
27 Dumbrava Roşie St
Phone 021 201 56 12;
021 201 56 15;
021 201 56 24;
021 201 56 21
Monday–Thursday 8.30–16.30,
Friday 8.30–14.30

### Belarus
55 Kiseleff Avenue
(Şoseaua Kiseleff)
Phone 021 223 17 76;
021 222 42 88
Monday–Friday
9.00–13:00, 14.00–18.00

### Belgium
58 Dacia Avenue
(Bulevardul Dacia)
Phone 021 210 29 69;
021 210 29 70;
021 210 29 80
Monday–Friday 9.00–12.30

### Bosnia and Herzegovina
12 Stockholm St
Phone 021 409 26 01;
021 409 26 06
Monday–Friday 9.00–17.00

### Brazil
40 Aviatorilor Avenue
(Bulevardul Aviatorilor)

Phone 021 230 11 30;
021 230 78 25;
021 230 11 16
Monday–Friday 9.00–17.00

### Bulgaria
5 Rabat St
Phone 021 230 21 50;
021 230 21 59
Monday–Friday
9.00–12.30, 13.00–17.00

### Canada
1–3 Tuberozelor St
Phone 021 307 50 00

### Chile
24 Griviţei Avenue
(Calea Griviţei)
Phone 021 312 72 39;
021 312 73 11;
021 312 72 39
Monday–Friday 9.00–16.00

### China
2 Nordului Avenue
(Şoseaua Nordului)
Phone 021 232 88 58;
021 232 17 32;
021 233 41 88
Monday–Friday 8.30–15.00

### Congo
14 Pache Protopopescu
Avenue (Bulevardul Pache
Protopopescu)
Phone 021 315 33 71
Monday–Friday 10.00–16.00

### Congo (Democratic Republic of)
50–54 Mihai Eminescu St
Phone 021 210 54 98;
0740 808 009
Monday–Friday 10.00–15.00

### Croatia
1 Dr. Burghelea St
Phone 021 313 03 74;
021 313 04 57
Monday–Friday 9.00–17.00

### Cuba
44–48 Mihai Eminescu St

Phone 021 211 87 39;
021 211 87 95;
021 211 86 71
Monday–Friday 9.00–17.00

### Cyprus
2 Petöfi Sándor St
Phone 021 223 04 55
Monday–Friday 09.00–17.00

### Czech Republic
11 Ion Ghica St
Phone 021 303 92 30/31/32
Monday–Friday 8.00–16.30

### Denmark
3 Dr. Burghelea St
Phone 021 300 08 00
Monday–Friday 9.00–16.00

### Egipt
67 Dacia Avenue
(Bulevardul Dacia)
Phone 021 211 09 38;
021 211 09 39
Monday–Friday 10.00–15.00

### Finland
2 Atena St
Phone 021 230 75 04;
021 230 75 45;
021 230 75 26
Monday–Friday 8.00–16.15

### France
13–15 Biserica Amzei St
Phone 021 303 10 00
Monday–Friday 8.30–13.00,
14.30–17.30

### Georgia
44–48 Mihai Eminescu St
Phone 021 210 06 02
Monday–Friday 9.00–18.00

### Germany
6–8 Cpt. Av. Gheorghe
Demetriade St
Phone 021 202 98 30;
021 230 25 80;
021 202 98 69;
021 202 98 30
Monday–Thursday
08.00–13.00; 13.30–17.00;
Friday 8.00–14.00

## Greece
1–3 Pache Protopopescu
Avenue (Bulevardul Pache
Protopopescu)
Phone 021 209 41 70
Monday–Friday 9.00–16.00

## Hungary
63–65 Jean-Luis Calderon St
Phone 021 312 00 73
Monday–Thursday 08.00–
16.30; Friday 8.00–14.00

## India
183 Mihai Eminescu St
Phone 021 211 54 51;
021 619 02 36
Monday–Friday 9.00–17.00

## Indonesia
10 Orlando St
Phone 021 312 07 42/43/44
Monday–Friday 9.00–13.00,
14.00–17.00

## Iran
39 Lascăr Catargiu Avenue
(Bulevardul Lascăr Catargiu)
Phone 021 312 04 93;
021 312 04 94;
021 312 04 95

## Iraq
6–8 Venezuela St
Phone 021 233 90 08;
021 233 90 09
Monday–Friday 9.00–15.00

## Ireland
50–52 Buzeşti St
Phone 021 310 21 31
Monday–Friday 9.30–12.30;
14.00–17.00

## Israel
1 Dimitrie Cantemir Avenue
(Bulevardul Dimitrie Cantemir)
Phone 021 318 94 16;
021 318 94 17
Monday–Friday 9.30–12.30

## Italy
9 Henri Coandă St
Phone 021 305 21 00
Monday–Friday 9.00–13.00

## Japan
4–8 Nicolae Titulescu Avenue
(Bulevardul Nicolae Titulescu)
nr. 4–8
Phone 021 319 18 90/91
Monday–Friday 9.00–12.30,
13.30–17.00

## Jordan
1 Dumbrava Roşie St
Phone 021 210 47 05;
021 210 80 80
Monday–Friday 9.00–15.00

## Kazakhstan
26 Giuseppe Garibaldi Str
Phone 021 107 10 83;
021 107 10 84
Monday–Friday 8.30–12.30,
14.30–18.30

## Kuwait
19A–19B Louis Blank St
Phone 021 315 44 44;
021 315 99 88
Monday–Friday 9.00–12.00

## Lebanon
16 Andrei Mureşanu St
Phone 021 230 92 05;
021 230 03 02
Monday–Friday 9.00–17.00

## Lithuania
51 Primăverii Avenue
(Bulevardul Primăverii)
Phone 021 311 59 97;
021 317 33 73
Monday–Thursday 8.00–17.00;
Friday 8.00–15.45

## Macedonia
144 Mihai Eminescu St
Phone 021 210 08 80
Monday–Friday 8.30–16.30

## Madagascar
9 Giuseppe Garibaldi St
Phone 021 210 52 72
Monday–Friday 9.00–13.00

## Malaysia
11 Drobeta St
Phone 021 211 38 01;
021 211 38 02
Monday–Friday 8.30–12.30,
13.30–16.30

## Mexico
124 Mihai Eminescu St
Phone 021 210 44 17;
021 210 47 28;
021 210 45 77
Monday–Friday 9.00–13.30,
14.00–17.00

## Moldova (Republic of)
40 Aleea Alexandru
Phone 021 230 04 74
Monday–Friday 8.30–12.30,
15.00–16.30

## Morocco
78 Dionisie Lupu St
Phone 021 317 41 24
Monday–Friday 9.00–16.00

## Netherlands
20 Aleea Alexandru
Phone 021 208 60 30
Monday–Thursday 8.30–13.00;
13.30–17.30; Friday 8.30–13.00;
13.30–15.00

## Nigeria
9 Orlando St
Phone 021 312 86 85;
021 312 79 37
Monday–Friday 8.30–16.30

## North Korea (Democratic People's Republic)
6 Nordului Avenue
(Şoseaua Nordului)
Phone 021 232 19 94
Monday–Friday 9.00–12.00;
14.00–17.00

## Norway
18 Atena St
Phone 021 306 98 00
Monday–Friday 9.00–16.00

## Pakistan
22 Barbu Delavrancea St
Phone 021 318 78 73;
021 318 7876
Monday–Friday 9.00–17.00

## Palestinian Territories
12 Eugen Lovinescu St
Phone 021 211 94 22
Monday–Friday 9.00–15 00

## Peru
29 Iacul Tei Avenue
(Bulevardul Lacul Tei)
Phone 021 211 18 19;
021 211 18 16
Monday–Friday 8.30–13.00

## Philippines
105–107 Carol Davila St
Phone 021 319 82 52;
021 319 82 54;
021 319 82 56
Monday–Friday 9.00–17.00

## Poland
23 Aleea Alexandru
Phone 021 308 22 00;
021 308 22 10;
021 308 22 46
Monday–Friday 9.00–16.00

## Portugal
55 Paris St
Phone 021 230 41 36;
021 230 41 18
Monday–Friday 9.30–12.30

## Qatar
10 A Venezuela St
Phone 021 230 47 41;
021 230 79 33
Monday–Friday 9.30–15.30

## Russia
6 Kiseleff Avenue
(Şoseaua Kiseleff)
Phone 021 222 16 52;
021 222 31.70;
021 222 31 68;

021 222 34 59
Monday–Friday 8.00–17.00

## Saudi Arabia
6 Polonă St
Phone 021 210 91 09;
021 210 92 21;
021 210 87 16
Monday–Friday 9.00–15.00

## Serbia
34 Dorobanţilor Avenue (Calea Dorobanţilor)
Phone 021 211 98 71;
021 211 98 72;
021 211 98 73;
021 210 03 59; (consulate)
021 211 49 80
Monday–Friday 8.30–16.00

## Slovakia
3 Oţetari St
Phone 021 300 61 00
Monday–Friday 8.15–16.00

## Slovenia
25 Teheran St
Phone 021 300 27 80

## Spain
43 Aleea Alexandru
Phone 021 318 10 77;
(consulate) 021 318 10 80
Monday–Friday 8.30–14.00

## South Africa
26–28 Ştirbei Vodă St
Phone 021 313 37 25;
021 313 37 35;
021 313 37 85;
0723 547 111
Monday–Friday

## South Korea (Republic of Korea)
14 Mircea Eliade Avenue
(Bulevardul Mircea Eliade)
Phone 021 230 71 98
Monday–Friday 9.00–12.30,
14.00–17.00

## Sweden
43 Kiseleff Avenue
(Şoseaua Kiseleff)

Phone 021 406 71 00
Monday–Thursday 08.30–
17.00; Friday 08.30–15.00;
(open for public) Tuesday–
Thursday 10.00–12.00

## Switzerland
16–20 Grigore Alexandrescu St
Phone 021 206 16 00;
021 206 16 10;
021 206 16 40
Monday–Thursday 8.00–12.30;
13.30–17.00; Friday 8.00–14.00;
(visas) Monday–Friday
8.30–11.00

## Syria
50 Lascăr Catargiu Avenue
(Bulevardul Lascăr Catargiu)
Phone 021 319 24 67;
021 319 24 69
Monday–Friday 9.00–15.30

## Thailand
12 Vasile Conta St
Phone 021 311 00 31;
021 311 00 67;
021 311 00 78
Monday–Friday 9.00–12.00,
13.00–17.00

## Tunisia
50–54 Mihai Eminescu St
Phone 021 210 11 97;
021 210 13 44

## Turkey
72 Dorobanţilor Avenue (Calea
Dorobanţilor)
Phone 021 206 37 00/04;
(consulate) 021 206 37 27/29
Monday–Friday 9.00–12.30;
14.00–18.00

## Ukraine
24 Aviatorilor Avenue
(Bulevardul Aviatorilor)
Phone 021 230 36 60;
021 230 36 68;
021 230 36 71;
021 230 36 69;
021 230 36 60 (consulate)
Monday–Friday 8.30–13.00;
14.30–17.45

## United Arab Emirates
4 Aleea Modrogan
Phone 021 231 76 76
Monday–Friday 9.00–15.00

## United Kingdom
24 Jules Michelet St
Phone 021 201 72 00;
021 201 72 69
Monday–Thursday 8.30–17.00;
Friday 8.30–16.00; (consulate)
Monday–Thursday 8.30–13.00;
14.00–17.00; Friday 8.30–13.30

## United States of America
4–6 Dr. Liviu Libescu Avenue
(Bulevardul Dr. Liviu Librescu)
Phone 021 200 33 00
Monday–Friday 8.00–17.00

## Vatican City State
5–7 Pictor Constantin Stahi St
Phone 021 313 94 90;
021 312 38 83
Monday–Friday 9.00–13.00;
15.00–17.00

## Venezuela
18 Pictor Mirea St
Phone 021 222 58 74;
021 222 43 11(consulate)
Program: Monday–Thursday
10.00–13.00; Friday 9.00–13.00

## Vietnam
13 C.A. Rosetti St
Phone 021 311 16 04;
021 311 03 34
Monday–Friday 9.00–12.00;
14.00–17.00

## CONSULATES

### Bulgaria
32 Vasile Lascăr St
Phone 021 318 79 78
Monday–Friday 10.00–12.00

### France
6 Intrarea Cristian Tell
Phone 021 303 10 00

### Greece
4–6 Ferdinand Avenue
(Bulevardul Ferdinand)
Phone 021 209 41 91/92

Monday–Friday 9.00–13.00

### Hungary
30 Ştefan Negulescu St
Phone 021 230 05 50;
021 230 05 51
Monday–Tuesday 8.30–11.30;
Thursday–Friday 8.30–11.30

### Italy
12 Arhitect Ion Mincu St
Phone 021 223 24 24;
021 223 33 13;
021 223 33 12
Monday–Friday 9.00–13.00

### Moldavia(Republic of)
8 Eroilor Avenue
(Bulevardul Eroilor)
Phone 021 410 98 27
Monday–Friday 8.30–12.30;
15.00–16.30

### Russia
4 Tuberozelor St
Phone 021 222 13 89;
021 222 15 56
Monday–Tuesdat,
Thursday–Friday 9.00–12.30

### San Marino
15 Unirii Avenue
(Bulevardul Unirii)
Phone 021 336 69 71

### United States of America
26 Nicolae Filipescu St
Phone 021 200 33 00
Monday–Friday 8.00–17.00

## Banks
### (headquarters)

### Alpha Bank Romania
Calea Dorobanţilor nr. 237B,
sector 1
Phone 021 209 21 00
Fax 021 231 65 70
E-mail: bbd@alphabank.ro

### ATE Bank
Calea Griviței nr. 24, sector 1
Phone 021 303 07 52
Fax 021 303 07 38
E-mail: ategt@ate.gr

### Banca C.R. Firenze
Bulevardul Unirii nr. 55,
bl. E4a, tronson 1, sector 3
Phone 021 201 19 30
Fax 021 201 19 31
E-mail: office@bancacrfirenze.ro

### Banca de Export-Import a României (EXIMBANK)
Splaiul Independentei nr. 15,
sector 5

Phone 021 405 33 33;
021 319 29 29;
0725 858 333
Fax: 021 405 33 88
E-mail: office@eximbank.ro

### Banca di Roma
Intrarea Murmurului nr. 2–4,
sector 1
Phone 021 232 08 18
Fax: 021 232 64 65
E-mail: bucharest@ro.bdroma.com

### Banca Italo Romena
Bulevardul Dimitrie Cantemir
nr. 1, bl. B2, sc.2, sector 4
Phone 021 317 13 11/14/15/17
Fax 021 317 13 16
E-mail: office@italo-romena.ro

### Banca Românească
Bulevardul Unirii nr. 35,
sector 3
Phone 021 305 90 00;
021 305 93 00
Fax 021 305 91 91
E-mail: office@brom.ro

### BANCPOST
Calea Vitan nr. 6–6A, sector 3
Phone 021 308 09 01;
0800 110 200
Fax 021 326 85 20
E-mail: sugestiiclienti@banc-post.ro

### Banca Comercială Română
Bulevardul Regina Elisabeta
nr. 5, sector 3
Call Center: 0801 0801 227
E-mail: bcr@bcr.ro,
contact.center@bcr.ro

### Banca Națională a României – BNR
Strada Lipscani nr. 25,
sector 3
Phone 021 313 04 10
021 315 27 50
Fax 021 312 38 31
E-mail: info@bnro.ro

### Banca Română pentru Dezvoltare – BRD
Bulevardul Ion Mihalache

nr. 1–7, Turn BRD, sector 1
Phone 021 301 41 88/23
Fax 021 301 41 04/05
E-mail: comunicare@brd.ro;
investor@brd.ro;
vocalis@brd.ro

### C.E.C. Bank
Calea Victoriei nr. 11–13,
sector 3
Phone 021 311 11 19
Fax 021 312 54 25
E-mail: office@cec.ro

### Citibank Romania
Bulevardul Iancu
de Hunedoara nr. 8, sector 1
Phone 021 210 18 50
Fax 021 203 55 65

### Credit Europe Bank
Bulevardul Timişoara nr. 26Z,
sector 6
Phone 021 406 40 00
Fax 021 317 20 66
E-mail: office@crediteurope-bank.ro

### Emporiki Bank – Romania
Str. Berzei nr.19, sector 1
Phone 021 310 39 55/57
Fax 021 310 39 91
E-mail: bank@emporiki.ro

### GarantiBank International NV
Str. Banu Antonache
nr. 40–44, Floreasca II
Business Center, sector 1
Phone 021 208 92 60
Fax 021 208 92 86
E-mail: info@garantibank.ro

### HVB Banca pentru Locuinţe
Str. Dr. Grigore Mora nr. 37,
sector 1
Phone 021 300 11 22
Fax 021 319 39 71
E-mail: office@hvblocuinte.ro

### ING Bank N.V.
Bulevardul Iancu
de Hunedoara
nr. 48, sector 1
Phone 021 209 15 24

# Banks | Cafés

Fax 021 222 14 01
Email contact@ing.ro

**Leumi Bank Romania**
Bulevardul Aviatorilor nr. 45,
sector 1
Phone 021 206 70 75/76/77
Fax 021 206 70 50
E-mail: office@leumi.ro

**Libra Bank**
Str. Grigore Mora nr. 11,
sector 1
Phone 021 208 80 00
Fax 021 230 65 65
E-mail: info@librabank.ro

**Millennium Bank**
Piața Presei Libere nr. 3–5,
clădirea City Gate, Turn Sudic,
sector 1
Phone 021 529 73 00;
0801 000 111
Fax 021 529 55 16
Email: office@millenniumbank.ro

**MKB ROMEXTERRA Bank**
Str. Armand Călinescu
nr. 2–4, Millennium Business
Center, et.11–13, sector 2
Call Center 0800 410 310
Fax 021 317 82 10
E-mail: info@romexterra.ro

**OTP Bank Romania S.A.**
Strada Buzești nr. 66–68,
sector 1
Phone 021 307 57 00
Fax 021 308 51 80
E-mail: office@otpbank.ro

**Piraeus Bank Romania**
Bulevardul Carol I nr. 34–36,
sector 2
Phone 021 303 69 69
Fax 021 303 69 09
E-mail: office@piraeusbank.ro

**ProCredit Bank**
Str. Buzești nr. 62–64,
sector 1
Phone 021 201 60 00
Fax 021 201 60 02
E-mail: headoffice@procredit-bank.ro

**Raiffeisen Bank**
Calea Floreasca, Clădirea Sky
Tower, nr. 246 C, sector 1
Phone 021 306 10 00
Fax 021 230 07 00
E-mail: centrala@rzb.ro

**RBS România
(fostă Abn Amro Bank)**
Str. Barbu Văcărescu
nr. 301–311, et. 1, sector 2
Phone 021 202 08 00
E-mail: client.service@rbs.com

**Romanian International
Bank**
Bulevardul Unirii 67, bl. G2A,
Tronson 1 și 2, sector 3
Phone 021 318 95 15
Fax 021 318 95 16/17
E-mail: office@roib.ro

**UniCredit Țiriac Bank**
Bulevardul Expoziției nr.1F,
sector 1
Phone 021 200 20 20
Fax 021 200 20 22
E-mail: office@unicredit.ro

## Cafés

**1001 Nopți –
Lounge & Club**
Str. Ion Brezoianu nr.18
Phone 0746 171 111

**1974 Niște Domni și Fiii**
Str. Covaci nr. 7
Phone 0723 629 306;
0721 551 099

**Academic Cafe Bar**
Bulevardul Regina Elisabeta
nr. 30
Phone 021 313 85 22;
0720 424 203;
0729 233 558

**Afternoons &
Coffee Spoons**
Str. Iacob Felix nr. 63–69
Phone 0731 343 095

**Aida Cafee**
Calea Victoriei nr. 16–20
Phone 0726 318 463

**Alsy Cafe – Romană**
Str. Biserica Amzei nr. 29
Phone 031 103 52 90;
0720 241 527

**Alsy Cafe – Unirii**
Bulevardul Unirii nr. 65
Phone 031 103 52 90;
0725 513 087

**Amber Cafe**
Str. Nerva Traian nr. 3A
Phone 021 200 62 70

**Aromaroma**
Str. Popa Tatu nr. 61
Phone 031 104 87 24;
0723 973 025;
0771 575 945

**Arts Concept Cafe**
Str. Doctor Turnescu nr. 1
Phone 0725 265 375

**Atelier Cafe – Șelari**
Str. Șelari nr. 7
Phone 021 318 28 54;
021 312 42 04

**Base Cafe**
Str. Șepcari nr. 22
Phone 0756 160 542

**Bernschutz & Co –
Grădina Icoanei**
Str. General Eremia
Grigorescu nr. 5
Phone 021 610 11 33;
0372 790 723

**Bernschutz&Co – Nistor 6**
Str. Ion Nistor nr. 6
Phone 021 310 47 88

**Blues Cafe**
Calea Victoriei nr. 6–20
Phone 021 312 63 36;
0722 530 415;
0723 520 643

**Bohemia Tea House**
Str. Poiana Narciselor nr. 1
Phone 0727 333 631

**Boulevard Cafe**
Bulevardul Gheorghe Şincai
nr. 9A
Phone 0735 155 357

**Bourbon Cocktails
& Coffee**
Bulevardul Decebal nr. 29
Phone 0771 056 193;
0726 555 333

**Brit C@Fe**
Calea Dorobanţilor nr. 14
Phone 021 307 96 57;
021 210 03 14;
021 307 96 00

**Café Verona**
Str. Pictor Arthur Verona
nr. 13–15
Phone 021 317 34 59;
0732 003 061;
0732 003 060

**Cafe Corner**
Bulevardul Timişoara nr. 26
Phone 021 430 14 68;
0788 008 070

**Cafe Deko**
Str. Smârdan nr. 30

**Cafe Du Pont**
Str. Cotroceni nr. 16
Phone 0726 279 857

**Cafe Klein**
Str. Smârdan nr. 11
Phone 021 313 93 15;
0213 139 316

**Cafe Milena**
Calea Moşilor nr. 308
Phone 021 212 08 55;
021 100 60 22

**Cafe Pink**
Bulevardul Decebal nr. 13
Phone 021 322 51 01

**Cafe-Nescafe (Plaza
Romania)**
Bulevardul Timişoara nr. 26
Phone 021 300 05 27

**Cafe-Nescafe (Vitan Mall)**
Calea Vitan nr. 55–59
Phone 021 326 55 50

**Cafeneaua Carada**
Str. Eugeniu Carada nr. 5–7
Phone 0766 358 654

**Cafeneaua Dalles**
Bulevardul Nicolae Bălcescu
nr. 18
Phone 031 805 24 91;
0730 003 826

**Cafeneaua Egipteană Valea
Regilor (Calea Victoriei)**
Calea Victoriei nr. 16–18–20
Phone 021 311 29 69

**Cafeneaua Smârdan**
Str. Smârdan nr. 18
Phone 0723 522 644

**Cafepedia (Piaţa Alba Iulia)**
Piaţa Alba Iulia nr. 2
Phone 021 320 26 00;
0728 853 854

**Cafepedia (Romană)**
Str. Pictor Arthur Verona nr. 2
Phone 021 320 26 00;
0721 102 101;
0728 853 854

**Caffe Caribe**
Bulevardul Decebal nr. 4
Phone 0747 124 470;
0741 589 039

**Caffe Cinema 3d –
Sala Mică Cinema Patria**
Bulevardul Gheorghe
Magheru nr. 12–14
Phone 021 316 92 66

**Caffe D'Arthe**
Str. Popa Nan nr. 7
Phone 0734 662 580

**Caffe Frappe**
Str. Mendeleev nr. 7–15
Phone 021 319 69 21

**Caffe Milano**
Bulevardul Dimitrie Cantemir
nr. 2–2 A
Phone 021 335 64 09;
0788 215 938;
0722 434 600;

**Caffe Tabiet Avrig**
Str. Avrig nr. 29
Phone 021 252 05 63

**Caffe & Latte**
Bulevardul Schitu Măgureanu
nr. 35
Phone 021 314 38 00;
021 314 38 34;
0744 333 100

**Casa Actorilor**
Str. General Nicolae Dona
nr. 18
Phone 0743 060 662

**Casuţa din Poveşti**
Str. Dr. Staicovici nr. 37
Phone 0733 811 620

**Ceai la Cotroceni**
Str. Dr. Gheorghe Marinescu
nr. 25
Phone 0721 669 535

**Ceainăria Tabiet**
Str. Gheorghe Ionescu Gion
nr. 9
Phone 0722 525 963

**Ceas Cafe**
Bulevardul Dacia nr. 22
Phone 0735 557 777;
0745 551 218;
0762 466 662

**Centro Bar & Lounge**
Calea Dorobanţilor nr. 5–7
Phone 021 201 50 30;
021 311 55 33/32

**Chocolat**
Calea Victoriei nr. 12
Phone 021 314 92 45

**City Cafe**
Piaţa Charles de Gaule nr. 15
Phone 0720 626 262

**Coffee Cabinet**
Bulevardul Ion Mihalache nr. 23
Phone 021 316 94 12

**Coffee Grind**
Calea Dorobanţilor nr. 20–28
Phone 021 211 67 00;

0726 696 395

**Coffee Right
(Aeroport Otopeni)**
Calea Bucureștilor nr. 224E
Phone 021 204 19 31

**Coffee Right (Alba Iulia)**
Piața Alba Iulia nr. 3
Phone 021 326 82 15;
0743 189 933

**Coffee Right
(Casa Presei Libere)**
Piața Presei Libere nr. 1
Phone 0743 189 263

**Coffee Right
(Gara de Nord)**
Piața Gara de Nord nr. 3
Phone 021 218 70 38

**Coffee Right (Lipscani)**
Str. Lipscani nr. 27
Phone 021 310 20 44

**Coffee Right
(Piața Victoriei)**
Piața Victoriei nr. 6
Phone 021 212 56 63

**Coffee Right (Unirii)**
Aleea Unirii nr. 27
Phone 021 336 60 24

**Coffee Sense Social
Beat Club**
Șoseaua Virtuții nr. 148
Phone 0788 555 702

**Cube Cafe**
Calea Dorobanți nr. 54
Phone 031 105 72 58;
021 210 77 66;
0767 655 523

**D'eight**
Strada Franceză nr. 2–4
Phone 021 311 40 10;
0721 333 533

**Dante Cafe**
Bulevardul Mihail
Kogălniceanu nr. 49
Phone 0743 688 722

**Dinette**
Str. Covaci nr. 6
Phone 021 311 77 55

**Favela**
Calea Moșilor nr. 160
Phone 0727 222 574

**Gio Cafe**
Str. Toma Caragiu nr. 3
Phone 021 313 97 40;
0730 030 764

**Glendale Cinema & Art
Cafe**
Șoseaua Cotroceni nr. 9
Phone 021 316 32 86;
0730 615 121/22

**Gloria Jean's Coffees
(Feeria)**
Șoseaua București–Ploiești nr.
44
Phone 021 310 69 81

**Gloria Jean's Coffees
(Plaza Romania)**
Bulevardul Timișoara nr. 26
Phone 021 317 63 10

**Gloria Jean's Coffees
(Vitan Mall)**
Calea Vitan nr. 55–59
Phone 021 321 13 40

**Godot Cafe Teatru**
Str. Blănari nr. 14
Phone 021 316 16 82;
0736 414 244

**Golden Falcon
Antique Cafe**
Str. Hristo Botev nr. 18–20
Phone 021 314 28 25

**Grădina OAR**
Str. Pictor Arthur Verona
nr. 19
Phone 021 650 20 20;
0743 027 981;
0766 741 791

**Grand Cafe Galleron**
Str. Nicolae Golescu nr. 18 A
Phone 021 312 45 65

**Greentea**
Str. Dr. Burghelea nr. 24
Phone 021 320 93 96;
021 320 93 96;
0749 090 202

**Happy Pub**
Str. Căderea Bastiliei nr. 36

**Hard Rock Cafe**
Șoseaua Kiseleff nr. 32
Phone 021 206 62 61

**Hashas Coffee & Longe**
Str. Vasile Lascăr nr. 24
Phone 0723 266 103;
0723 639 022

**High Heels Cafe
(Plaza Romania)**
Bulevardul Timișoara nr. 26
Phone 021 230 70 40;
031 100 25 99;
0723 898 852

**Hobby Café**
Str. Negustori nr. 34
Phone 0771 760 238,
0724 288 850

**Hobby Caffe & Shop**
Str. Jean-Louis Calderon
nr. 58
Phone 0731 006 699

**I.O Caffe Bar**
Str. Demetru I. Dobrescu
nr. 5
Phone 021 315 60 98

**Il Cantuccio Cafe**
Str. Mitropolit Nifon
Phone 021 337 45 67;
0721 251 823

**Inbox Bar**
Str. Lascăr Catargiu nr. 6
Phone 0745 113 552

**Indie Club**
Str. Inişor nr. 2
Phone 0735 527 464;
0728 825 777

**J'ai Bistrot**
Calea Griviţei nr. 55
Phone 031 426 20 47

**Jessie's Caffe**
Drumul Taberei nr. 24
Phone 0733 194 150

**Kartell Cafe**
Str. Smârdan nr. 7
Phone 0749 057 773;
0749 057 770

**La Cinci Grădina cu Ceai**
Str. Olimpului nr. 13
Phone 0734 847 594

**La Galette**
Piaţa Montreal nr. 10
Phone 021 202 17 22;
021 318 30 00

**La Mandragora**
Str. Mendeleev nr. 29
Phone 021 319 75 92

**La Metoc**
Str. Popa Rusu nr. 21
Phone 0732 522 789

**La Mode Cafe & More**
Str. George Enescu nr. 21
Phone 021 367 22 30

**Lautrec**
Str. Iancu Cavaler de Flondor
nr. 2

Phone 021 252 16 16;
0723 910 170

**Legere Cafe**
Piaţa Rossetti nr. 5
Phone 0730 534 373

**Lente & Cafea**
Str. General Praporgescu
nr. 31
Phone 031 102 06 61;
021 310 74 24

**Librarie Cafenea Ifb**
Bulevardul Dacia nr. 77
Phone 021 316 38 36;
021 316 3837;
021 316 38 38

**Londophone Pub**
Str. Zalomit nr. 2
Phone 0744 629 499

**Margo Lounge Caffe**
Str. Lipscani nr. 29–33
Phone 0723 199 977

**Metropolis Cafe**
Bulevardul Alba Iulia nr. 13
Phone 0743 165 139

**Meu Café**
Bulevardul Mircea Vodă
nr. 34
Phone 031 425 59 11;
0771 602 784;
0771 602 789

**Minigolf Coffee
(Parcul Floresca)**
Phone 0730 316 993

**Minigolf Coffee
(Parcul Herăstrău)**
Phone 0730 316 992

**Minigolf Coffee
(Parcul Tineretului)**
Phone 0730 316 798

**Monkaff Roasting House**
Calea Floreasca nr. 111–113
Phone 031 425 95 94;
0771 795 281

**Noi Art Cafe**
Piaţa Alba Iulia nr. 7
Phone 031 104 70 63;
0728 873 268

**Nova Brasilia**
Str. Radu Beller nr. 6
Phone 021 231 55 40

**Ok Cafe**
Str. Mămulari nr. 2
Phone 021 311 11 03;
021 312 60 79;
0721 659 543;
0744 659 814;
0755 037 205

**Orient Cafe**
Calea Victoriei nr. 16–20
Phone 021 310 26 24;
0733 758 358

**Orient Expres**
Calea Victoriei nr. 16–20 (Pasaj Villacrosse)
Phone 0733 758 358

**Palatul Ghika**
Str. Doamna Ghica nr. 5
Phone 0735 444 422

**Pardon Cafe**
Str. Sibiu nr. 4
Phone 0744 310 166

**Pascucci Caffe**
Calea Dorobanţi nr. 140 A
Phone 021 222 00 42;
0756 166 111 (for events)

**Piano Cafe**
Bulevardul Iancu
de Hunedoara nr. 29F
Phone 021 230 45 42

**Plach Friends & Coffee**
Bulevardul Dacia nr. 153–155
Phone 0730 448 080;
0771 674 095

**Ramayana Café**
Str. Baldovin Pârcălabul nr. 11
Phone 021 317 16 81;
0788 595 595

# Cafés | Cultural centers and institutes

**Rendez-Vous Floreasca**
Calea Floreasca nr. 102
Phone 021 230 88 90;
021 230 88 91;
0720 070 286

**Rendez-Vous Quinet**
Str. Edgar Quinet nr. 8–10
Phone 021 230 88 90;
021 230 88 91;
0723 541 998

**Retro Cafe & Tea**
Str. Câmpia Libertății nr. 46
Phone 0727 634 926;
0764 992 992;
0756 158 158

**Rooms Cafe**
Str. Mendeleev nr. 28–30
Phone 0730 076 667

**Sala de Lectură – Ceainăria Teatrul Act**
Calea Victoriei nr. 126, etaj 2
Phone 021 312 00 42;
0724 360 755

**Secret Cafe**
Bulevardul Decebal nr. 12
Phone 021 326 06 03;
0722 297 451;
0721 732 738

**Serendipity**
Str. Dumbrava Roșie nr. 12
Phone 021 211 31 00;
0743 283 342,
0733 300 424

**Silence Cafe**
Str. Căderea Bastiliei nr. 19
Phone 021 317 41 37

**Smoking Cafe**
Șoseaua București–Ploiești,
nr. 42D
Phone 0771 67 40 95;
0730 448 080

**Tecafi**
Str. Doamnei nr. 9

**Triangle d'Or**
Bulevardul Ion Mihalache
nr. 92
Phone 0722 645 646

**Turabo Cafe (City Mall)**
Șoseaua Olteniței nr. 2
Phone 031 105 90 24;
0726 887 226

**Turabo Cafe (Romană)**
Str. Episcopiei nr. 6
Phone 021 327 69 62;
031 105 90 24;
0726 887 226

**Turabo Cafe (Universitate)**
Str. Ion Ghica nr. 3
Phone 021 313 66 22;
031 105 90 24;
0722 732 141

**Turabo Cafe (Vitan)**
Calea Vitan nr. 6
Phone 031 105 90 24;
021 337 69 62

**Underworld**
Str. Colței nr. 48
Phone 0732 050 550

**Uranus Cafe**
Șoseaua Progresului
nr. 151–171

**Van Gogh Grand Café**
Str. Smârdan nr. 9
Phone 031 107 63 71

**Vecchio 1812**
Str. Covaci nr. 16
Phone 031 430 95 77

**Veda Lounge**
Str. Octav Cocărăscu nr. 45
Phone 0721 065 402;
0745 222 226

**Verde Café**
Str. Domnița Ruxandra nr. 15
Phone 031 100 00 38;
0731 30 88 23

**Vibe Café**
Str. Ion Ghica nr. 3
Phone 0722 677 777

**Vienna Cafe**
Calea 13 Septembrie nr. 90
Phone 021 403 19 01;
021 403 30 99

**Voyage Cafe**
Str. Gabroveni nr. 9
Phone 0720 889 753;
0727 374 148

**White Caffe**
Bulevardul Decebal nr. 7
Phone 0754 040 000

**Wings Club**
Str. Mihai Eminescu nr. 127
Phone 0724 076 246

**Woodstock**
Str. Traian nr. 141
Phone 0744 422 279

**Zaze Caffe**
Bulevardul Dimitrie Cantemir
nr. 22

**Zebra Caffe**
Bulevardul Octavian Goga
nr. 8
Phone 031 800 55 57;
0721 092 076

**Zu Cafe**
Str. Daniel Danielopolu nr. 2
Phone 021 232 02 83;
0766 598 583

## Cultural centers and institutes

**ArCuB**
Str. Batiștei nr. 14
Phone 021 319 26 91;
021 319 26 90

**Artasia – Academia de Arte Asiatice**
Str. Negru Vodă nr. 4
Phone 0720 722 153

**Asociația Erudio**
Str. Paris, nr. 14, et. 2
Phone 031 107 61 55

**Atelierul de Producție / Param Pam Pam**
Splaiul Unirii nr. 160

Phone 0726 967 600;
0723 930 101

**Ateneul Român**
Str. Benjamin Franklin nr.1
Phone 021 315 68 75

**Bell Bucharest**
Bulevardul Dacia nr. 87
Phone 021 313 90 95;
0752 446 612

**Biblioteca Academiei Române**
Calea Victoriei nr. 125
Phone 021 212 82 84;
021 212 82 85

**Biblioteca Metropolitană Mihail Sadoveanu**
Str. Take Ionescu nr. 4
Phone 021 316 83 00;
021 316 83 03/04/05

**British Council**
Calea Dorobanților nr. 14
Phone 021 307 96 00

**Casa de Cultură a Studenților**
Calea Plevnei nr. 61
Phone 021 315 25 42;
021 315 40 55

**Casa de Cultură Friedrich Schiller**
Strada Batiștei nr. 15
Phone 021 319 26 88

**Centrul Ceh**
Str. Ion Ghica nr. 11
Phone 021 309 92 30

**Centrul Cultural Petőfi Sándor**
Str. Zalomit nr. 6
Phone 021 314 98 80

**Centrul Cultural al M.I.R.A.**
Str. Mihai Vodă nr. 17
Phone 021 314 62 19

**Centrul Cultural European**
Str. Lipscani nr. 53
Phone 021 315 89 80

**Centrul Cultural Metropolitan al Primăriei 1**
Bulevardul Poligrafiei nr. 4
(ADP, near Casa Presei)
Phone 0751 405 213

**Centrul Cultural Mihai Eminescu**
Str. Arh. Hârjeu nr. 61
Phone 021 322 69 57

**Centrul Cultural pentru UNESCO Nicolae Bălcescu**
Str. 11 Iunie nr. 41
Phone 021 336 43 40

**Centrul Cultural Maghiar**
Str. Orlando nr. 8
Phone 021 210 48 84

**Centrul de Cultură Arhitecturală**
Str. Jean-Louis Calderon nr. 48

**Centrul de Introspecție Vizuală**
Str. Biserica Enei nr. 16
Phone 021 314 22 98

**Centrul de Limbi Străine Ariel**
Str. Pitar Moș nr. 7–13
Phone 021 318 15 86;
021 318 15 85

**Centrul de Limbi Străine B. Smart**
Bulevardul Timișoara nr. 31
și Bulevardul Unirii nr. 78
Phone 0722 223 136 (english);
0727 691 276 (other languages); 0743 170 757 (for
children)

**Centrul de Limbi Străine Fides**
Bulevardul Hristo Botev nr. 1
Phone 021 313 47 85 / 86

**Centrul de Limbi Străine Teachers Indeed**
Piata Amzei, nr. 10–22
Phone 0753 161 209;
0731 589 546

**Centrul Lingua Franca**
Str. I.L. Caragiale nr. 22
Phone 0722 745 123

**Centrul Metropolitan pentru Tineret**
Bulevardul Poligrafiei nr. 4

**Centrul Național al Dansului**
Bulevardul Nicolae Bălcescu nr. 2
Phone 021 318 86 76;
021 319 73 82

**Centrul Național de Artă Tinerimea Română**
Str. Johann Gutenberg nr. 19
Phone 021 315 81 65,
fax 021 312 19 62

**Conacul Anthropoesis**
Str. Mircea Vulcănescu nr. 19

**Echo – Cursuri de Limbi Străine și Traduceri – Foișorul de Foc**
Str. Traian nr. 169
Phone 021 252 39 55;
021 252 38 99

**Echo – Cursuri de Limbi Străine și Traduceri – Moșilor**
Str. Dimitrie Onciul nr. 33
Phone 021 252 33 55;
021 252 01 15

**Euro-Training**
Șoseaua Orhideelor nr. 27–29
Phone 021 311 79 78;
021 312 00 59;
0722 287 495

**Fundația Calea Victoriei**
Str. Popa Soare nr. 40
Phone 021 321 30 22;
0723 167 892;
0735 863 847

**Global English**
Str. Decebal nr. 9
Phone 0724 030 492

**Goethe Institut**
Str. Tudor Arghezi nr. 8–10
Phone 021 312 02 31;
021 311 97 62 / 82

**Institutul Cervantes**
Str. Marin Serghiescu nr. 12
Phone 021 210 47 77

**Institutul Cultural Român**
Aleea Alexandru nr. 38
Phone 031 710 06 06

**Institutul Francez**
Bulevardul Dacia nr. 77
Phone 0374 125 200;
Cursuri: 0374 125 209;
Campus France: 0374 125 243

**Institutul Irecson**
Calea Victoriei nr. 2
Phone 0724 239 585

**Institutul Italian de Cultură Vito Grasso**
Aleea Alexandru nr. 41
Phone 021 231 08 80, int.103

**Institutul Polonez**
Str. Popa Savu nr. 28
Phone 021 224 45 56

**International House**
Str. Lânăriei nr. 93–95
Phone 021 335 44 90;
021 335 81 97

**JCC București – Centrul Comunitar Evreiesc**
Str. Popa Soare nr. 18
Phone 021 320 26 08;
0728 457 777;
0728 457 777

**Labomba – Centrul Comunitar pentru Educație și Artă Activă Rahova-Uranus**
Calea Rahovei nr. 194

**Lexis Schools Of Languages – Barbu Văcărescu**
Str. Mozart nr. 1B
Phone 021 231 82 41

**Lexis Schools of Languages – Kogălniceanu**
Intrarea Ursulețului nr. 1
Phone 021 315 10 06

**Lexis Schools of Languages – Mărășești**
B-dul Mărășești nr. 31
Phone 021 223 07 88

**Lexis Schools of Languages – Mihai Bravu**
Șoseaua Mihai Bravu nr. 247
Phone 021 317 95 37;
021 317 94 09

**Lexis Schools of Languages – Olteniței**
Șoseaua Olteniței nr. 38 A
Phone 021 332 61 26

**Lexis Schools of Languages – Pache Protopopescu**
Bulevardul Pache Protopopescu nr. 10
Phone 021 310 26 29

**Lexis Schools of Languages – Rahova**
Str. Mihail Sebastian nr. 1–3
Phone 021 456 02 52

**Bucharest**

**Lexis Schools
of Languages –
Titan**
Aleea Calistrat Hogaş nr. 45 B
Phone 021 340 41 59

**Lexis Schools
of Languages –
Unirii**
Str. Bucur nr. 4–6
Phone 021 330 44 25

**Liceul de Coregrafie
Floria Capsali**
Str. Căpitan Preoţescu nr. 9
Phone 021 336 37 92

**Lingua Transcript**
Bulevardul Nicolae Bălcescu
nr. 36
Phone 021 312 08 82;
0722 333 081

**Ministerul Culturii
şi Patrimoniului Naţional**
Piaţa Unirii nr. 22
Phone 021 224 25 10

**Muzeul Memorial
C.C. Nottara**
Bulevardul Dacia nr. 105
Phone 021 210 38 23

**Palatul Naţional al Copiilor**
Bulevardul Tineretului
nr. 8–10
Phone 021 330 40 83;
021 330 40 89

**Palatul Universul**
Str. Brezoianu nr. 23

**Reflectart**
Str. Parfumului nr. 13

**Road Language Centre –
English Cafe**
Str. Dr. Staicovici nr. 4
Phone 021 312 90 36;
0721 287 790

**Shakespeare School
of English**
Str. Eufrosin Potecă nr. 42 A
Phone 021 252 24 79;
0755 132 228

**Societatea Română
de Radiodifuziune**
Str. General Berthelot
nr. 60–64
Phone 021 222 22 41

**Tangotangent**
Str. Pache Protopopescu nr. 30
Phone 0741 131 319

**Tradumond**
Str. Ştirbei Vodă nr. 105
Phone 021 312 91 95;
0722 527 097
0744 636 033

**Turbohalle – Centrul
Cultural Neconvenţional**
Bulevardul Iuliu Maniu
nr. 220B

**Universitatea de Ştiinţe
Agronomice şi Medicină
Veterinară**
Str. Mărăşti nr. 59

**Universitatea Populară
Ioan I. Dalles**
Bulevardul Nicolae Bălcescu
nr. 18
Phone 021 314 66 37

**WASP – Working Art
Space & Production**
Str. Ion Minulescu nr. 67–93

## Cinemas

**Băneasa Drive In Cinema**
Şoseaua Bucureşti–Ploieşti nr.
42D
Phone 021 306 55 05

**Cinema City – Cotroceni**
Str. Vasile Milea nr. 4
Phone 021 407 00 00

**Cinema City Sun Plaza**
Calea Văcăreşti nr. 391
Phone 021 386 06 00

**Cinema Corso**
Bulevardul Elisabeta nr. 27
Phone 021 315 13 34

**Cinema Glendale Studio**
Str. Cotroceni nr. 9
Phone 021 316 32 86

**Cinema Gloria**
Bulevardul Bucovina nr. 6
Phone 021 324 46 75

**Cinema Patria**
Bulevardul Gh. Magheru
nr. 12–14
Phone 021 316 92 66

**Cinema Scala**
Bulevardul Gh. Magheru
nr. 2–4
Phone 021 316 67 08

**Cinema Studio**
Bulevardul Gh. Magheru
nr. 29
Phone 021 316 55 26

**Cinemapro**
Str. Ion Ghica nr. 3
Phone 031 824 13 60

**Cinemateca – Sala Eforie**
Str. Eforie nr. 2
Phone 021 313 04 83

**Cinemateca – Sala Union**
Str. Ion Câmpineanu nr. 21
Phone 021 313 92 89

**Cityplex**
Şoseaua Olteniţei nr. 2
Phone 021 319 82 26

**Eurocinema – Tinerimea
Română**
Str. Gutenberg nr. 19
Phone 021 315 81 65;
0722 578 929

**Garden Cinema**
Str. Doamna Ghica nr. 5
Phone 021 302 30 33;
0735 444 422

**Grand Cinema Digiplex**
Şoseaua Bucureşti–Ploieşti nr.
42D
Phone 021 306 55 05

# Cinemas | Clubs

**Hollywood Multiplex**
Calea Vitan nr. 55–59
Phone 021 327 70 20; 021
327 70 21; 021 327 70 22

**Movieplex**
Bulevardul Timişoara nr. 26
Phone 021 431 00 00;
031 407 83 00

**NCRR (Noul Cinematograf al Regizorului Român)**
Str. Monetăriei nr. 3
Phone 0213 129 875

**Romtelecom Imax**
Bulevardul Vasile Milea nr. 4
Phone 021 407 00 00

**Sala Elvira Popescu**
Bulevardul Dacia nr. 77
Phone 0374 125 216

**The Light Cinema**
Şoseaua Progresului nr. 151–171
Phone 021 369 97 97;
021 369 97 40

**Uranus 144 – Cinema în aer liber**
Str. Uranus nr. 144
Phone 0727 794 737;
0722 334 455

## Clubs

**1001 Nopţi – Lounge & Club**
Str. Ion Brezoianu nr. 18
Phone 0746 171 111

**Absolut Party Bar**
Str. Covaci nr. 6
Phone 0784 237 789;
0784 237 789

**Acqua Club**
Str. Mihai Eminescu nr. 89
Phone 0728 330 565

**Ageless Club**
Calea Şerban Vodă nr. 213

**Alexander Club**
Calea Victoriei nr. 91–93

Phone 0786 663 211;
0721 790 589

**Allure**
Calea Floreasca nr. 110
Phone 0744 501 155;
0726 649 085

**Anton Pub**
Str. Şepcari nr. 22

**Arcade Cafe**
Str. Smârdan nr. 30
Phone 021 314 50 66;
0727 257 022;
0722 777 674

**Armada Club**
Str. Soarelui nr. 4–6
Phone 0721 276 232

**Arrogance Club**
Calea Victoriei nr. 16–18
Phone 021 312 70 27;
0744 323 712

**Art Jazz Club**
Bulevardul Nicolae Bălcescu nr. 23 A
Phone 0731 645 918

**Attraction Club**
Str. Agricultori nr. 16
Phone 0731 578 887;
0757 952 474

**B52**
Str. 11 Iunie nr. 50
Phone 0753 315 563

**Babylon Club – City Of Sin**
Str. Nerva Traian nr. 27
Phone 0733 763 361

**Bamboo**
Str. Tuzla nr. 50
Phone 0723 266 266;
0726 266 266

**Baraka – Skate Park Herăstrău**
Şoseaua Nordului nr. 1

**Barca Herăstrău**
Şoseaua Nordului nr. 7–9
Phone 0722 399 228

**Barfly**
Str. Olteni nr. 3
Phone 0721 652 899;
0720 566 110

**Barocco Bar**
Str. Domniţa Anastasia nr. 10
Phone 0755 028 028;
0740 114 132

**Bastards**
Str. Lipscani nr. 28
Phone 0745 764 842

145

**Bellagio Club**
Şoseaua Ştefan cel Mare
nr. 31
Phone 0722 323 324

**Big Mamou**
Splaiul Independenţei nr. 2
Phone 0724 671 108;
0744 520 149

**Blue Club (R3)**
Splaiul Independenţei nr. 290
Phone 021 316 27 39;
021 222 88 21

**Bonton by Marie Celeste**
Şoseaua Nordului nr. 1
Phone 0745 999 111;
0745 999 222

**Cafeneaua Actorilor Universitate**
Bulevardul Nicolae Bălcescu
nr. 2
Phone 0721 900 842

**Chat Noir Club**
Str. Blănari nr. 5
Phone 0745 113 552;
0740 100 797

**Cliche Club & Lounge**
Str. Smârdan nr. 41
Phone 0729 056 254

**Club 99 – The Comedy Club**
Bulevardul Dacia nr. 99
Phone 0733 500 301

**Club A**
Str. Blănari nr. 14
Phone 021 316 16 67

**Club Antiqum**
Str. Jean-Louis Calderon
nr. 33

**Club Kuky Cafe**
Splaiul Unirii nr. 176

**Club Loft**
Bulevardul Iancu
de Hunedoara nr. 55

**Club Makondo**
Str. Mircea Eliade nr. 18
Phone 021 311 56 10

**Club Maxx**
Splaiul Independenţei nr. 290
Phone 0722 647 337

**Club Maya**
Calea Moşilor nr. 138
Phone 0769 778 644

**Club Molotov**
Str. Vasile Conta nr. 18

**Club One**
Şoseaua Orhideelor nr. 6
Phone 0729 112 582

**Club Princess**
Str. Ghercu Constantin
nr 24
Phone 0720 535 383;
0720 535 382

**Clubul Prometheus**
Piaţa Naţiunilor Unite nr. 3–5
Phone 021 336 66 38

**Clubul Ţăranului**
Bulevardul Kiseleff nr. 3
Phone 021 310 80 48

**Colors**
Str. Lipscani nr. 19

**Complex Herăstrău**
Şoseaua Nordului nr. 7–9
Phone 021 232 21 28

**Control**
Str. Constantin Mille nr. 4

**Coyote Cafe**
Calea Victoriei nr. 40–50
Phone 021 311 34 87;
0724 011 135

**Cuando Club**
Str. Academiei nr. 35–37
Phone 0722 505 085

**Cuando Summer Lounge**
Şoseaua Nordului nr. 3
Phone 0722 505 085

**Daimon Club**
Str. Piscului nr. 10
Phone 0722 207 100;
0731 300 833

**Damage Club**
Calea Victoriei nr. 18–20
Phone 0727 547 147;
0735 118 598

**Deja Vu**
Bulevardul Nicolae Bălcescu
nr. 25
Phone 021 311 23 22;
0721 918 279

**Downtown Bar & Cafe**
Str. Mendeleev nr. 23–24
Phone 021 314 86 06

**Dreams Club**
Str. Mihai Eminescu nr. 89
Phone 0753 333 378;
0753 333 325

**Dumars Light**
Splaiul Independenţei nr. 290
Phone 031 105 79 45;
0733 386 277

**El Comandante Grande**
Str. Viitorului nr. 26
Phone 0728 556 043

**El Comandante Junior**
Str. Lipscani nr. 43
Phone 0728 555 043

**El Comandante Primer**
Str. Sfântul Ştefan nr. 13
Phone 0729 733 042

**El Dictador**
Str. Sfântul Dumitru nr. 3
Phone 0729 041 043

**Elements**
Şoseaua Nordului nr. 7–9
Phone 0734 123 456;
0733 102 686

**Elephant Pub & Live Music**
Str. Gabroveni nr. 16

**Eleven**
Bulevardul Nicolae Bălcescu
Phone 0751 111 115

**Energiea**
Str. Brezoianu nr. 4
Phone 0736 374 432

**ENTOURAGE**
Şoseaua Nordului nr. 7–9

**Expirat**
Str. Lipscani nr. 5,
Phone 0733 974 728,
after 4 p.m.

**Fabrica**
Str. 11 Iunie nr. 50
Phone 021 335 03 23;
0753 227 422

**Fat Cat Club**
Str. Gabroveni nr. 24

**Favela**
Calea Moşilor nr.160
Phone 0727 222 574

**Fire Club**
Str. Gabroveni nr. 12
Phone 0732 166 604

**Frame Club**
Bulevardul Magheru nr. 38 B
Phone 021 211 01 44;
0730 117 703

**Fratelli**
Str. Nicolae Golescu nr. 5
Phone 021 311 66 76

**Fratelli Studios**
Str. Glodeni nr. 1–3
Phone 021 311 66 76

**Funky Lounge**
Bulevardul Decebal nr. 9
Phone 0755 155 155

**Funky Lounge Herăstrău**
Herăstrău Park, Pescăruş
Entrance
Phone 0744 450 450

**Fusion Arena**
Str. Traian Popovici nr. 79–91
Phone 0732 037 872

**Gaia Boutiqueclub**
Str. Banu Antonache
nr. 40–44
Phone 0723 610 933

**Gala Wine**
Str. Icoanei nr. 32
Phone 021 210 40 39

**Glass Garden**
Str. Şelari nr. 9–11
Phone 0744 360 005;
0744 808 915

**Glow Club Cafe**
Str. Spineni nr. 18
Phone 0721 170 560

**Golden Plum**
Şoseaua Bucureşti–Târgovişte,
km 23
Phone 021 350 06 11;
0733 691 451;
0740 142 622

**Gossip**
Calea Floreasca nr. 169
Phone 0729 44 88 66

**Graffiti Club**
Str. Albac nr. 25
Phone 021 231 79 79

**Green Hours 2**
Bulevardul Ştefan cel Mare
nr. 7–9
Phone 0788 452 485

**Green Hours 22 Jazz Cafe**
Calea Victoriei nr. 120
Phone 0788 452 485;
0722 234 356

**Happy Pub**
Str. Căderea Bastiliei nr. 36

**Heaven & Hell Bar**
Str. Occidentului nr. 1
Phone 0753 118 107;
0723 195 719

**Hot Shots**
Str. Cercului nr. 3 A
Phone 0726 050 619;
0724 355 554

**Icon**
Calea Floreasca nr. 111–113
Phone 0721 260 011

**Inbox Bar**
Str. Lascăr Catargiu nr. 6
Phone 0745 113 552

**Indie Club**
Str. Inişor nr. 2
Phone 0735 527 464;
0728 825 777

**Iron City**
Str. Blănari 21
Phone 0730 879 021;
0721 223 343

**Jet Set Events Hall**
Bulevardul Libertăţii nr. 1
Phone 0735 298 286

## Jukebox Club
Str. Turturelelor nr. 11
Phone 021 322 66 10;
021 323 70 83

## Kanto Club
Str. Nerva Traian nr. 25 A
Phone 0760 034 466;
0786 755 217

## Kristal Glam Club
Str. J.S. Bach nr. 2
Phone 021 231 21 36;
0722 795 184

## Kulturhaus
Str. Sfânta Vineri nr. 4
Phone 021 313 55 92

## La Muse
Str. Lipscani nr. 53
Phone 021 310 64 34;
0734 000 236;
0745 024 217

## Legacy
Str. Lipscani nr. 56
Phone 0726 130 859

## Legere Live
Piața Rossetti nr. 5
Phone 0730 534 373

## Londophone Pub
Str. Zalomit nr. 2
Phone 0744 629 499

## Ludic
Str Colței nr. 50
Phone 0745 658 342;
031 438 01 79

## Malibu Club
Bulevardul Mihai Bravu nr. 32
Phone 021 231 32 23;
0722 284 857

## Mândală Club
Str. Paleologu nr. 20
Phone 0214 120 135;
0732 026 279

## Metropolis lii
Piața Unirii nr. 1
Phone 0743 165 139

## Modern
Str. Mihai Eminescu nr. 127
Phone 021 300 00 00

## Mojo
Str. Gabroveni nr. 14
Phone 0760 263 496

## Mon Amour & Mon Cher Club
Șoseaua Nordului nr. 79
Phone 0726 683 896

## Music Club (Live Music)
Str. Bărăției nr. 31
Phone 0720 887 115

## Oasis Sport & Leisure – Club
Str. Străulești nr. 4
Phone 021 667 02 11;
0723 731 899

## Obey Club
Str. Lipscani nr. 18
Phone 0726 093 215

## Octopus Lounge & Club
Str. Șelari nr. 9–11
Phone 0768 988 888

## Old City – Lipscani Beer Garden
Str. Lipscani nr. 45
Phone 0729 377 774

## Old School
Calea Plevnei nr. 61
Phone 021 313.26.88;
0744 105 445

## Oldies Club
Str. Ion Câmpineanu nr. 16
Phone 0723 666 551

## Onx Club
Splaiul Independenței nr. 290
Phone 0744 520 025

## Open Pub
Str. Tunari nr. 65
Phone 0746 484 765

## Opium Stage
Calea Victoriei nr. 16–20
Phone 021 312 70 27;
0727 062 001

## Opium Studio
Str. Horei nr. 5
Phone 0727 062 001

## Other Side
Str. Lipscani nr. 5
Phone 0733 974 728,
after 4 p.m.

## Our Evolution
Str. Covaci nr. 16
Phone 0722 571 572

## Panic
Str. Academiei nr. 19

## Passage Club
Calea Victoriei nr. 52
Phone 0757 048 784;
0722 327 223

## Q Pub
Str. Mendeleev nr. 35
Phone 021 316 80 45;
0722 518 612

## Qub Club
Calea Victoriei nr. 91–93
Phone 0732 863 681

## Revenge
Str. Șelari nr. 9–11
Phone 0722 331 226

## Rooms Club
Str. Mendeleev nr. 28–30
Phone 0730 076 667

## Salsa 3
Str. Mihai Eminescu nr. 89
Phone 0728 725 723

## Salsa 5 / Guantanamo Club
Str. Tăbăcari nr. 7
Phone 0723 531 841

## Shade Club
Bulevardul Magheru nr. 24
Phone 0731 060 606

## Silver Afterhours
Str. Gabroveni nr. 20
Phone 0721 745 837

## Soho
Str. Sfântul Ștefan nr. 6
Phone 0728 877 576

**Soho Studio**
Str. Şelimbăr nr. 1
Phone 0733 748 502

**Spice Club**
Calea Victoriei nr. 21–23
Phone 021 312 01 36

**Studio Bar**
Str. Colonel Iosif Albu
nr. 62 B
Phone 0740 353 385;
0746 418 343;
0762 635 935

**Studio Martin**
Bulevardul Iancu
de Hunedoara nr. 41
Phone 0722 399 228

**Stuf Vama Veche**
Str. Berzei 25 A
Phone 021 316 22 42;
0745 694 791;
0724 788 388

**Tan Tan Club**
Bulevardul Carol nr. 61
Phone 0720 826 826

**Tephra**
Str. Domniţa Anastasia nr. 14
Phone 0722 120 271

**The Artist Studio**
Str. Şelimbăr nr. 1
Phone 0758 111 179

**The Barrel British Pub**
Str. Smârdan nr. 27
Phone 0726 412 646

**The Blu'zz**
Str. General Ipătescu nr. 4
Phone 0728 880 808;
0722 548 111

**The Dj's**
Str. Mihai Eminescu nr. 156
Phone 0752 028 469

**The Drunken Lords**
Str. Şelari nr. 3–5
Phone 031 424 54 63;
0736 238 815

**The Embassy –
Hanul cu Tei**
Str. Lipscani nr. 63
Phone 0723 528 242;
0727 571 371

**The Gate Club**
Str. Primo Nebiolo nr. 1
Phone 0728 434 283

**The Gin Factory**
Str. Lipscani nr. 37
Phone 021 311 38 36

**The Jack Pub & Rock**
Str. Sg. Marcu Ion nr. 23
Phone 021 725 50 35;
0743 153 441

**The Legend**
Str. Colţei nr. 50
Phone 021 310 96 11;
0722 766 510;
0769 757 520;
0749 800 459

**The Office**
Str. Tache Ionescu nr. 2
Phone 021 211 67 48;
0745 110 064

**The Player**
Str. Primo Nebiolo nr. 7
Phone 0720 734 734

**The Silver Church Club**
Calea Plevnei nr. 61
Phone 021 313 55 92;
0723 379 026

**The Vault Club**
Str. Lipscani nr. 29–33
Phone 0723 199 977

**Tralala Club**
Str. Lipscani nr. 43

**Tribute Club**
Calea Victoriei nr. 118
Phone 0728 742 883

**Turabo Society Club**
Str. Olteţului nr. 30
Phone 0755 111 777;
0744 313 444

**Underworld Club**
Str. Colţei nr. 48
Tel. 0732 050 550

**Velvet Club**
Str. Ştirbei Vodă nr. 4
Phone 021 312 70 04;
021 315 92 41

**Vertigo Club**
Str. Blănari nr. 21
Phone 0730 471 746

**Voyage Club**
Str. Gabroveni nr. 9
Phone 0720 889 753;
0727 374 148

**Weiss Beer Garden**
Str. Uverturii nr. 132
Phone 0733 582 852

**Wings Club**
Str. Mihai Eminescu nr. 127
Phone 0724 076 246

**Woodstock**
Str. Traian nr. 141
Phone 0744 422 279

**Zoom Cafe & Club**
Str. Colţei nr. 44
Phone 0726 825 331

## Non stop pharmacies

### District 1

**Alicat**
Bulevardul Aerogării nr. 32
Phone 021 232 41 99

**Dona**
Bulevardul Magheru nr. 32–34
Phone 021 316 54 07

**Farmadex**
Bulevardul Nicolae Titulescu
nr. 119
Phone 021 250 37 25

**HelpNet**
Str. Ion Mihalache nr. 92
Phone 031 405 04 59

**Sensiblu – 1 Mai**
Bulevardul Ion Mihalache
nr. 92
Phone 021 224 18 68

**Sensiblu – Dorobanți 2**
Str. Radu Beller nr. 6
Phone 021 233 89 61

**Sensiblu – Magheru**
Bulevardul Nicolae Bălcescu
nr. 7
Phone 021 305 73 14

**Sensiblu Amzei**
Piața Amzei nr. 10–22
Phone 021 308 85 79

**Sensiblu Berzei**
Str. Berzei nr. 50bis
Phone 021 212 64 01

**Sensiblu Dorobanți**
Cal. Dorobantilor nr. 65
Phone 211 11 27

**Sensiblu Dristor**
Șoseaua Mihai Bravu
nr. 311–313, bl. SB1
Phone 021 346 46 50

## District 2

**Dami-mar**
Bulevardul Carol I nr. 59
Phone 021 315 61 37

**Dami-mar**
Șoseaua Colentina nr. 1
Phone 021 242 52 90

**Dami-mar**
Șoseaua Colentina nr. 26
Phone 021 240 52 94

**Dami-mar**
Șoseaua Pantelimon nr. 117
Phone 021 250 31 92

**Farmadex**
Calea Moșilor nr. 280
Phone 021 211 95 60

**Farmadex**
Calea Moșilor nr. 280
Phone 021 211 95 60

**Farmadex**
Șoseaua Pantelimon nr. 291
Phone 0744 650 078

**Flora**
Bulevardul Basarabia nr. 55
Phone 021 255 50 72

**HelpNet**
Șoseaua Mihai Bravu nr. 128,
bl. D24
Phone 031 405 04 46

**Meta-farm**
Șoseaua Iancului nr. 33
Phone 021 250 21 18

**Sensiblu Doamna Ghica**
Str. Doamna Ghica nr. 8, bl. 2
Phone 021 242 52 48

**Sensiblu Obor**
Șoseaua Mihai Bravu nr. 2
Phone 021 252 68 99

**Sensiblu Ștefan cel Mare I**
Șoseaua Ștefan cel Mare
nr. 22B, bl. 24A
Phone 021 212 31 11

**Sensiblu Ștefan Cel Mare II**
Șoseaua Ștefan cel Mare
nr. 48, bl. 35A
Phone 021 211 32 83

**Sf. Mina**
Șoseaua Pantelimon nr. 285
Phone 021 255 34 56

**Simart Farm Foisor**
Bulevardul Ferdinand nr. 31
Phone 021 252 58 67/68

## District 3

**Dona**
Calea Vitan nr. 199
Phone 021 344 26 17

**Med Farm Lipscani**
Bulevardul I.C. Brătianu
nr. 34
Phone 021 315 23 09

**Sensiblu**
Calea Călărașilor nr. 113,
bl. 1B, sc. A
Phone 021 315 31 59

**Sensiblu 1 Decembrie**
Bulevardul 1 Decembrie 1918
nr. 31–33
Phone 021 345 23 97

**Sensiblu Mihai Bravu**
Șoseaua Mihai Bravu nr. 288
Phone 021 320 98 75

**Sensiblu Rosetti**
Bulevardul Carol I nr. 23
**Sensiblu Titan**
Şoseaua Câmpia Libertăţii
nr. 46, bl. 52
Phone 021 302 99 53
**Sensiblu Unirii**
Piaţa Unirii, nr. 1
(Unirea Shopping Center)
Phone 021 303 02 67
**Sensiblu Victoriei**
Calea Victoriei nr. 12A
Phone 021 315 31 60

**Titan**
Bulevardul Nicolae
Grigorescu nr. 20
Phone 021 340 21 02

**Titan**
Bulevardul Nicolae
Grigorescu nr. 20
Phone 021 340 21 02

## District 4

**4EM Farm**
Şoseaua Olteniţei nr. 12,
bl. D2
Phone 021 332 45 40;
021 332 13 00

**Dona**
Şoseaua Giurgiului nr. 123
Phone 021 450 62 67

**Dona**
Bulevardul Obregia nr. 31
Phone 021 460 31 92

**Drogheria Silvester**
Str. Reşiţa nr. 20, bl. A19,
sc. B, ap. 16
Phone 021 423 41 21

**HelpNet**
Bulevardul Unirii nr. 24
Phone 031 405 04 57

**Sensiblu Giurgiului**
Şoseaua Giurgiului
nr. 118–120
Phone 021 629 20 24

**Sensiblu Obregia**
Bulevardul Al. Obregia nr. 6,
bl. M1
Phone 021 460 30 72

**Tineretului**
Bulevardul Şincai nr. 2
Phone 021 252 58 68

**York Farm**
Bulevardul Constantin
Brâncoveanu nr. 110B

## District 5

**HelpNet**
Str. 13 Septembrie nr. 126
Phone 031 405 04 63

**SensiBlu – Alexandriei**
Şoseaua Alexandriei nr. 78
Phone 021 404 80 83

## District 6

**Crângaşi**
Calea Crângaşi nr. 30, bl. 50
Phone 021 221 40 88

**Help Net Moghioroş**
Str. Braşov nr. 21
(Piaţa Moghioroş)
Phone 031 405 06 81

**Orizont**
Drumul Taberei nr. 18
Phone 021 413 25 55

**Royal Blue**
Str. Virtuţii nr. 9
Phone 021 430 34 88

**Sensiblu Drumul Taberei 1**
Drumul Taberei nr. 80–82,
bl. C16
Phone 021 402 80 78

**Sensiblu Drumul Taberei 2**
Drumul Taberei nr. 96, bl. 521
Phone 021 777 32 84

**Sensiblu Ghencea**
Str. Vlădulescu Cristea nr. 2,
bl. C62
Phone 021 413 10 22

**Sensiblu Militari 1**
Bulevardul Iuliu Maniu
nr. 17–29
**Sensiblu Militari 2**
Bulevardul Iuliu Maniu nr. 14
Phone 021 430 34 52;
021 434 34 45

## Art galleries

**Annart Gallery**
Str. Mahatma Ghandi nr. 1
Phone 031 437 95 33

**115 – Galerie de Artă
Digitală**
Str. Mihai Eminescu nr. 115
Phone 021 210 19 69

**418 Contemporary Art
Gallery**
Intrarea Armaşului nr. 12
Phone 021 211 78 33;
0747 480 630

**Ambra Decor**
Str. Academiei nr. 7
Phone 0788 250 248;
0788 250 248

**Anaid Art Gallery**
Str. Slobozia nr. 34
Phone 021 337 11 87

**Art Concept Atelier
PNŢ-CD**
Bulevardul Carol nr. 24
Phone 0722 142 070

**Art Decoronica**
Str. Batiştei nr. 16
Phone 0745 064 830

**Art Point – Galerie, Atelier,
Studio**
Bulevardul Regina Maria nr. 2
Phone 0723 013 857

**Artmark – Galerii de Artă
şi Casă de Licitaţie**
Str. Log. Luca Stroici nr. 18
Phone 021 210 30 16;
021 210 30 15

**Atelier 35**
Str. Şelari nr. 13
Phone 0726 704 334

**Atelier Cafe – Gabroveni**
Str. Gabroveni nr. 24
Phone 021 312 42 04

**Atelier Cafe – Şelari**
Str. Şelari nr. 7
Phone 021 318 28 54;
021 312 42 04

**Atelier David Sandu**
Str. Smârdan nr. 30
Phone 0721 451 693;
0723 582 599

**Atelier Hag**
Str. Maria Rossetti nr. 53
Phone 021 222 54 47;
0721 261 242

**Atelier în Tranziţie**
Str. Edgar Quinet nr. 8

**Atelierul de Creaţie Sultana**
Calea Griviţei nr. 403, bl. R,
sc. B
Phone 021 668 18 22;
0723 339 352;
0724 044 624

**Back Space / Open Studio**
Str. Iacob Negruzzi nr. 28

**Casa Brătianu**
Str. Visarion nr. 4–6

**Centrul Artelor Vizuale (Căminul Artei)**
Str. Biserica Enei nr. 16
Phone 021 312 67 66

**Draft One – Galeria de Proiecte**
Piaţa Concordiei nr. 4

**Fotocabinet**
Str. Lipscani nr. 41
Phone 0726 694 005

**Fractart**
Calea Călăraşi nr. 173
Phone 021 323 52 38;

021 323 52 39;
0722 630 159

**Galeria "26" / Ota**
Str. Dr. Staicovici nr. 26
Phone 0721 840 723

**Galeria A.P.P.**
Pavilionul B – Aleea Artiştilor –
Parcul Herăstrău
Phone 0720 933 616;
0720 933 641

**Galeria 2 Meta**
Str. Sfinţii Apostoli nr. 37A
Phone 031 805 21 23;
0771 602 769

**Galeria Allianz-Ţiriac**
Str. Căderea Bastiliei
nr. 80–84
Phone 021 208 22 22

**Galeria Anticariat 9**
Calea Victoriei nr. 12
Phone 021 314 47 02

**Galeria Anticariat Curtea Veche**
Strada Franceză nr. 54
Phone 021 312 23 57;
0744 351 649

**Galeria Apollo**
Bulevardul Nicolae Bălcescu
nr. 2
Phone 021 313 50 10

**Galeria Art Room**
Şoseaua Pipera–Tunari nr. 2
Phone 021 208 37 68

**Galeria Arte**
Strada Episcopiei nr. 2–4

**Galeria Artis**
Bulevardul Nicolae Bălcescu
nr. 2

**Galeria Atelier 030202**
Str. Sfânta Vineri nr. 11

**Galeria Basil**
Str. Dionisie Lupu nr. 46
Phone 031 805 97 57;
0726 186 188

**Galeria C. Piliuţă**
Calea Victoriei nr. 208
Phone 021 212 99 79

**Galeria Cărtureşti**
Str. Pictor Verona nr. 13
Phone 021 212 19 22

**Galeria Ceramică 7**
Str. Hanul cu Tei (Lipscani)

**Galeria Colors Art**
Str. Puțul lui Zamfir nr. 22–24
(Piața Dorobanți)
Phone 021 211 57 28;
0724 120 277

**Galeria de Artă a Municipiului București (GAMB)**
Str. Academiei nr. 15

**Galeria de Artă Ana**
Str. Emil Pangrati nr. 25
Phone 021 231 11 80;
0747 118 558

**Galeria de Artă Bucureștii Vechi – Micul Paris**
Str. Dionisie Lupu nr. 47
Phone 0720 933 641

**Galeria de Artă Casa Vernescu**
Calea Victoriei nr. 133
Phone 021 311 97 44

**Galeria de Artă și Antichități Hanul cu Tei**
Str. Lipscani nr. 63–65
Phone 021 313 01 81;
021 315 56 63;
0727 221 491;
0744 328 200

**Galeria Degradee**
Str. Naum Râmniceanu nr. 5

**Galeria Dialog**
Str. Chiristigiilor nr. 11–13

**Galeria Etaj 3/4**
Bulevardul Nicolae Bălcescu
nr. 2
Phone 021 313 02 50

**Galeria Fundației / Baku Art Gallery**
Str. Dem I. Dobrescu nr. 11
Phone 021 307 29 77;
021 307 29 78

**Galeria Gabriela Călinoiu**
Str. Virgil Pleșoianu nr. 94
Phone 0721 949 740

**Galeria Galateea**
Calea Victoriei nr. 132
Phone 021 659 38 14

**Galeria Karousel**
Str. George Călinescu nr. 5A
Phone 0742 055 888

**Galeria Laika**
Str. Christian Tell nr. 21, et.1, ap. 2
Phone 0723 320 931

**Galeria Luchian 12**
Str. Pictor Ștefan Luchian
nr. 12
Phone 021 315 68 02;
0723 397 645

**Galeria Mensualart 25**
Str. Gr. Alexandrescu nr. 41
Phone 0722 375 771

**Galeria Mora**
Str. Grigore Mora nr. 39
Phone 021 316 55 41

**Galeria Nemțoi**
Calea Victoriei nr. 126
Phone 021 312 98 00

**Galeria Nit**
Str. Șelari nr. 13
Phone 021 312 67 15

**Galeria Nouă**
Str. Academiei nr. 15
Phone 021 322 81 59;
0744 357 007

**Galeria Octav Doicescu – UAR**
Calea Victoriei nr. 126
Phone 021 310 91 94

**Galeria Orizont**
Bulevardul Nicolae Bălcescu
nr. 23 A
Phone 021 315 89 22

**Galeria Orizont M**
Bulevardul Nicolae Bălcescu
nr. 23 A
Phone 021 312 40 55

**Galeria Pogany**
Bulevardul Nicolae Bălcescu
nr. 2
Phone 021 312 70 12;
0722 516 508;
0722 353 757

**Galeria Posibilă**
Str. Popa Petre nr. 6
Phone 021 211 79 33

**Galeria Recycle Nest**
Str. Icoanei nr. 17
Phone 0720 226 682

**Galeria Senso**
Bulevardul Unirii nr. 15
Phone 021 201 09 00

**Galeria și Centrul de Artă Euterpe**
Strada Duzilor nr. 5
Phone 0727 857 747

**Galeria Simeza**
Bulevardul Gheorghe Magheru nr. 20
Phone 021 659 75 80

**Galeria Una**
Str. Budișteanu nr. 10
Phone 021 212 88 64

**Galeriile Artexpo – TNB**
Bulevardul Nicolae Bălcescu
nr. 2
Phone 021 311 51 47

**H'art Gallery**
Str. Mihai Eminescu
nr. 105–107
Phone 021 210 83 51

**Ht003 Gallery**
Str. Hanul cu Tei nr. 22
Phone 021 313 01 81;
021 315 56 63;
0727 221 491;
0744 328 200

**If Gallery**
Str. Tokyo nr. 1

**Ivan Gallery**
Str. Dr. Dimitrie Grecescu
nr. 13
Phone 0721 261 242

**Melenia Art Gallery**
Str. Constantin Daniel nr. 3
Phone 021 315 77 50;
0732 834 757

**Moir**
Bulevardul Iancu de
Hunedoara nr. 64
Phone 0374 036 827;
0742 356 762

**Palatul Parlamentului –
Sala de Expoziţii
Constantin Brâncuşi**
Str. Izvor nr. 3
Phone 021 402 14 28

**Pavilion Unicredit**
Bulevardul Nicolae Titulescu
nr. 1
Phone 031 103 41 31

**Point Contemporary**
Str. Icoanei nr. 15
Phone 0756 056 100

**Romulus Art Gallery**
Str. Romulus nr. 8
Phone 021 322 40 23;
0741 239 470

**Sala Dalles**
Bulevardul Nicolae Bălcescu
nr. 18

**Salonul de Proiecte**
Calea Moşilor nr. 62–68, et. 2
Phone 021 313 91 15

**SI Gallery**
Str. Jean-Louis Calderon
nr. 26

**Studio Arte**
Str. Episcopiei nr. 2–4
Phone 0721 482 297

**Studio R**
Str. Pandele Ţăruşanu nr. 4 bis

**Sun Art Studio**
Str. Ioan Florescu nr. 13
Phone 0761 448 924

**Tc Art Gallery**
Str. Lipscani nr. 63–65
Phone 0788 433 490

**Val House**
Str. Gabroveni nr. 24
Phone 021 312 42 04

**Veroniki Art**
Intrarea Murmurului nr. 2–4
Phone 021 232 98 44

**Victoria Art Center**
Calea Victoriei nr. 12C
Phone 031 102 05 12

**Wagner Maison
de la Porcelaine**
Str. Dr. Staicovici nr. 19
Phone 0722 521 174;
0728 306 619

**Wagner – Arte Frumoase
şi Poveşti**
Bulevardul Carol nr. 39
Phone 0723 191 656;
0722 521 174

## Hotels

**Amphitryon**
Str. Ardeleni nr. 2–4
Phone 021 201 65 10;
021 201 65 12

**Angelo Airport Hotel**
Calea Bucureştilor nr. 283
Phone 021 203 65 00

**Antheus**
Str. Abrud nr. 1
Phone 021 223 43 13;
031 816 72 51

**Armonia**
Calea Moşilor nr. 112
Phone 021 312 04 77

**Astoria**
Bulevardul Dinicu Golescu nr. 27
Phone 021 212 66 54

**Athénée Palace Hilton**
Str. Episcopiei nr. 1–3
Phone 021 303 37 77

**Banat**
Piaţa Rossetti nr. 5
Phone 021 313 10 56;
021 313 10 57

**Băneasa Parc Hotel**
Şoseaua Bucureşti–Ploieşti
nr. 69
Phone 021 231 32 54

**Best Western Parc**
Bulevardul Poligrafiei nr. 3–5
Phone 021 549 20 00

**Best Western Plus Mari
Villa Bucharest**
Str. Balta Doamnei nr. 44–50
Phone 021 566 66 66

**Bucharest Comfort Suites**
Bulevardul Nicolae Bălcescu
nr. 15
Phone 021 310 28 84/85/86;
0744 587 838;
0746 167 216

**Capitol**
Calea Victoriei nr. 24
Phone 021 315 80 30

**Capşa**
Calea Victoriei nr. 36
Phone 021 313 40 38

**Caro**
Bulevardul Barbu Văcărescu
nr. 164 A
Phone 021 208 61 00

**Carpaţi**
Str. Matei Millo nr. 16
Phone 021 315 01 40

**Casa Locato**
Bulevardul Ion Mihalache
nr. 125
Phone 021 224 44 46;
0726 178 178;
0745 398 636

**Casa Victor**
Str. Emanoil Porumbaru nr. 44
Phone 021 222 57 23

**Central**
Str. Ion Brezoianu nr. 13
Phone 021 315 56 35;
021 315 56 36

**Centre Ville Aparthotel**
Str. Lutherană nr. 2–4
Phone 021 312 70 70

**Class**
Str. Gârlei nr. 30A
Phone 021 233 28 14;
021 233 28 15

**Club Citroniers**
Str. Odăii nr. 137A
Phone 021 315 16 66;
0722 333 443

**Complex Confort Rin**
Calea Bucureștilor nr. 255A
Phone 021 350 41 10 / 16

**Crowne Plaza Bucharest**
Bulevardul Poligrafiei nr. 1
Phone 021 224 00 34

**Crystal Palace**
Str. Cpt. Aviator Alex.
Șerbănescu nr. 18–20
Phone 021 233 20 30

**Dacia**
Str. Matei Basarab nr. 19
Phone 021 228 13 20;
021 228 13 30

**Dalin**
Bulevardul Mărășești
nr. 70–72
Phone 021 335 55 41

**Diplomat**
Bulevardul Poligrafiei
nr. 73–75
Phone 021 311 87 62

**Duke**
Bulevardul Dacia nr. 33
Phone 021 317 41 86;
021 317 41 87;
021 317 41 88

**El Greco**
Str. Jean-Louis Calderon
nr. 16
Phone 021 315 81 31

**Elizeu**
Str. Elizeu nr. 11–13
Phone 021 319 17 35;
021 319 17 34;
0722 550 139

**Erbas**
Str. Av. Alex. Șerbănescu
nr. 27
Phone 021 232 69 31;
021 232 68 56;
021 232 68 57

**Euro Hotels International (Polizu)**
Str. Gheorghe Polizu nr. 4
Phone 021 316 88 39;
021 317 99 71 / 75

**Euro Hotels International (Triumf)**
Bulevardul Mareșal Averescu
nr. 32–34
Phone 021 224 46 96;
021 224 43 63

**Flanders**
Str. Ștefan Mihăileanu
nr. 20–22
Phone 021 327 65 72

**Floreta de Aur**
Str. Aviator Popa Marin nr. 2
Phone 021 230 64 96

**Gallery**
Drumul Sării nr. 31 A

Phone 021 411 41 85;
0740 005 545

**Golden Tulip Bucharest**
Piața Victoriei nr. 166
Phone 021 212 55 58

**Golden Tulip Times**
Bulevardul Decebal nr. 19
Phone 021 316 65 18

**Green Forum Business**
Str. Pictor Iscovescu nr. 19
Phone 021 316 95 95

**Hanul lui Manuc**
Strada Franceză nr. 62–64
Phone 021 313 14 15

**Helios**
Str. Iulia Hașdeu nr. 16
Phone 021 310 70 83;
021 310 70 84

**Helvetia**
Piața Charles de Gaulle nr. 13
Phone 021 223 05 66

**Herăstrău**
Șoseaua Nordului nr. 7–9
Phone 021 232 96 66;
021 203 99 20

**Horoscop**
Bulevardul Dimitrie Cantemir
nr. 2
Phone 021 335 40 31;
021 336 62 42

**Hostel Wonderland**
Str. Colţei nr. 48
Phone 0729 199 393

**Hotel Christina**
Str. Ion Slătineanu nr. 13
Phone 021 210 73 03;
0731 009 999

**Hotel Confort (Otopeni)**
Calea Bucureştilor nr. 255 A
Phone 021 350 41 10;
021 350 41 16

**Hotel Confort (Traian)**
Str. Traian nr. 55
Phone 021 308 31 53;
021 308 31 54

**Hotel Dan**
Bulevardul Dacia nr. 125
Phone 021 210 39 58;
0727 59 95 99

**Howard Johnson Grand Plaza**
Calea Dorobanţilor nr. 5–7
Phone 021 201 50 00

**Ibis Nord**
Calea Griviţei nr. 143
Phone 021 222 27 22

**Ibis Palatul Parlamentului**
Str. Izvor nr. 82–84
Phone 021 222 27 22

**Intercontinental**
Bulevardul Nicolae Bălcescu nr. 4
Phone 021 310 20 20

**Irisa**
Str. Banu Manta nr. 24
Phone 021 223 49 65;
021 223 49 67

**Johann Strauss**
Str. Johann Strauss nr. 1
Phone 021 230 57 35

**JW Marriott**
Calea 13 Septembrie nr. 90
Phone 021 403 10 00

**Lev Or**
Str. Occidentului nr. 25
Phone 021 319 09 00

**Lido**
Bulevardul Magheru nr. 38–40
Phone 021 314 49 30

**Marna**
Str. Buzeşti nr. 3
Phone 021 310 70 74;
021 310 70 76

**Minerva**
Str. Gheorghe Manu nr. 2–4
Phone 021 318 12 81;
021 311 15 51

**Mioriţa Hostel**
Str. Lipscani nr. 12
Phone 021 312 03 61;
0742 102 316

**Monte-Nelly**
Str. Corbeni nr. 30
Phone 021 211 09 79

**Nh Bucharest**
Bulevardul Mircea Vodă nr. 21
Phone 021 300 05 45

**Novotel**
Calea Victoriei nr. 37B
Phone 021 308 85 00

**Opera**
Str. Ion Brezoianu nr. 37
Phone 021 312 48 57

**Parliament**
Str. Izvor nr. 106
Phone 021 411 99 90

**Passion Club**
Str. Valea Oltului nr. 117A
Phone 021 444 36 68;
0743 048 701

**Phoenicia Grand Hotel**
Str. Cpt. Aviator Alex. Şerbănescu nr. 87
Phone 021 300 08 88;
031 100 20 47

**Pullman Hotel**
Piaţa Montreal nr. 10
Phone 021 318 30 00;
021 316 25 00

**Radisson Sas**
Calea Victoriei nr. 63–81
Phone 021 311 90 00

**Ramada Majestic**
Calea Victoriei nr. 38–40
Phone 021 310 27 20;
021 312 19 67

**Relax Comfort**
Bulevardul Nicolae Bălcescu nr. 22
Phone 021 311 02 10;
021 311 02 11;
021 311 02 12;
0746 167 217;
0746 167 221

**Rembrandt**
Str. Smârdan nr. 11
Phone 021 313 93 15

**Residence Oliviers**
Str. Clucerului nr. 19
Phone 021 223 19 78;
0723 671 657

**Rin Grand Hotel**
Şoseaua Vitan–Bârzeşti nr. 7D
Phone 031 106 11 38

**Snagov Club**
Str. Nufărului nr. 13
Phone 021 352 60 79

**Stil**
Str. Nicolae Caramfil nr. 63
Phone 021 233 39 90

**Suisse Hotel**
Strada Jiului nr. 49
Phone 021 224 62 75;
021 224 62 76

**Sunset**
Bulevardul Iuliu Maniu nr. 594
Phone 021 316 12 03

**Tempo**
Str. Armand Călinescu nr. 19
Phone 21 310 12 16;
021 310 12 41

**Tiny Club Hotel**
str. Căuzaşi nr. 27
Phone 021 232 72 61;
021 232 72 62

**Triumf**
Soseaua Kiseleff nr. 12
Phone 021 222 31 72

**Unique**
str. Căderea Bastiliei nr. 35
Phone 021 319 45 91;
021 311 81 96;
0724 678 849

**Yourhotels Kogălniceanu**
Calea Plevnei nr. 10
Phone 021 315 56 10;
021 315 57 90;
0745 041 042

## Ice rings and swimming pools

**Cişmigiu Ice ring**
M–T: 10.00–21.00
F–S: 10.00–24.00
Sunday: 10.00–21.00
*Entrance fee*
M–T: 10 lei/2h
F–Sunday: 15 lei/2h

**Kiseleff Ice Park**
M–F: 10.00–22.00
S: 9.00–24.00
Sunday: 9.00–22.00
*Entrance fee*
M–F (till 4 p..): 10 lei.
after 4 p.m.: 15 lei
F–Sunday (after 4 p.m.): 15 lei

**Titan Ice ring**
M–F: 10.00–22.00
S–Sunday: 8.00–23.00
*Entrance fee*
M–F: 10 lei
S–Sunday: 15 lei

**Parc Bazilescu Ice ring**
M–F: 10.00–21.30
*Entrance fee*
10 lei/1h 30 min

**Parc Herăstrău Ice ring**
M–T: 10.00–21.00
F–S: 10.00–24.00
Sunday: 10.00–21.00
*Entrance fee*
M–F (till 4 p.m.): 10 lei
M–F (after 4 p.m.)
S–Sunday: 15 lei

**Floreasca Ice ring**
M–Sunday: 10.00–24.00
*Entrance fee*: 15 lei

**Drumul Taberei Ice ring**
M–T: 12.00–23.00
F: 12.00–24.00
S.: 9.00–24.00
Sunday: 9.00–23.00
*Entrance fee*
M–F: 10 lei
S–Sunday: 15 lei

**Fun Park Băneasa Ice ring**
In front of mall Băneasa
Shopping Center
M–F: 10.00–24.00
S–Sunday: 10.00–24.00
*Entrance fee*: 15 lei

**Parc Tineretului Ice ring**
In the park Palatului Copiilor
M–T: 10.00–21.00
F–S: 10.00–24.00
Sunday: 10.00–21.00
*Entrance fee*: 10 lei

**Parc Plumbuita Ice ring**
In Colentina neighbourhood
M–T: 11.00–22.30
F–S: 10.00–23.30
Sunday: 10.00–21.30
*Entrance fee*
M–T:10 lei/h
F–S: 15 lei/h

**The Champs Ice ring**
Liberty Center, second floor
Open all year long
M–T: 10.00–22.00
F–Sunday: 10.00–24.00
*Entrance fee*
M–T: 13 lei/45 min
F–Sunday: 16 lei/45 min

**Cotroceni On Ice**
In Afi Palace Cotroceni mall

M–T: 10.00–24.00
F: 10.00–2.00
S: 11.00–2.00
Sunday: 11.00–24.00
*Entrance fee*
Children
M–F (10.00–17.00): 8 lei
M–T (17.00–24.00): 10 lei
F (17.00–24.00), S and Sunday: 12 lei
Teenagers (13–17 years)
M–F (10.00–17.00): 10 lei
M–T (17.00–24.00): 12 lei
F(17.00–24.00), S and
Sunday: 15 lei
Adults
M–F (10.00–17.00): 12 lei
M–T (17.00–24.00): 15 lei
F (17.00–24.00), S and Sunday: 18 lei

**Drumul Taberei Swimming pool**
Drumul Taberei nr. 115

**Bleu Ciel Piscine**
Bd. Giuseppe Verdi nr. 2

**Giuleşti Piscine**
Str. Giuleşti nr. 240

**Tineretului Swimming pool**
Bd. Primo Nebiolo nr. 1

**Apa Nova Swimming pool**
Str. Ţărmului nr. 9

**Mediterana Swimming pool**
Str. Călugăreni

**IDM Club Piscine**
Strada Independenţei nr. 319B

**Complex Sportiv Naţional Lia Manoliu Swimming pool**
Bd. Basarabia nr. 37–39

**Clubul Sportiv Dinamo Swimming pool**
Bd. Ştefan cel Mare nr. 7–9

**Hotel Intercontinental Swimming pool**
Bd. Nicolae Bălcescu nr. 4

**Daimon Sport Club Swimming pool**
Str. Piscului nr. 10

**Club White Swimming pool**
Bd. Mircea Eliade nr. 16

Bucharest

**Ambasad'or Swimming pool**
Drumul Odăii nr. 34–36

**SUN Sensations Swimming pool**
Calea Văcărești nr. 391

**Aqua del Mar Swimming pool**
Str. Rezervelor nr. 70

**Water Park**
Bd. Bucureștilor nr. 255A

**Bamboo Pool**
Str. Tuzla nr. 50

**Titan Cara Swimming pool**
Bd. Nicolae Grigorescu

**Uverturii Swimming pool**
Str. Dreptății nr. 12

**Ciurel Dâmbovița Swimming pool**
Șoseaua Virtuții nr. 3

**Copiilor (Văcărești) Swimming pool**
Str. Pridvorului nr. 25

**Orhideea SPA**
Calea Plevnei nr. 145B

**Pescariu Sports & SPA**
Str. Glodeni nr. 3

**Barletto Club Swimming pool**
Str. Oltețului nr. 30

## Restaurants, pastry shops and fast food

**1001 Nopți**
Str. Ion Brezoianu nr. 18
Phone 0746 171 111

**18 Lounge**
Piața Presei Libere nr. 3–5
Phone 021 267 26 66;
0733 501 401

**A. Ro club**
Bulevardul Carol nr. 31–33
Phone 021 317 81 95

**Adagio**
Str. Știrbei Vodă nr. 50
Phone 021 310 44 02;
0722 812 834

**Agapitos (Dorobanți)**
Calea Dorobanților nr. 99
Phone 021 231 91 93

**Agapitos (Rossetti)**
Str. Jean-Louis Calderon
nr. 1–5
Phone 021 315 39 14

**Agapitos (Unirii)**
Bulevardul Corneliu Coposu
nr. 4
Phone 021 326 60 95;
0723 640 902

**Agra Palace**
Bulevardul Pipera–Tunari
nr. 47
Phone 021 350 31 14

**Ai Sapori**
Complex Romexpo-Pavilion
nr. 13
Phone 0731 335 335

**Aladdin**
Str. Constantin Boșianu nr. 21
Phone 021 335 19 01;
0728 636 227

**Ali Baba**
Șoseaua Mihai Bravu nr. 213
Phone 021 327 48 10;
0722 707 208

**Alice**
Șoseaua Mihai Bravu
nr. 123–135
Phone 021 250 70 85;
0744 486 465;
0726 312 850

**Allegro Club**
Bulevardul Nicolae Grigorescu
nr. 20 A
Phone 021 340 49 50;

0751 055 536;
0744 649 177

**Ambasad'or**
Drumul Odăii nr. 34–36
Băneasa–Otopeni
Phone 0372 755 460

**Ambianța Restaurant**
Str. Basarabilor nr. 10
Phone 021 685 45 04;
0722 214 894

**American Beer House**
Drumul Taberei nr. 92
Phone 021 444 17 77/78

**Ana Rustic Pantelimon**
Aleea Hobița nr. 1
Phone 021 250 50 76;
0721 989 577;
0731 013 225;
0788 982 679

**Ana-Pan**
Str. Locotenent Aviator
Radu Beller nr. 8
Phone 021 230 67 00

**Ana-Pan (Dorobanți)**
Str. Dorobanților nr. 134
Phone 021 233 22 36

**Ana-Pan (Titulescu)**
Șoseaua Nicolae Titulescu
nr. 81–87
Phone 021 223 46 86

**Anatolia**
Bulevardul Lacul Tei nr. 145
Phone 021 710 22 27;
0720 047 541

**Andros Grup**
Str. Antiaeriană nr. 5
Phone 021 411 96 75;
0744 885 033;
0740 530 245

**Angel's**
Str. Paris nr. 52
Phone 021 231 90 44;
0723 264 357

**Angelique**
Str. Mântuleasa nr. 6

Phone 021 327 25 23;
0731 120 430

**Anytime**
Str.11 Iunie nr. 75
Phone 021 335 81 43;
0723 166 069

**Aquarium**
Str. Alecu Russo nr. 4
Phone 021 211 28 20

**Arcade**
Str. Ion Cantacuzino nr. 8
Phone 021 260 29 60;
0726 799 799

**Art@Bari Lounge
& Restaurant**
Bulevardul George Coșbuc
nr. 69
Phone 021 33 66 111

**Asami**
Calea Victoriei nr. 17
Phone 021 312 47 85;
021 312 47 86

**Asia**
Bulevardul Decebal nr. 12
Phone 021 201 50 30;
0722 641 966

**Avalon-Contemporary
Restaurant**
Calea Dorobanți nr. 5–7
Phone 021 201 50 30

**Avantgarde Restaurant**
Str. Nerva Traian nr. 3 A (Hotel
Tulip Inn)
Phone 021 200 62 70

**Aysha Lebanese**
Str. Puțul lui Zamfir nr. 26
Phone 021 230 41 81

**Azzurro**
Drumul Taberei nr. 122
Phone 021 411 70 66;
021 440 01 06;
0721 596 999;
0723 147 438

**Balthazar**
Str. Dumbrava Roșie nr. 2
Tel. 021 212 14 60 / 61

**Baraka Lounge**
Parcul Herăstrău
Phone 0729 167 627

**Barka Saffron**
Str. Aviator Sănătescu nr. 1
Phone 021 224 10 04;
0745 003 660

**Basilicum**
Str. Popa Savu nr. 7
Phone 021 222 67 79;
0721 373 440

**Bavaria Restaurant**
Str. Al. Ioan Cuza nr. 73–75
Phone 021 223 02 58;
0723 358 555

**Beciul Boierilor**
Str. Știrbei Vodă nr. 129
Phone 0788 033 054;
0744 374 951

**Bel Mondo**
Str. Covaci nr. 6
Phone 0725 966 636

**Bellagio**
Str. Vrejului nr. 21
Phone 021 344 06 61;
0769 402 506;
0726 081 427

**Bellini (Tineretului)**
Str. Lânăriei nr. 6
Phone 0723 100 101

**Benihana**
Calea Dorobanți nr. 5–7
Phone 021 201 50 30

**Best Chef**
Șoseaua Pipera nr. 2
Phone 021 313 23 83;
0727 880 528;
0722 587 589

**Best Corner**
Bulevardul Timișoara nr. 21
Phone 021 413 41 96;
0728 202 063

**Biboche Pizza**
Livrare la domiciliu
Phone 021 337 77 33;

0723 377 377;
0743 377 377

**Bistro Ateneu**
Str. Episcopiei nr. 3
Phone 021 212 77 88

**Bistro Bella Notte Cafe**
Str. Doctor Staicovici nr. 4
Phone 021 781 45 56;
0721 123 553

**Bistro La Taifas**
Str. Gheorghe Manu nr. 16
Phone 021 212 77 88

**Bistro Montignac**
Str. George Enescu nr. 10
Phone 031 102 07 54;

**Bistro Opereta By
Cafeneaua Actorilor**
Bulevardul Nicolae Bălcescu
nr. 2
Phone 0731 498 792;
0721 900 842

**Bistro Royal Cafe**
Str. Episcopiei nr. 1–3
Phone 021 303 37 77

**Bistro Tirebouchon**
Str. Lascăr Catargiu nr. 27
Phone 021 367 24 13

**Blanduziei**
Str. Academiei nr. 2
Phone 021 315 28 12

**Bolivar**
Str. Salcâmilor nr. 9
Phone 0720 878 601

**Bolta Rece**
Str. Emanoil Porumbaru nr. 62
Phone 021 222 72 58;
0722 527 077

**Braseria Corso**
Braseria Nicolae Bălcescu
nr. 4
Phone 021 310 20 20

**Brasserie Crowne Plaza**
Bulevardul Poligrafiei nr. 1
Phone 021 224 00 34

**Brauhaus**
Str. Smârdan nr. 41
Phone 0725 523 081

**Brio Restaurant**
Str.Traian nr. 147
Phone 0766 304 830

**Brioche Dorée – Sun Plaza**
Calea Văcăreşti nr. 391
Phone 021 780 70 99

**Bruxelles**
Str. Chile nr. 10
Phone 021 231 22 83;
0723 526 445

**Bucureştiul Insular**
Str. Mihail Georgescu nr. 24
Phone 0770 220 709;
021 326 30 36

**Buona Fortuna**
Bulevardul Aviatorilor nr. 19
Phone 021 260 04 32

**Burebista**
Calea Moşilor nr. 195
Phone 021 210 97 04

**Burebista Vânătoresc**
Str. Batiştei nr. 14
Phone 021 211 89 29

**Business Land**
Bulevardul Regina Maria
nr. 43
Phone 021 336 64 07;
021 335 43 21;
0722 250 811

**Byblos**
Str. Nicolae Golescu nr. 14–16
Phone 021 313 20 91

**Cade**
Calea Dorobanţilor nr. 159
Phone 0728 133 513

**Caesar Pizza**
Str. C.F. Robescu nr. 15
Phone 021 316 53 02;
0721 22 37 27;
0743 22 37 27;
0760 08 90 80

**Cafe Boheme Restaurant**
Str. Căderea Bastiliei nr. 11
Phone 021 317 25 08

**Cafeneaua Actorilor
de Vară**
Lacul din Parcul Tineretului
Phone 0724 147 432

**Caffe & Latte**
Str. Schitu Măgureanu nr. 35
Phone 0213 143 800;
0744 333 100

**Cantina Mariachi**
Mall Vitan, et. 2
Phone 021 321 46 62

**Capri Restaurant**
Bulevardul Iuliu Maniu nr. 484
Phone 021 311 51 53 / 54;
0730 094 662

**Capriccio**
Str. Icoanei nr. 18
Phone 021 211 12 35

**Capricciosa**
Bulevardul Ion Ionescu
de la Brad nr. 2
Phone 021 230 11 92;
021 233 06 35;
0722 224 799

**Caredy – Casa
Ardelenească**
Str. Sofia nr. 1
Phone 021 230 27 69

**Caro Restaurant**
Str. Barbu Văcărescu nr. 164 A
Phone 021 208 61 00

**Carre Restaurant**
Bulevardul Dinicu Golescu
nr. 3
Phone 021 311 84 12;
0726 751 032

**Caru' Cu Bere**
Str. Stavropoleos nr. 3–5
Phone 021 313 75 60;
0730 022 021

**Casa Adam**
Str. Alexandriei nr. 21F
Phone 0731 266 279

**Casa Alba**
Aleea Privighetorilor nr. 1–3
Phone 021 230 52 03;
021 230 45 25

**Casa Alsy**
Str. Popa Lazăr nr. 5
Phone 021 252 54 14;
0732 334 334

**Casa Arcaşului**
Calea Şerban Vodă nr. 276 C
Phone 021 336 51 04;
0745 670 564;
0726 307 736

**Casa Capşa**
Calea Victoriei nr. 36
Phone 021 313 40 38

**Casa di David**
Şoseaua Nordului nr. 7–9
Phone 021 232 47 15

**Casa di'Angelo**
Bulevardul Camil Ressu
nr. 70 A
Phone 031 102 42 55;
0726 179 994;
0767 545 223;
0771 794 940

**Casa Dicos**
Str. Avrig nr. 76
Phone 021 252 00 80;
0744 570 782

**Casa Doina**
Şoseaua Kiseleff nr. 4
Phone 021 222 67 17

**Casa Doina la Parc**
Bulevardul Poligrafiei nr. 3–5
Phone 021 549 25 41

**Casa Elisabeta**
Str. Ion Neculce nr. 63
Phone 021 225 18 85;
0723 536 799

**Casa Enache**
Str. Grigore Alexandrescu
nr. 106
Phone 021 210 18 33;
0728 957 931

**Casa Gorjană**
Str. Domnița Anastasia nr. 13
Phone 021 315 64 29;
0722 171 999

**Casa Iancului
(Foișorul de Foc)**
Str. Popa Nan nr. 16
Phone 021 252 29 56

**Casa Iancului (Iancului)**
Str. Sarafinești nr. 2
Phone 021 256 97 98

**Casa Jienilor**
Str. Făinari nr. 5
Phone 021 212 19 51;
0722 916 111

**Casa Latină (Panduri)**
Șoseaua Panduri nr. 71
Phone 021 410 20 20;
0728 999 393

**Casa Latină (Traian)**
Str. Traian nr. 2
Phone 021 320 51 07;
0723 112 237

**Casa M**
Str. Grigore Gafencu nr. 19–23
Phone 021 233 26 32;
0723 037 157

**Casa Madan**
Str. Principatele Unite nr. 19A
Phone 0728 499 017;
0722 401 579

**Casa Mica**
Str. Popovăț nr. 76
Phone 021 223 85 38;
0749 114 663

**Casa Montefiore**
Str. Radu Vodă nr. 28A
Phone 021 212 21 13;
0728 302 431

**Casa Mov Bar & Grill**
Str. Drumul între vii nr. 3
Phone 021 344 21 24;
0724 356 637

**Casa Myt**
Drumul Taberei nr. 4
Phone 021 410 05 20

**Casa Oamenilor de Știință**
Piața Lahovari nr. 9
Phone 021 211 35 21

**Casa Pache**
Bulevardul Pache Protopopescu
nr. 28
Phone 021 252 50 95;
0724 292 270

**Casa Restaurant**
Intrarea Spătarului nr. 4
Phone 021 317 22 65;
0740 257 595

**Casa Romană**
Calea Văcărești nr. 230
Phone 021 330 86 20;
021 330 86 47

**Casa Românească**
Calea București nr. 285 A
Phone 021 350 15 10;
0744 689 920

**Casa Rustic**
Str. Valea Oltului nr. 113–115
Phone 021 444 79 29;
0724 447 822

**Casa Select**
Str. Drobeta nr. 23
Phone 021 210 16 51

**Casa Știrbey**
Str. Știrbei Vodă nr. 118–120
Phone 0729 142 174

**Casa Țărănească Elite**
Piața C.A. Rosetti nr. 5
Phone 0213 124 930;
0729 178 189

**Casa Veche**
Str. George Enescu nr. 15–17
Phone 021 315 78 97;
021 312 58 16;
0721 237 727

**Casa Vernescu**
Calea Victoriei nr. 133
Phone 021 311 97 44

**Casablanca**
Str. Tache Ionescu nr. 29
Phone 021 212 51 58

**Centre Ville Le Bistro**
Str. Luterană nr. 4
Phone 021 312 70 70

**Cercul Militar Național**
Str. Constantin Mille nr. 1–3
Phone 021 314 37 35

**Cerisiers**
Str. Alexandru
Constantinescu nr. 33
Phone 021 224 50 44;
0372 150 600

**Champions**
Calea 13 Septembrie nr. 90
Phone 021 403 19 17

**Charme**
Str. Smârdan 12
Tel. 021 311 19 22

**Cheers Restaurant**
Str. Dimitrie Racoviță nr. 18
Phone 021 315 33 96;
0727 300 444

**Chez Marie**
Str. Dionisie Lupu nr. 48
Phone 031 107 20 33;
0730 344 810

**Chocolat**
Calea Victoriei nr. 12 A
Phone 021 314 92 45

**Christie's**
Str. Aaron Florian nr. 3A
Phone 021 318 65 68;
0722 216 337;
0767 291 697

**Churrascaria Carnivore**
Str. Gârlei nr. 1
Phone 021 233 55 55

**Cimma**
Str. Teiuș nr. 43
Phone 0214 209 844;
0722 542 358

**City Grill Carrefour Orhideea**
Splaiul Independenței nr. 210
Phone 021 318 87 18

**City Grill Lipscani**
Str. Lipscani nr. 12
Phone 021 314 24 89;
0729 62 62 62

**City Grill Oracle Tower**
Calea Floreasca nr. 175
Phone 021 232 49 79;
0727 543 333

**City Grill Primăverii**
Bulevardul Primăverii nr. 3
Phone 021 233 98 18;
0726 62 62 62

**City Grill Shopping Center Băneasa**
Șoseaua București–Ploiești nr. 44 A
Phone 021 310 69 79;
0721 333 742

**City Grill Titulescu**
Șoseaua Nicolae Titulescu nr. 4–8
Phone 021 311 74 50;
0729 64 26 42

**City Pizza**
Str. Mihai Eminescu nr. 190
Phone 021 211 41 14;
0720 733 687;
0751 639 377

**Clasic (Kogălniceanu)**
Bulevardul Kogălniceanu nr. 22
Phone 0213 156 194

**Clasic (Rossetti)**
Str. Jean-Louis Calderon nr. 18
Phone 021 317 21 19;
0743 563 118;
0765 327 555

**Classa Di T**
Calea Floreasca nr. 111–113
Phone 031 405 05 97;
0722 111 121

**Club 99**
Bulevardul Dacia nr. 99
Phone 0733 500 301

**Club Antiqum**
Str. Jean-Louis Calderon nr. 33

**Club Contele Dracula**
Splaiul Independenței nr. 8 A
Phone 021 312 13 53

**Coin Vert**
Str. Constantin Sandu Aldea nr. 75
Phone 021 319 24 39;
0721 331 465

**Constance (Tei)**
Str. Doamna Ghica nr. 6
Phone 021 243 36 49

**Constance (Victoriei)**
Str. Doctor Felix nr. 101
Phone 021 316 93 03

**Continental**
Calea Victoriei nr. 56
Phone 021 312 01 32;
021 313 36 94;
021 314 53 48

**Cor'tile**
Str. Dr. Felix nr. 75
Phone 021 311 53 10;
0728 334 965

**Coral**
Șoseaua Pantelimon nr. 247
Phone 021 255 10 80;
0723 290 582;
0743 034 668

**Crama Culmea Veche**
Str. Culmea Veche nr. 2
Phone 021 311 11 32;
0743 003 071

**Crystal Palace**
Str. Aviator Alexandru Șerbănescu nr. 18–20
Phone 021 233 20 30;
021 208 62 60

**Cucina**
Calea 13 Septembrie nr. 90
Phone 021 403 19 02

**Cupola**
Calea 13 Septembrie nr. 90
Phone 021 403 19 03

**Cuptorul cu Lemne**
Bulevardul Pache Protopopescu nr. 63
Phone 021 252 24 14;
0728 323 985

**Da Mario**
Str. Agricultori nr. 113
Phone 021 321 31 79;
031 805 75 44;
0723 996 811

**Dacia**
Bulevardul Basarabia nr. 72
Phone 0745 204 866;
0742 958 948

**Dacia – RRT**
Str. Matei Basarab nr. 19
Phone 031 228 13 31

**Dada Bistro**
Str. Matei Voievod nr. 94 bis
Phone 021 252 31 59;
0729 997 405

**Daddy Restaurant**
Bulevardul Regina Elisabeta
nr. 25
Phone 021 312 55 24;
0728 128 291

**Daily**
Str. Tunari nr. 67–69
Phone 021 610 62 18;
0755 112 787;
0753 270 000;
0741 097 974

**Daniela**
Str. Strãduinţei nr. 1
Phone 021 460 31 25

**Dantes**
Str. Radu Beller nr. 11
Phone 021 231 08 97;
0728 388 888;
0729 166 088

**Danubio**
Bulevardul Iuliu Maniu
nr. 432–442
Phone 021 319 82 08;
0788 137 415

**De Gustibus**
Str. Pictor Marcel Iancu nr. 10
Phone 021 211 14 49;
0744 520 106

**Dealu Mare**
Calea Floreasca nr. 19
Phone 021 230 12 82

**Decebal Rustic**
Bulevardul Decebal nr. 17
Phone 021 321 67 00;
0723 515 009;
0724 891 819

**Decebal Steak House**
Bulevardul Barbu Vãcãrescu
nr. 51

Phone 0724 891 819;
0723 515 009

**Derby Restaurant & Bar**
Bulevardul Eroii Sanitari nr. 49 A
Phone 021 410 85 45;
0722 500 361

**Deutschland**
Str. Radu Beller nr. 1
Phone 021 230 43 84;
0722 500 361

**Die Deutsche Kneipe**
Str. Stockholm nr. 9
Phone 021 233 94 62;
0722 284 560

**Dines – Fast Food**
Rondul Coşbuc
Phone 021 336 72 00;
0722 077 971

**Dinette**
Str. Covaci nr. 6
Phone 021 311 77 55

**Divan**
Strada Francezã nr. 46–48
Phone 021 312 30 34

**Don Taco**
Str. Doctor Felix nr. 101
Phone 021 316 94 52

**Doya**
Str. Amiral Vasile Urseanu nr. 1
Phone 021 650 00 75;
0720 510 736

**Dressing Room Cafe**
Bulevardul Decebal nr. 13
Phone 031 417 94 34

**El Bacha (Alba Iulia)**
Str. Alba Iulia nr. 6
Phone 021 269 13 12;
0722 833 333

**El Bacha (Pipera)**
Str. Drumul Bisericii nr. 11
Phone 021 316 47 70;
0722 811 111

**El Greko**
Bulevardul Decebal nr. 17
Phone 021 326 80 98

**El Torito**
Str. Iancu Cãpitanu nr. 30
Phone 021 252 66 88;
0728 176 059

**Escargot**
Str. Toamnei nr. 101
Phone 021 201 71 33;
0746 795 029

**Etiquette**
Str. Traian nr. 139
Phone 021 320 19 02;
0724 573 090

**Exile**
Str. Sofia nr. 15
Phone 021 260 07 24;
0741 937 664

**Expres Pizza**
Str. Lotru nr. 11
Phone 021 224 31 32;
0724 474 992;
0742 074 992

**Fabio Pizza
(Barbu Vlãdoianu)**
Str. Barbu Vlãdoianu nr. 46
Phone 021 311 71 22;
021 311 71 74;
0726 816 733;
0741 765 480

**Fabio Pizza (Traian)**
Str. Traian 42
Phone 021 322 07 22;
021 322 07 23;
0732 835 458;
0744 458 241

**Fakhreldine**
Calea 13 Septembrie nr. 90
Phone 021 403 31 03;
021 403 35 03

**Favela**
Calea Moşilor nr. 160
Phone 0727 222 574

**Fibrio Restaurant**
Str. Marcel Andreescu nr. 11
Phone 021 230 02 49;
0727 342 746

**Figaro**
Str. Radu Beller nr. 11
Phone 212 310 897;
0745 005 500

**Flanders**
Str. Ştefan Mihăileanu nr. 20
Phone 021 327 65 72

**Floreta de Aur**
Str. Aviator Popa Marin nr. 2
Phone 021 230 64 96

**Four Seasons**
Str. Vasile Lascăr nr. 81
Phone 021 212 29 92;
0722 216 666

**Friends**
Str. Tudor Vianu nr. 11
Phone 021 230 24 13;
0727 479 540

**Frufru**
Str. Batiştei nr. 1–3
Phone 021 222 11 11

**Gallo Nero Restaurant**
Bulevardul Decebal nr. 12
Phone 021 326 81 28;
0726 544 889

**Ginger**
Calea Griviţei nr. 194
Phone 021 223 47 15;
0752 167 403

**Gladiola**
Calea Călăraşi nr. 135
Phone 021 323 50 43

**Golden Blitz Center**
Şoseaua Nicolae Titulescu 10
Phone 021 316 50 50

**Golden Falcon**
Str. Hristo Botev nr. 18–20
Phone 021 314 28 25/33

**Hanul Haiducilor**
Str. Pridvorului nr. 25
Phone 021 330 72 07

**Hanul Hangiţei**
Str. Gabroveni nr. 16
Phone 021 314 70 46;
021 336 62 83

**Hanul lui Manuc**
Strada Franceză nr. 62–64
Phone 021 313 14 11;
021 313 14 15

**Harbin**
Str. Paltin nr. 12
Phone 021 322 57 28

**Hard Rock Cafe**
Bulevardul Kiseleff nr. 32 C
Phone 021 206 62 61

**Haveli**
Str. Episcopul Radu nr. 3
Phone 021 211 03 90;
0721 721 640

**Herăstrău**
Şoseaua Nordului nr. 7–9
Phone 021 232 21 28;
021 232 96 66

**Hong Kong**
Calea Griviţei nr. 81
Phone 021 310 71 30;
0727 834 877

**Hotel Christina Restaurant**
Str. Ion Slătineanu nr. 13
Phone 021 210 73 03;
0731 009 999

**Il Cantuccio**
Str. Fabrica de Chibrituri nr. 2
(formely La Pergola)
Phone 021 337 45 67;
0721 251 823

**Il Corso**
Str. Mănăstirea Caşin nr. 1
Phone 0788 692 146;
0724 205 484

**Il Forno**
Bulevardul Dacia nr. 110
Phone 021 211 50 84;
0728 669 056

**Il Gattopardo Blu**
Calea Victoriei nr. 115
Phone 021 319 65 95

**Il Giardino Oliviers**
Str. Clucerului nr. 19
Phone 021 223 19 78 (int. 204);
0721 678 992

**Il Magnifico**
Str. Olteni nr. 9A
Phone 021 327 04 54

**Imperial**
Calea Moşilor nr. 123
Phone 021 313 39 26;
021 312 28 56

**In Spayer Bistro**
Str. Batiştei nr. 24A

**Insieme**
Str. Toamnei nr. 85
Phone 021 210 15 56

**Intim**
Str. Aviator Mircea Zorileanu nr. 89
Phone 021 319 26 38

**Irisa**
Str. Banu Manta nr. 24
Phone 021 223 49 65;
021 223 49 66/67/68

**Izvorul Rece**
Str. Pache Protopopescu nr. 11
Phone 021 311 24 26

**Jadoo Restaurant**
Str. Nicolae Racotă nr. 3
Phone 021 222 05 02;
0724 365 583

**Jasmine**
Bulevardul Poligrafiei nr. 3–5
Phone 021 549 20 00;
021 315 20 00

**Jeff De Bruges**
Calea Moşilor nr. 199
Phone 021 211 96 24

**Jubile – The Ballroom**
Şoseaua Pipera nr. 50
Phone 0730 733 240

**Jukebox Club Restaurant**
Str. Turturelelor nr. 11
Phone 021 322 66 10;
021 323 70 83

**Jumbo Vietnamese Food (Ştefan cel Mare)**
Bulevardul Ştefan cel Mare nr. 26

Phone 031 103 56 36;
0730 20 11 11

**Jumbo Vietnamese Food (Sun Plazza)**
Calea Văcărești nr. 391
Phone 0722 215 511

**Karishma**
Str. Iancu Căpitanu nr. 36
Phone 021 252 51 57

**KFC – Băneasa**
Băneasa Shopping City,
parter, șoseaua București–
Ploiești nr. 42D
Phone 021 361 15 78;
021 361 15 79;
0751 190 433

**KFC – Beldiman**
Bulevardul Regina Elisabeta
nr. 23
Phone 021 316 99 98;
0751 190 449

**KFC – City Mall**
Șoseaua Olteniței nr. 2,
City Mall, et. 2
Phone 021 311 94 00;
0741 134 456

**KFC – Colentina**
Carrefour Colentina (Șoseaua
București–Voluntari)
Phone 021 241 40 58;
0740 121 909

**KFC – Cora–Granitul**
Galeria Comercială Esplanada
(Cora – Granitul
Shopping Center)
Phone 021 255 27 10;
0740 12 19 08

**KFC – Feeria**
Centrul Comercial Feeria
Băneasa (Șoseaua București –
Ploiești nr. 44 A )
Phone 021 310 69 72;
0749 27 54 36

**KFC – Gara de Nord**
Gara de Nord,
Exit Grivița

Phone 021 310 87 68;
0754 081 781

**KFC – Liberty Center**
Liberty Center, e. 2,
Șoseaua Progresului
nr. 151–171
Phone 021 369 97 09;
0754 081 798

**KFC – Magheru**
Bulevardul Magheru nr. 28–30
Phone 021 312 00 23;
0740 12 19 04

**KFC – Mall Vitan**
Calea Vitan nr. 55–59,
București Mall, et. 2
Phone 021 327 75 12;
0740 12 19 05

**KFC – Orhideea**
Centrul Comercial Orhideea
Phone 021 316 29 67;
0740 12 19 07

**KFC – Plaza România**
Bulevardul Timișoara nr. 26,
Plaza România, et. 2
Phone 021 317 63 61;
0740 12 19 11

**KFC – Unirii**
Unirea Shopping Center,
Călărași
Phone 021 312 5 842;
0740 12 19 06

**Korea House**
Str. Bârgăului nr. 13
Phone 021 667 21 19;
0749 272 192

**Kyoto**
Calea Dorobanți nr. 79A
Phone 021 610 79 50;
0723 312 459

**L'harmattan**
Strada Franceză nr. 56
Phone 021 314 12 50;
0723 248 810

**La 100 de Beri**
Str. Covaci nr. 8
Phone 0784 246 046

**La 2 lei**
Str. Delea Nouă nr. 32
Phone 021 311 88 18;
021 321 00 35;
0722 659 293;
0768 556 315;
0766 231 783

**La Belle Epoque**
Str. Aviator Radu Beller nr. 6
Phone 021 230 07 70

**La Boema**
Șoseaua Vitan–Bârzești nr. 7D
Phone 031 106 11 11 (int.
345); 0731 111 000

**La Bucătaru**
Str. Liviu Rebreanu nr. 1
Phone 021 324 19 85;
0720 215 274

**La Bucur**
Bulevardul Gheorghe Șincai
nr. 1–1A
Phone 0744 181 060;
0745 351 635

**La Casa Roz**
Str. Apusului nr. 12
Phone 031 250 35 43;
021 434 05 94;
0721 542 909

**La Cave de Bucharest**
Str. Mărgelelor nr. 139–143
Phone 0746 254 444;
0749 074 405

**La Cena**
Str. Maria Rossetti nr. 1
Phone 021 211 67 17;
0730 210 014

**La Cocoșatu**
Str. Neagoe Vodă nr. 52A
Phone 021 232 87 96;
0726 224 444

**La Dolce Vita**
Str. Occidentului nr. 44
Phone 021 310 86 94;
0744 388 659

**La Fattoria**
Şoseaua Nordului nr. 7–9
Phone 031 104 63 38;
0729 994 995;
0729 881 005

**La Gil**
Bulevardul Aerogării nr. 21
Phone 021 232 91 05;
021 232 36 51;
0722 534 117

**La Gogoşaru**
Str. Turda nr. 53
Phone 021 222 30 68

**La Gondola**
Str. Nicolae Caranfil nr. 2C
Phone 021 232 12 60;
0372 783 897;
0752 356 356

**La Historia de Argentina**
Str. Viitorului nr. 26
Phone 0724 396 043

**La Historia de Cuba**
Str. Sfântul Ştefan nr. 13
Phone 0785 273 875

**La Historia de Sudamerica**
Str. Sfântul Dumitru nr. 3
Phone 0722 626 043

**La Italieni**
Str. Traian nr. 168
Phone 021 323 21 35;
021 320 14 14;
0742 730 832

**La Mama (Ateneu)**
Str. Episcopiei nr. 9
Phone 021 312 97 97;
0721 526 262

**La Mama
(Carrefour Orhideea)**
Splaiul Independenţei
nr. 210–213
Phone 021 220 33 95;
0724 505 605

**La Mama (Muncii)**
Str. Delea Veche nr. 51
Phone 021 320 52 13;
0723 292 846

**La Mama (Piaţa Alba Iulia)**
Piaţa Alba Iulia nr. 2
Phone 021 320 20 00;
0728 853 853

**La Mama (Shopping
Center Băneasa)**
Şoseaua Bucureşti – Ploieşti
nr. 44A
Phone 021 319 42 46;
0729 526 262

**La Mama
(Ştefan Cel Mare)**
Str. Barbu Văcărescu nr. 3
Phone 021 212 40 86;
0723 292 863

**La Mandragora**
Str. Mendeleev nr. 29
Phone 021 319 75 92

**La Matache**
Str. Haralambie Botescu nr. 2
Phone 021 310 73 27/37;
021 311 26 24;
0740 407 478;
0727 070 715

**La Nostalgia**
Str. Primo Nebiolo nr. 1
Phone 021 224 46 41;
0722 236 775

**La Nova**
Calea Floreasca nr. 242–246
Phone 021 233 08 76;
021 233 08 77

**La Provence**
Str. Barbu Văcărescu
Phone 021 243 17 77

**La Radu Capivox**
Şoseaua Kiseleff nr. 32
Phone 021 224 43 72;
0728 222 410;
0728 222 442

**La Radu
(Moxa Bistro-Pizzerie)**
Str. Sfinţii Voievozi nr. 38
Phone 021 212 03 66;
0728 222 411;
0744 305 239

**La Radu (Parcul Carol)**
Parcul Carol
Phone 021 335 11 13;
0728 222 438

**La Radu
(Piaţa Presei Libere)**
Şoseaua Kiseleff nr. 32
(Parc Herăstrău)
Tel. 0728 222 446

**La Radu (Voinţa)**
Şoseaua Pipera nr. 38
(Clubul Sportiv Voinţa)
Phone 031 805 58 95;
0728 222 422;
0763 726 095;
0734 974 584

**La Roată**
Str. Nicolae Iorga nr. 21
Phone 0722 381 904;
0744 655 091

**La Rocca**
Str. Theodor Aman nr. 36
Phone 0744 574 004

**La Şosea**
Bulevardul Timişoara nr. 82
Phone 0788 700 824;
0721 845 265

**La Templu**
Calea Dorobanţi nr. 127–129
Phone 021 230 50 72;
0720 407 005;
0763 617 164

**La Tortilla**
Str. Ion Mihalache nr. 23
Phone 021 310 55 29

**La Villa**
Str. Alexandru Constantinescu
nr. 65
Phone 021 224 15 05;
021 224 15 55;
0749 284 821

**la'teral**
Splaiul Unirii nr. 6
Phone 021 455 44 00

**Laguna Blu**
Str. Gârlei nr. 1
Phone 021 233 02 17;
0730 013 900

**Laleaua**
Şoseaua Pantelimon
nr. 358–362
Phone 021 255 50 31;
0744 305 368

**Lautrec**
Str. Iancu Cavaler de Flondor
nr. 2
Phone 021 252 16 16;
0723 910 170

**L'esperance**
Str. Clucerului nr. 86
Phone 021 222 71 81;
0744 647 357

**Le Drakkar**
Strada Franceză nr. 6
Phone 021 312 40 13;
0723 389 347;
0722 422 338;
0722 602 117

**Le Gourmand**
Str. Delea Nouă nr. 2
Phone 021 322 30 40;
0733 644 444;
0728 582 257;
0729 012 349;
0728 879 112

**Legacy**
Str. Lipscani nr. 56
Phone 0726 130 859

**Les Oliviades**
Piaţa Montreal nr. 10
Phone 021 224 30 00

**Liliana**
Bulevardul Ion Mihalache
nr. 115–117
Phone 021 224 23 41

**Livada cu Vişini**
Str. Grigore Alexandrescu nr. 77
Phone 021 610 41 51;
0723 183 222;
0723 200 778

**Locanta Jariştea**
Str. George Georgescu nr.
50–52
Phone 021 3 353 338;
0722 605 564;
0744 240 126;
0721 961 936

**Long Xuan**
Calea Dudeşti nr. 198
Phone 021 320 26 66;
0761 929 019

**Maccheroni**
Str. Alexandru Donici nr. 14
Phone 021 210 29 36;
0724 072 372;
0722 259 360

**Madrigal Steak House**
Bulevardul Nicolae Bălcescu
nr. 4
Phone 021 310 20 20;
0724 242 806

**Malagamba**
Str. Sfântul Dumitru nr. 2
Phone 021 313 33 89;
0748 502 543

**Mamma Leone**
Str. Povernei nr. 22
Phone 021 311 46 06;
0724 417 497;
0743 072 008

**Mândală Club**
Str. Paleologu nr. 20
Phone 021 412 01 35;
021 311 06 01;
0732 026 279

**Margo Lounge Restaurant**
Str. Lipscani nr. 29–33
Phone 0723 199 977

**Maverick**
Drumul Taberei nr. 18
Phone 021 413 08 45

**Menuet Restaurant**
Str. Nicolae Golescu nr. 14
Phone 021 319 94 94;
021 312 01 43;
0751 146 871

**Mesogios**
Str. Jean-Louis Calderon nr. 49
Phone 021 317 13 55;
021 313 49 51;
0727 239 239

**Metropolitan**
Str. Avram Iancu nr. 7A
Phone 021 311 47 57;
0722 256 090;
0788 728 767

**Mica Elveţie – St. Moritz**
Str. Sandu Aldea nr. 64
Phone 021 224 50 17

**Micul Prânz**
Str. Tudor Vianu nr. 50
Phone 0788 355 366

**Minion Dragon House**
Piaţa Amzei nr. 1
Phone 021 314 77 00;
021 310 96 91

**MJU**
Str. Vasile Lascăr nr. 29
Phone 021 313 00 15;
021 313 00 16

**Moara Mariei**
Str. Blănari nr. 14
Phone 021 315 64 94

**Mon Cheri**
Str. Tudor Ştefan nr. 16
Phone 021 231 09 08;
0748 750 029;
0744 569 363

**Monte Carlo**
Bulevardul Schitu Măgureanu
nr. 23
Phone 021 313 13 44;
031 425 21 95

**Mulanruj Dining Room**
Str. Şelari nr. 9–11
Phone 0748 881 084

**Museum**
Str. Doctor Clunet nr. 15
Phone 021 411 91 28

**Mythos**
Str. Costache Negri nr. 28
Phone 021 410 23 76;

0727 392 938;
0724 349 268;
0786 748 894

**Nan-Jing**
Str. Gheorghe Manu nr. 2–4
Phone 021 318 12 85;
021 650 60 10;
0726 103 407

**New York Pizza**
Bulevardul Camil Ressu nr. 76
Phone 021 348 34 59;
0729 881 660;
0766 552 564;
0722 659 755;
0740 659 752

**Nicoreşti**
Str. Toamnei nr. 14
Phone 021 211 24 80;
021 211 13 34

**Noblesse Restaurant**
Str. Paris nr. 47A
Phone 021 230 54 06/28;
0721 855 333

**Noel**
Str. Crăciun nr. 25
Phone 021 210 60 00;
0744 494 709

**Oasis Sport & Leisure**
Str. Străuleşti nr. 4
Phone 021 667 02 11;
0723 731 899

**Olive Garden**
Str. Tudor Vianu nr. 11
Phone 021 230 26 30;
0730 337 928

**One Club şi Restaurant**
Str. Matei Voievod nr. 79
Phone 021 252 20 92;
0732 988 911

**Opera**
Str. Doctor Lister nr. 1
Phone 021 411 63 30

**Oraşul Interzis**
Str. Silvestru nr. 3
Phone 031 425 47 47;

031 425 47 48;
0720 993 333;
0722 252 421

**P.P. 59**
Str. Pache Protopopescu nr. 59
Phone 021 252 52 59;
0745 777 294;
0744 777 296

**Pan Veneţia**
Şoseaua Pantelimon nr. 254
Phone 021 255 00 99

**Panoramic**
Str. Aviator Mircea Zorileanu
nr. 89
Phone 021 319 26 38;
0722 336 733

**Paparazzi**
Bulevardul Aviatorilor nr. 31
Phone 021 222 64 22;
0788 958 127

**Parco Dei Principi**
Şoseaua Nordului nr. 7–9
Phone 0788 457 930;
0788 457 932/933

**Pars**
Str. Făinari nr. 25
Phone 021 222 49 23;
0723 595 233

**Passion**
Str. Valea Oltului nr. 117 A
Phone 021 444 36 67;
0743 048 701

**Passo Doble**
Str. Avram Iancu nr. 7A
Phone 021 311 47 57;
0722 256 090;
0788 728 767

**Pasta Fresca**
Str. Doctor Staicovici nr. 4
Phone 021 781 45 56

**Pasticceria Giuseppina**
Şoseaua Ştefan cel Mare nr. 6
Phone 0730 283 947

**Patiseria Fadel**
Str. Jean-Louis Calderon nr. 56
Phone 0722 919 132

**Patisseria
Parisienne-Valerie**
Şoseaua Pipera nr. 4
Phone 021 232 95 48;
0745 654 993

**Patru Anotimpuri**
Şoseaua Nordului nr. 7–9
Phone 021 232 01 34;
0726 33 00 22

**Patyan – Imperial Chinese
Restaurant**
Calea Victoriei nr. 163
Phone 0726 566 366

**Pekin**
Calea Victoriei nr. 16–20
Phone 021 310 31 60;
0723 233 169;
0769 414 020

**Perla**
Calea Dorobanţilor nr. 98
Phone 021 230 12 80;
0744 565 686

**Persia**
Str. Avalanşei nr. 21
Phone 021 330 30 10;
0723 210 295;
0788 300 311

**Pescăruş**
Bulevardul Aviatorilor nr. 1
Phone 021 230 46 40

**Petit**
Str. Olteni nr. 3
Phone 0753 315 577

**Petrecerile Delice –
Cook & Fun**
Piaţa Montreal nr. 10
Phone 031 228 11 39;
0721 101 767

**Phileas Fogg**
Calea Vitan nr. 55–59
Phone 021 327 75 10

**Philippe Bar & Bistro**
Str. C.A. Rossetti nr. 26
Phone 021 317 41 28;
0722 526 110

**Photo Cake**
Str. Obolului nr. 9
Phone 021 324 51 47;
0729 737 619

**Piatra Albă**
Drumul Taberei nr. 68
Phone 021 440 33 35;
0723 132 765

**Piccolo Mondo**
Str. Clucerului nr. 9
Phone 021 223 22 25;
021 222 57 55;
0722 205 020

**Piticot (Rahova)**
Str. Petre Ispirescu nr. 77
Phone 021 420 66 70;
0726 714 863

**Pizza del Baba Novacco**
Str. Baba Novac nr. 1
Phone 021 648 07 71;
0721 741 753;
0786 070 101

**Pizza din Tei**
Str. Petricani nr. 22
Phone 021 243 14 32;
0734 151 161;
0768 099 077;
0756 828 282

**Pizza e Pasta**
Șoseaua Fundeni nr. 120
Phone 021 241 30 83;
0722 480 231

**Pizza Hut (Dorobanți)**
Calea Dorobanți nr. 5–7
Phone 021 201 17 55;
021 203 90 39

**Pizza Hut (Moșilor)**
Calea Moșilor nr. 219
Phone 021 210 60 33

**Pizza Hut (Plaza România)**
Bulevardul Timișoara nr. 26
Phone 021 317 62 63

**Pizzeria Dado**
Șoseaua Virtuții nr. 1
Phone 0724 464 441

**Pizzeria Romană**
Str. Știrbei Vodă nr. 20A
Phone 021 300 74 28;
0740 048 048

**Plevnei**
Calea Plevnei nr. 145
Phone 021 316 66 07

**Point Blank Lite**
Bulevardul Schitu Măgureanu
nr. 6
Phone 031 805 42 80

**Privileg Catering**
Bulevardul Biruinței nr. 54
Phone 021 200 54 64;
0722 321 133

**Providence**
Bulevardul Unirii nr. 7
Phone 031 432 94 45/46;
0744 913 638;
0735 038 838;
0767 437 342

**Pub D'eight**
Strada Franceză nr. 2–4
Phone 021 311 40 10;
0721 333 533

**Puțin din Tot**
Str. Pache Protopopescu nr. 25
Phone 021 252 27 07

**Qian-Bao**
Intrarea Baba Novac nr. 2
Phone 0722 622 865;
0788 836 206

**Quadri Ristorante**
Calea Floreasca nr. 45
Phone 021 231 85 31;
0749 999 499

**Quattro Stagioni (Aviatorilor)**
Bulevardul Mareșal Prezan nr. 1
Phone 021 222 72 22;
0723 196 380

**Quattro Stagioni (Herăstrău)**
Șoseaua Nordului nr. 7–9
Phone 021 233 37 81;
0722 110 022

**Rasputin House**
Bulevardul Decebal nr. 1
Phone 0721 233 826

**Rateș**
Str. Vasile Lascăr nr. 206
Phone 021 211 20 25;
0752 541 101;
0720 579 555

**Raymond's**
Str. Walter Mărăcineanu nr. 1–3
Phone 021 316 14 34

**Residence – Olivers**
Str. Clucerului nr. 19
Phone 021 223 19 78

**Restaurant Crângași (La Nașu)**
Șoseaua Crângași nr. 87
Phone 021 221 42 85;
0722 257 923;
0728 984 754/755

**Restaurant Dumbrava**
Calea Văcărești nr. 460
Phone 0742 064 891;
0763 434 475

**Restaurant Intermacedonia**
Șoseaua Mihai Bravu nr. 95–105
Phone 021 252 20 10;
021 252 21 90

**Restaurant Maxim**
Str. General Berthelot nr. 44
Phone 031 438 37 57

**Restaurant Piccadilly**
Str. Voinicului nr. 7
Phone 021 321 48 90;
0729 881 671

**Restaurant Planet**
Str. Fluierului nr. 18
Phone 021 253 23 21;
0722 291 367

**Restaurant Poem**
Aleea Suter nr. 23–25
Phone 213 363 377

**Restaurant Rustic Dines**
Parcul Carol
Phone 021 336 24 74;

0723 634 741;
0723 670 900

**Restaurant Tulin**
Str. Pictor Constantin Stahi nr. 2
Phone 021 314 40 01;
0762 212 675

**Restaurant Vatra**
Str. Brezoianu nr. 23–25
Phone 021 315 83 75;
0721 200 800

**Restaurant Viţă Nobilă**
Bulevardul Decebal nr. 13
Phone 021 323 24 32;
0722 640 131

**Restaurant Xanadu**
Str. Sfântul Ştefan nr. 20
Phone 021 315 06 53;
0722 62 17 17

**Restaurant-Pizzerie Horoscop**
Bulevardul Dimitrie Cantemir nr. 20
Phone 021 335 72 65

**Ristorante Da Giulio**
Str. Popa Stoica Farcaş nr. 29
Phone 021 323 52 40;
0721 444 422

**Riviera Restaurant**
Bulevardul Basarabia nr. 23
Phone 021 321 19 96

**Roberto's**
Str. Episcopiei nr. 1–3
Phone 021 303 37 37 (int. 6760);
021 303 37 77

**Rodon**
Str. Jean-Louis Calderon nr. 16
Phone 021 315 81 41;
021 315 81 31;
021 315 90 00

**Românaşul**
Str. Icoanei nr. 15
Phone 021 211 33 26;
0721 261 600;
0722 161 974

**Romantica Pub**
Str. Rădulescu Motru nr. 22
Phone 0727 311 984

**Rossetya**
Str. Dimitrie Bolintineanu nr. 9
Phone 031 805 91 99;
0748 220 220

**Ruby Tuesday (Decebal)**
Bulevardul Decebal nr. 4
Phone 021 323 78 71

**Ruby Tuesday (Mall Vitan)**
Calea Vitan nr. 55–59
Phone 021 320 36 73

**Sabattini**
Str. Witing nr. 4
Phone 021 314 55 00;
0722 366 480

**Safir House**
Bulevardul Barbu Văcărescu nr. 39
Phone 021 210 45 92

**Sale e Pepe**
Str. Luterană nr. 3
Phone 021 315 89 89

**Sallmen**
Str. General Dimitrie Salmen nr. 9
Phone 021 642 52 26;
0742 785 087;
0726 625 802

**Salt Pub**
Str. Blănari nr. 21
Phone 021 314 22 14;
0732 162 345

**Sangria**
Str. Căderea Bastiliei nr. 78
Phone 021 211 22 76;
0722 510 583;
0728 984 668

**Şarpele Roz**
Calea Victoriei nr. 163
Phone 0742 582 728

**Select Club**
Aleea Alexandru nr. 18
Phone 021 230 21 20;

021 230 03 84;
021 230 04 92;
0722 244 131

**Selena Blue**
Str. Sfântul Ştefan nr. 21
Phone 0723 034 445;
0724 119 618

**Sensazioni Ristorante**
Str. Fabrica de Glucoză nr. 21
Phone 021 324 24 36

**Shadow**
Str. Cătinei nr. 18
Phone 0749 101 682

**Shanghai Garden**
Şoseaua Pipera–Tunari nr. 2
Phone 021 269 13 12;
0724 724 751;
0723 323 458

**Shift**
Str. Eremia Grigorescu nr. 17
Phone 021 211 22 72;
0733 927 862

**Shorley**
Str. Econom Cezărescu nr. 50
Phone 021 312 43 12

**Siam Thai Restaurant**
Str. Amiral Vasile Urseanu nr. 1
Phone 021 210 94 35;
0732 388 146

**Silva**
Calea Floreasca nr. 145
Phone 021 230 73 17;
0724 241 966;
0722 324 399

**Silviu's**
Str. Louis Pasteur nr. 44
Phone 021 410 91 84;
0721 292 526

**Simbio Restaurant**
Str. Şelari nr. 18
Phone 021 310 27 00

**Smart's**
Str. Alexandru Donici nr. 14
Phone 021 211 90 35;
021 230 00 71

**Snack Attack (Amzei)**
Str. Amzei nr. 7–9
Phone 021 312 48 76

**Snack Attack (Batiştei)**
Str. Batiştei nr. 17
Phone 031 620 12 43

**Snack Attack (Dorobanţi)**
Str. Andrei Mureşan nr. 28
Phone 031 620 12 37

**Snack Attack (Magheru)**
Str. Câmpineanu nr. 10
Phone 021 620 12 39

**Snack Attack
(Piaţa Alba Iulia)**
Piaţa Alba Iulia
Phone 031 620 03 11

**Snack Attack (Pipera)**
Str. Dimitrie Pompei nr. 3
Phone 021 232 62 29;
031 620 03 15

**Snack Attack (Polonă)**
Şoseaua Ştefan cel Mare nr. 8
Phone 031 620 12 45

**Snack Attack (Victoriei I)**
Calea Victoriei nr. 224
Phone 031 620 12 35

**Snack Attack (Victoriei II)**
Calea Victoriei nr. 12A
Phone 031 620 12 77

**Snagov Club**
Str. Nufărului nr. 1B
Phone 021 352 60 79;
0372 746 861

**Soccer Cafe Restaurant**
Calea Floreasca nr. 45
Phone 021 230 44 42

**Sorriso Take Away**
Intrarea Iacob Felix nr. 59
Phone 021 317 65 35;
021 316 53 58

**Spazio**
Str. Ştefan Marinescu nr. 2–8
Phone 0727 677 667,
0765 542 786;
0733 660 736/732/731

**Springtime
(Carrefour Colentina)**
Şoseaua Colentina
nr. 426–426A
Phone 021 230 44 96

**Springtime
(Carrefour Militari)**
Autostrada Bucureşti – Piteşti
km 11
Phone 021 230 44 96

**Springtime (Cora Militari)**
Bulevardul Iuliu Maniu nr. 19
Phone 021 407 55 00

**Springtime
(Cora Pantelimon)**
Şoseaua Vergului nr. 21
Phone 021 230 44 96

**Springtime (Floreasca)**
Calea Floreasca nr. 113B
Phone 021 231 86 78

**Springtime (Gara de Nord)**
Piaţa Gării de Nord nr. 1–3
Phone 021 230 44 96

**Springtime
(Piaţa Alba Iulia)**
Piaţa Alba Iulia, bl. H2

Phone 021 230 44 96

**Springtime
(Plaza România)**
Bulevardul Timişoara nr. 26
Phone 021 230 44 96

**Springtime
(Ştefan cel Mare)**
Şoseaua Ştefan cel Mare nr. 42
Phone 021 230 44 96

**Springtime (Unirii)**
Piaţa Unirii nr. 1
Phone 021 230 44 96

**Springtime (Universitate)**
Str. Academiei nr. 3–5
Phone 021 230 44 96

**Springtime (Victoriei)**
Piaţa Victoriei, bl. A6
Phone 031 405 78 62

**Springtime (Vitan Mall)**
Calea Vitan nr. 55–59
Phone 021 230 44 96

**St. George**
Strada Franceză nr. 44
Phone 021 317 10 87;
0747 111 000

**Stadio Sports Bar**
Str. Ion Câmpineanu nr. 11
Phone 021 312 24 92;
0731 333 311

**Stadion**
Str. Costache Negri nr. 38
Phone 021 411 29 79;
0744 248 490;
0765 215 336

**Stil**
Str. Nicolae Caramfil nr. 63
Phone 021 233 39 90

**Suvenir**
Bulevardul Dacia nr. 147
Phone 021 211 22 60;
0788 878 788

**Taj**
Calea 13 Septembrie
nr. 127–131
Phone 021 410 18 20;
0748 133 300

**Tasty Fish**
Str. General Berthelot nr. 50
Phone 021 311 00 95;
0761 119 137

**Taverna Cappuccini**
Bulevardul Camil Ressu nr. 41
Phone 0726 748 600;
0726 307 767

**Taverna La Butoaie**
Phone Liviu Rebreanu nr. 6
Tel. 021 340 73 05

**Taverna La Gigi**
Str. Piscului nr. 16
Phone 021 331 07 50;
0788 472 725

**Taverna Sârbului**
Str. Tipografilor nr. 31
Phone 021 490 60 50/51/52;
0727 353 353;
0721 353 353

**Taverneria La Gigi**
Str. Uruguay nr. 11
Phone 021 222 06 07;
0722 220 607

**Templul Soarelui
(Colentina)**
Str. Vasile Lascăr nr. 205
Phone 021 212 29 55;
0729 883 663;
0723 743 878;
0745 476 693;
0760 989 669

**Templul Soarelui (Foişor)**
Str. Dimitrie Onciul nr. 17
Phone 021 211 16 93;
0729 883 663;
0723 743 878;
0745 476 693;
0760 989 669

**Templul Soarelui
(Mihai Eminescu)**
Str. Mihai Eminescu nr. 151
Phone 021 211 16 93;
0729 883 663;
0723 743 878;
0745 476 693;
0760 989 669

**Terasa Doamnei**
Str. Doamnei nr. 9
Phone 021 314 64 81;
0723 605 438

**Terasa Musafir**
Calea Rahovei nr. 196A
Phone 0752 218 555

**The Gin Factory**
Str. Lipscani nr. 37
Phone 021 311 3836

**The Grill House**
Str. Matei Voievod nr. 90
Phone 0767 796 263;
0765 369 858;
0760 445 012

**The Harbour**
Piaţa Amzei nr. 10–12
Phone 021 319 72 57;
0724 388 686

**The Left Hand**
Str. Panait Iatropol nr. 4
Phone 727 277 300

**Tic-Tac**
Str. Constantin Brâncuşi nr. 11

Phone 021 324 95 54;
0722 459 539

**Tineretului**
Bulevardul Tineretului nr. 1
Phone 021 330 35 12

**Tom**
Bulevardul Ion Mihalache
nr. 128
Phone 021 224 20 54;
0722 305 306

**Torega**
Str. Mihai Eminescu nr. 93
Phone 021 210 12 03;
0722 299 624

**Trafalgar Pub & Restaurant**
Str. David Emanuel nr. 4
Phone 021 211 31 51

**Traffic Pub & Restaurant**
Bulevardul Burebista nr. 2
Phone 021 322 59 45

**Traffic Pub & Restaurant 2**
Str. Vasile Lascăr nr. 216
Phone 021 210 77 99

**Trattoria Belucci**
Str. Fundeni nr. 120 B
Phone 0768 488 775

**Trattoria Il Calcio (fostă
Hard Rock Cafe & Pizza)**
Drumul Taberei nr. 32
Phone 0722 886 151

**Trattoria Il Carnevale**
Str. Christian Tell nr. 1–3
Phone 021 311 45 30;
0745 055 219;
0723 601 321

**Trattoria Buongiorno**
Bulevardul Lascăr Catargiu
nr. 56
Phone 021 317 43 63;
0722 446 766

**Trattoria del Tatoli**
Calea Victoriei nr. 26
Phone 021 315 33 99;
0724 77 66 55

**Trattoria Il Calcio (Amzei)**
Str. Mendeleev nr. 14
Phone 021 312 24 30;
0722 134 299

**Trattoria Il Calcio (Delea Veche)**
Str. Delea Veche nr. 36
Phone 0726 010 383

**Trattoria Il Calcio (Floreasca)**
Calea Floreasca nr. 118–120
Phone 0728 639 906

**Trattoria Il Calcio (Herăstrău)**
Șoseaua Nordului nr. 7–9
Phone 0724 706 665

**Trattoria Il Calcio (Phoenicia)**
Str. Alexandru Șerbănescu nr. 87
Phone 0728 339 931

**Trattoria Il Calcio (Pipera)**
Str. Erou Iancu Nicolae nr. 12–26
Phone 0723 076 520

**Trattoria Roma**
Str. Mihai Eminescu nr. 114–116
Phone 021 210 81 57;
0722 323 734

**Trattoria Verdi (Amzei)**
Str. Mendeleev nr. 29
Phone 0736 623 447

**Trattoria Verdi (Aviatorilor)**
Bulevardul Aviatorilor nr. 19
Phone 021 422 250 98;
0731 333 11

**Trattoria Verdi (Camera de Comerț)**
Str. Mircea Vodă nr. 34
Phone 0724 718 950

**Trattoria Verdi (Lahovari)**
Str. Tache Ionescu nr. 29
Phone 0736 623 446

**Trattoria Verdi (Piața Alba Iulia)**
Str. Popa Nan nr. 140
Phone 021 320 20 32;
0731 333 410

**Trattoria Verdi (Tineretului)**
Str. Piscului nr. 10
Phone 0735 555 221

**Trattoria Verdi (Titan)**
Str. Postăvaru nr. 84
Phone 0731 315 513

**Trattoria Verdi (Universitate)**
Str. Toma Caragiu nr. 3
Phone 0736 623 444

**Trattoria Xanadu**
Str. Postăvaru nr. 98A
Phone 021 345 15 86;
0726 212 114

**Unico Vero**
Str. Viitorului nr. 8
Phone 021 212 33 38

**Uptown**
Str. Rabat nr. 2
Phone 021 231 40 77

**Urbanesc**
Str. Ștefan Luchian nr. 17
Phone 021 313 77 16

**Valencia – Casa Spaniolă**
Str. Doctor Leonte nr. 12
Phone 021 312 81 96;
0722 204 884;
0723 231 584

**Vama Veche km. 0**
Str. Cristofor Columb nr. 13
Phone 021 211 64 46;
0744 671 213;
0745 866 066

**Varr – The House of Tastes**
Str. Silvestru nr. 67
Phone 021 210 30 39

**Vecchio 1812**
Str. Covaci nr. 16
Phone 031 430 95 77

**Vilacrosse Bistro**
Str. Eugen Carada nr. 7
Phone 0744 796 894;
0745 146 263;
0788 263 883

**Villa Rodizio**
Str. Ion Luca Caragiale nr. 32
Phone 021 211 80 78;
0758 818 841;
0755 041 480;
0755 041 481

**Violeta's Vintage Kitchen**
Str. Batiștei nr. 23
Phone 021 310 06 81;
0722 525 643;
0724 900 757

**Viv**
Str. Lipscani nr. 45
Phone 0750 100 000

**Vogue**
Str. George Enescu nr. 25
Phone 021 313 12 99;
0721 208 435

**Waterloo Taverne**
Str. Traian nr. 188
Phone 021 320 35 88;
0744 526 048;
0740 171 090

**Whispers Pub & Restaurant**
Str. Brezoianu nr. 4
Phone 021 314 29 01;
0722 439 097

**White Horse**
Str. George Călinescu nr. 4A
Phone 021 231 27 95

**Wu Xing**
Str. Cartojani nr. 2
Phone 021 222 21 26;
0740 222 122

**Yesterday**
Str. Econom Cezărescu nr. 8
Phone 021 340 85 85;
0720 552 818

**Yin-Yang**
Str. Puțul lui Zamfir nr. 38

Phone 021 231 41 32;
021 231 41 34;
0723 310 903

**Zafferano**
Str. Popa Savu nr. 29
Phone 021 222 72 10;
0728 777 678

**Zet**
Str. Vatra Luminoasă nr. 97
Phone 021 337 01 15;
021 337 49 00;
021 250 93 10

## Police stations

### Sector 1
Secţia nr. 1
Bulevardul Lascăr Catargiu
nr. 22
Phone 021 212 56 84
Secţia nr. 2
Str. Arhitect Ion Mincu nr. 15
Phone 021 222 96 01
Secţia nr. 3
Str. General Berthelot nr. 34
Phone 021 313 89 02
Secţia nr. 4
Str. Ion Neculce nr. 6
Phone 021 222 41 58
Secţia nr. 5
Bd Bucureştii Noi nr. 54
Phone 021 667 56 98

### Sector 2
Secţia nr. 6
Str. Paul Greceanu nr. 36
Phone 021 210 43 35
Secţia nr. 7
Str. Teiul Doamnei nr. 3
Phone 021 242 26 44
Secţia nr. 8
Şoseaua Mihai Bravu nr. 137
Phone 021 250 69 79
Secţia nr. 9
Şoseaua Pantelimon nr. 290
Phone 021 255 24 33

### Sector 3
Secţia nr. 10
Strada Stelea Spătarul nr. 13–15

Phone 021 313.69.45
Secţia nr. 11
Calea Vitan nr. 43
Phone 021 321 72 12
Secţia nr. 12
Str. Prof. Şt. S. Nicolau nr. 2
Phone 021 324 50 15
Secţia nr. 13
Str. Ciucea nr. 2
Phone 021 345 07 90
Secţia nr. 23
Str. Rodnei nr. 52
Phone 021 256 05 66

### Sector 4
Secţia nr. 14
Str. Oiţelor nr. 10
Phone 021 336 23 03
Secţia nr. 15
Str. E. Racoviţă nr. 2
Phone 021 461 00 71
Secţia nr. 16
Str. Stoian Militaru nr. 103
Phone 021 332 44 34
Secţia nr. 26
Bulevardul Metalurgiei nr. 89
Phone 021 683 21 08

### Sector 5
Secţia nr. 17
Str. Grigore Ţăranu nr. 10
Phone 021 410 90 02
Secţia nr. 18
Str. Constantin Miculescu
nr. 14–16
Phone 021 335 17 57
Secţia nr. 19
Str. Amurgului nr. 17
Phone 021 423 38 91
Secţia nr. 24
Str. Bazaltului nr. 17
Phone 021 332 49 03

### Sector 6
Secţia nr. 20
Str. George Mihail Zamfirescu
nr. 52
Phone 021 212 60 32
Secţia nr. 21
Str. Dezrobirii nr. 37

Phone 021 434 01 88
Secţia nr. 22
Str. Braşov nr. 19
Phone 021 413 10 20
Secţia nr. 25
Str. Aleea Callatis nr. 1A
Phone 021 444 19 06

## Hospitals

**Spitalul de Oftalmologie**
Piaţa Lahovari nr. 1
Phone 021 659 42 10

**Spitalul Clinic al
Constructorilor**
Str. Sf. Dumitru nr. 2
Phone 021 638 60 70;
021 315 29 41

**Spitalul Clinic Caritas**
Str. Traian nr. 29
021 323 22 50;
021 323 22 52

**Spitalul Clinic de
Ortopedie Foişor**
Bulevardul Ferdinand nr. 35
Phone 021 252 00 57;
021 635 13 87

**Spitalul Clinic Dr.
Cantacuzino**
Str. Ion Movilă nr. 5–7
Phone 021 210 71 00

**Spitalul Clinic Griviţa**
Bulevardul Ion Mihalache
nr. 37–39
Phone 021 222 35 19;
021 222 39 60

**Spitalul Clinic N. Malaxa**
Şoseaua Vergului nr. 12
Phone 021 255 54 05

**Spitalul Clinic pentru
Studenţi**
Str. C. Pascal nr. 25
Phone 021 314 41 91

**Spitalul Clinic Sf. Ioan**
Şoseaua Vitan–Bârzeşti
Phone 021 334 50 75

**Spitalul Colentina**
Șoseaua Ștefan cel Mare
nr. 21
Phone 021 210 32 45;
021 210 54 85

**Spitalul Colțea**
Bulevardul I.C. Brătianu nr. 1
Phone 021 314 27 44

**Spitalul de Chirurgire Plastică Reparatorie**
Calea Griviței nr. 218
Phone 021 224 09 47

**Spitalul de Copii Grigore Alexandrescu**
Bulevardul Iancu
de Hunedoara nr. 30–32
Phone 021 650 40 46

**Spitalul de Copii Marie Curie**
Bulevardul Constantin
Brâncoveanu nr. 20
Phone 021 682 41 60

**Spitalul de Copii Caraiman**
Str. Caraiman nr. 33A
Phone 021 224 07 83

**Spitalul de Copii Cotroceni**
Splaiul Independenței nr. 200
Phone 021 638 54 40

**Spitalul de Copii Victor Gomoiu**
Bulevardul Basarabia
Phone 021 323 22 30;
021 324 78 87

**Spitalul de Dermatologie**
Str. Șerban Vodă nr. 216
Phone 021 337 49 99

**Spitalul de neumoftiziologie**
Șoseaua Ștefan cel Mare nr. 11
Phone 021 210 39 36;
021 210 34 94

**Spitalul de neumoftiziologie**
Șoseaua Alexandrei nr. 145
Phone 021 420 38 45

**Spitalul de Recuperare Neuromotorie pentru Copiii**
Str. Marin Pazon nr. 2
Phone 021 345 21 95

**Spitalul de Stomatologie**
Calea Plevnei nr. 19
Phone 021 314 25 09;
021 315 52 17

**Spitalul de Urgență**
Calea Floreasca nr. 8
Phone 021 317 01 21

**Spitalul de Urologie Carol Davila**
Calea Griviței nr. 4
Phone 021 650 70 96

**Spitalul Dr. Bagdasar**
Șos. Berceni nr. 12
Phone 021 461 05 02

**Spitalul Elias**
Bulevardul Mărăști nr. 17
Phone 021 224 06 71

**Spitalul Emilia Irza**
Bulevardul Lacul Tei nr. 120
Phone 021 242 27 13

**Spitalul Filantropia**
Bulevardul Ion Mihalache
nr. 11
Phone 021 659 31 30

**Spitalul Fundeni**
Șoseaua Fundeni nr. 258
Phone 021 240 20 20

**Spitalul Militar Central**
Str. Mircea Vulcănescu nr. 88
Phone 021 637 51 25

**Spitalul de Obstetrică și Ginecologie Giulești**
Calea Giulești nr. 5
Phone 021 637 50 25;
021 637 25 54

**Spitalul de Obstetrică și Ginecologie Polizu**
Str. Gheorghe Polizu nr. 38–52
Phone 021 650 20 47

**Spitalul Parhon**
Bulevardul Aviatorilor nr. 34–36
Phone 021 230 20 40;
021 230 26 60

**Spitalul Sf. Pantelimon**
Șoseaua Pantelimon nr. 340
Phone 021 255 40 90

**Spitalul Titan**
Bulevardul Basarabia nr. 49
Phone 021 324 33 12

**Spitalul Universitar București**
Splaiul Independenței nr. 169
Phone 021 637 29 00

**Spitalul Victor Babeș**
Șoseaua Mihai Bravu nr. 281
Phone 021 323 41 10;
021 323 41 11

**Spitalul Witing**
Str. Witing nr. 37
Phone 021 637 60 81

## Theatres

**Club UNITER – Le Theatre**
Str. George Enescu nr. 2–4
Phone 021 318 28 74

**Clubul Copiilor Sector 5 (Studioul de Teatru Mihai Eminescu)**
Str. Năsăud nr. 93
Phone 021 423 01 78

**Compania de Teatru Dell'Arte**
Bulevardul Kiseleff nr. 3
Phone 0721 261 370;
0727 784 870

**Compania de teatru passe-partout dp.**
Str. Lipscani nr. 53
Phone 021 315 89 80;
0723 643 439

**La Scena**
Calea Călărași 55,
Phone 021 320 35 67
0727 795 380

**Lorgean Theatre**
Str. Şipotul Fântânilor nr. 4
Phone 0723 246 870

**Opera Comică pentru Copii**
Calea Giuleşti nr. 16
Phone 021 319 28 19;
0733 673 067

**Opera Naţională**
Bulevardul Mihail
Kogălniceanu nr. 70–72
Phone 021 313 18 57;
021 314 69 80

**Studioul de Arte Scenice
şi Vizuale Center Stage**
Splaiul Independenţei nr. 70
Phone 021 311 80 32;
0724 000 012

**Studioul Internaţional
de Teatru UNESCO
André-Louis Perinetti**
Bulevardul Magheru nr. 27,
etajul II
Phone 031 405 69 10;
0724 295 668

**Teatrul Act**
Calea Victoriei nr. 126
Phone 021 310 31 03;
0723 103 103

**Teatrul Apropo**
Str. Foişorului nr. 160
Phone 0765 450 549

**Teatrul Arca**
Calea Călăraşi nr. 55
Phone 031 402 47 24;
0727 795 380

**Teatrul Bulandra –
Sala Liviu Ciulei**
Bulevardul Schitu Măgureanu
nr. 1
Phone 021 314 75 46

**Sala Toma Caragiu**
Str. J. L. Calderon nr. 76A
Phone 021 212 05 27

**Teatrul de Comedie**
Str. Sfântul Dumitru nr. 2
Phone 021 315 91 37

**Teatrul de Comedie –
Sala Nouă**
Str. Sfânta Vineri nr. 11
Phone 021 315 91 37

**Teatrul de pe Lipscani
(Sala Rapsodia)**
Str. Lipscani nr. 53
Phone 021 315 89 80

**Teatrul de Revistă
Constantin Tănase**
Calea Victoriei nr. 33–35
Phone 021 315 56 78;
021 312 10 29;
021 314 19 79

**Teatrul de Vară –
Grădina Cinema Capitol**
Str. Constantin Mille nr. 13

**Teatrul de Vară Herăstrău**
Parcul Herăstrău

**Teatrul Elisabeta**
Bulevardul Regina Elisabeta
nr. 45
Phone 0749 093 093

**Teatrul Evreiesc de Stat**
Str. Iuliu Barasch nr. 15
Phone 021 323 45 30;
0721 332 436

**Teatrul Excelsior**
Str. Academiei nr. 28
Phone 021 315 97 36;
0760 262 313

**Teatrul fără Frontiere**
Str. Albac nr. 15
Phone 021 231 90 70;
0727 866 673

**Teatrul Foarte Mic**
Bulevardul Carol I nr. 21
Phone 021 314 09 05

**Teatrul în Culise**
Piața Națiunilor Unite nr. 3–5
Phone 021 320 20 59

**Teatrul Ion Creangă**
Bulevardul Magheru nr. 27
Phone 021 317 85 90

**Teatrul Logos**
Str. Vișinilor nr. 17
Phone 021 350 47 98;
0771 585 547

**Teatrul Luni
de la Green Hours**
Calea Victoriei nr. 120
Phone 0788 452 485

**Teatrul Masca**
Bulevardul Uverturii nr. 70–72
Phone 021 430 50 69

**Teatrul Mic**
Str. Constantin Mille nr. 16
Phone 021 314 70 81

**Teatrul Mignon**
Bulevardul Hristo Botev nr. 1
Phone 0726 243 907
0747 047 399

**Teatrul Montage**
Calea Călărașilor nr. 94
Phone 021 322 52 26;
0722 341 779;
0722 782 039

**Teatrul Național
de Operetă Ion Dacian**
Bulevardul Nicolae Bălcescu
nr. 2
Phone 021 315 15 02;
021 314 11 87

**Teatrul Național
I.L. Caragiale**
Bulevardul Nicolae Bălcescu
nr. 2
Phone 021 314 71 71

**Teatrul Nottara**
Bulevardul Gheorghe
Magheru nr. 20
Phone 021 317 41 01

**Teatrul Odeon**
Calea Victoriei nr. 40–42
Phone 021 314 72 34

**Teatrul Studențesc Podul**
Calea Plevnei nr. 61

**Teatrul Țăndarică –
Sala Lahovari**
Str. Eremia Grigorescu nr. 24
Phone 021 315 23 77

**Universitatea Națională
de Artă Teatrală
și Cinematografică
I.L. Caragiale**
Str. Matei Voievod nr. 75–77
Phone 021 252 74 57;
021 252 80 20

**Unteatru**
Str. Ilfov nr. 1,
Phone 0745 784 747

# Index

Index

# Selected Street Index

# Acknowledgements

We would like to thank the following institutions: Bucharest Municipal Hall for supporting the publication of this guide and for making publictransport and tourist-trail maps available to us; the Romanian National Museum of Art and the Romanian National Museum of History for help in editing the texts and for permission to reproduce photographs. We also thank the Peasant Museum and the Museum of Romanian Literature for making photographs available to us.

We are grateful to all those who granted permission to use photographs in their archives: Villa Rodizio, Burebista Vânătoresc, Taj, Sangria, and Crama Domnească restaurants; Radisson Blu, Howard Johnson Grand Plaza, and Athénée Palace Hilton hotels; Grand Café Galleron; Cărturești Tearoom; and Ark Underground Club.

**Picture credits**
Septimiu Slicaru, Cristina Mihală, Andreea Stoica, Bogdan Mitea, Mihai Potârniche, Ionuț Tarcea, MNAR, MNIR (photo ing. Marius Amarie), Muzeul Literaturii Române, Muzeul Țăranului Român, Burebista Vânătoresc, Villa Rodizio, Taj, Sangria, Grădina Verona, Ark Underground Club, Radisson Blu Hotel, Athénée Palace Hilton.

PAS

LAROMET 304

MOGOSOAIA 460    PIATA PRESEI 304

Str. Jandarmeriei    261

STRAND
STRAULESTI
97 205

Sos. Gh. Ionescu Sisesti
205

CHITILA 422

LAROMET
20 304 460

CARTIER
DAMAROAIA
24 331

MEZES
112

DRIDU

MAGAZIILE
16 FEBRUARIE
162

MEZES
45

Sos. Chitilei
43 422

Str. Pajurei    65 66

PIATA
PRESEI
41 42

CARTIER
GIULESTI-SARBI
163

DEPOUL
GIULESTI

CLABUCET
300 422

Bd. Expozitiei

CARTIER
16 FEBRUARIE
11

Cal. Giulesti

BANU
MANTA

GARA
BASARAB
35

ZURBAUA 421

COMPLEX
COMERCIAL
MILITARI
138

CARTIER
ROSU
106

APUSULUI

BD. REGIEI

SEMANATOAREA
601

GARA
DE NORD

GARA
DE NORD    SF.

CARREFOUR
137

LICEUL
INDUSTRIAL
TRANSPORTURI
62

MASTER
61 178

Bd. Iuliu Maniu

PASAJ
LUJERULUI
106

Bd. Iuliu Maniu

PIATA
LEUL
139

VASILE
PARVAN

COMPLEX
COMERCIAL
WEST PARK
236

Bd. Preciziei

DEPOUL
MILITARI
8 25 35

DEPOUL
MILITARI

Bd. Timisoara

Bd. Timisoara

CET VEST
MILITARI
47 136 221

CARTIER
BRANCUSI
168

VALEA IALOMITEI
90 91 93

Drumul Taberei

Bd. 1 Mai

Bd. Ghencea

VALEA ARGESULUI
69 71 173 268

VALEA OLTULUI
105 368 385

Bd. Ghencea

GHENCEA
41 47
126 185 221 302
427 453

Prel. Ghencea
122

DEPOUL
ALEXANDRIA
32 96 226 226
303 438

PIATA
RAHOVA

CARTIERUL LATIN
122

CIMITIRUL
GHENCEA 3
185

AUTOBAZA
ALEXANDRIA

DEPOUL
ALEXANDRIA

CARTIER
FORTUNA
302

Sos. Alexandria
303 438

BACAU
117

BRAGADIRU 438

ZETARILOR
4 & 23
139 141 323

PECINISCA
303

C.F.R.
PROGRESUL
7 25

DUMITRANA 427
VARTEJU 453

## KEY

— Tram line
— Trolley line
— Bus line
⊚ Public transport terminus
■■■ Exploatation units
— Tram lines in work

# PUBLIC TRANSPORT

# Metro Map

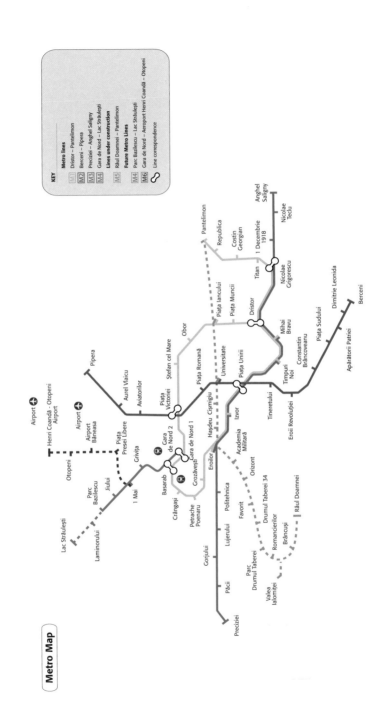

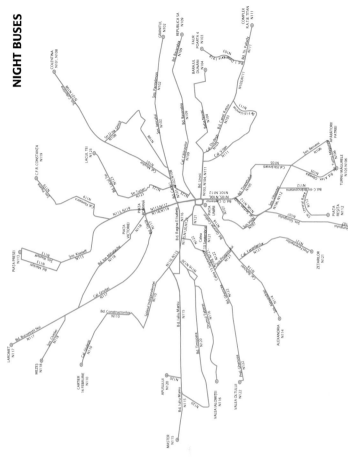

## Night buses

The intervals at which buses run are as follows:

- Between 11 p.m. and 1 a.m., buses every 30 minutes
- Between 1 a.m. and 5 a.m., buses every 60 minutes
- Between 5 a.m. and 6 a.m., buses every 30 minutes

RATB bus passes are valid on night buses.

Public transport passes issued for one or two routes are valid only for the corresponding night bus routes. The Unirii II office (at the terminus of the no. 32 tram line, Regina Maria Boulevard) that issues and renews public transport passes is also open between 10.30 p.m. and 6 a.m.

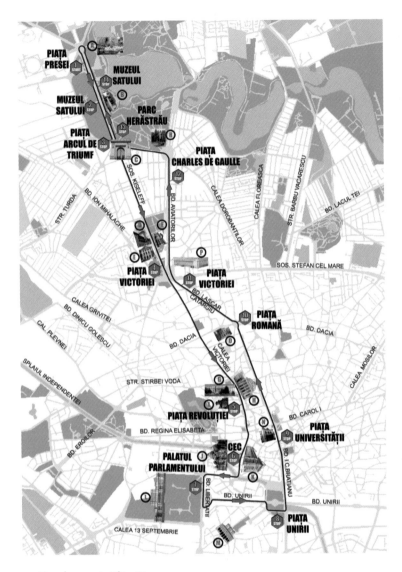

## Bucharest City Tour
### Programme 10.00–22.00
Buses every 15 min.
Tour length: approx. 50 min.
Ticket valid 24h after first validation. Tickets can be purchased on the bus, RATB centres (programme 6.00–20.30), and the Unirii Centre (programme 6.00–20.30, 22.00–6.00)
Price: adults 25 lei, children aged 17–14 10 lei, children under 7 free.
It is obligatory to validate your ticket each time you board the vehicle.
Audio presentation in English and Romanian.

# Monasteries and churches around Bucharest

**T1**: Terminal Ghencea – Piaţa Presei Libere – M-rea Căldăruşani – M-rea Balamuci

**T2**: Terminal Sf. Vineri – Piaţa Presei Libere – M-rea Căldăruşani – M-rea Balamuci

**T3**: Terminal Ghencea – Sf. Vineri – Granitul – M-rea Cernica – M-rea Pasărea

**T4**: Terminal Piaţa Presei Libere – Sf. Vineri – M-rea Cernica – M-rea Pasărea

**T7**: Terminal Piaţa Presei Libere – Ghencea – Biserica Adormirea Maicii Domnului Călugăreni – Biserica Sf. Ilie Călugăreni – Biserica Sf. Ilie Hulubeşti

**T9**: Terminal Piaţa Presei Libere – Ghencea – Biserica Sf. Gheorghe Brăniştari – Parcul Natural Comana

**T9\***: Terminal Sf. Vineri – Ghencea – Biserica Sf. Gheorghe Brăniştari – Parcul Natural Comana

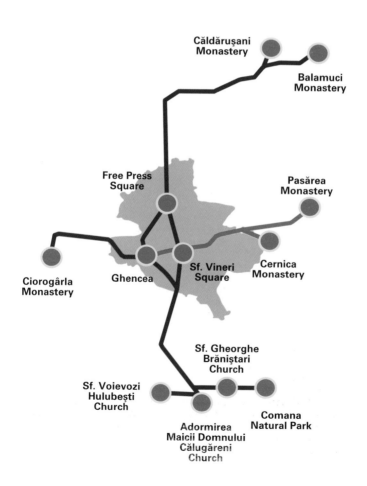

**LITERA**

O.P. 53. C.P. 212 București, România
tel.: 021 319 63 93, 031 425 16 19, 0752 548 372
E-mail comenzi@litera.ro

Ne puteți vizita la

**Bucharest. Illustrated Guide**

© 2013 Editura Litera

Publisher: Vidrașcu și fiii

Text: Ioana Gruenwald, Teodora Stanciu
Translated by: Alistair Ian Blyth
Editors: Andreea Stoica, Ilieș Câmpeanu
Proof reader: Georgiana Enache
Cover: Teodor Pricop
Layout and prepress: Teodor Pricop

Descrierea CIP a Bibliotecii Naționale a României
GRUENWALD, IOANA
    Bucharest.Illustrated Guide / Ioana Gruenwald,
Teodora Stanciu;  trad.: Alystar Ian Blyth - București:
Litera; 2013
    Index
    ISBN 978-606-686-562-3

I. Stanciu, Teodora
II. Blyth, Ian Alystar (trad.)

913(498 Buc.)(084)

Printed at R. A. „Monitorul Oficial"